_p172_

GROW RICH
WITH
MUTUAL
FUNDS

Without a Broker

Stephen Littauer

Dearborn
Financial Publishing, Inc.

While a great deal of care has been taken to provide accurate and current information, the ideas, suggestions, general principles and conclusions presented in this text are subject to local, state and federal laws and regulations, court cases and any revisions of same. The reader is thus urged to consult legal counsel regarding any points of law—this publication should not be used as a substitute for competent legal advice.

Publisher: Kathleen A. Welton
Associate Editor: Karen A. Christensen
Senior Project Editor: Jack L. Kiburz
Editorial Assistant: Kristen G. Landreth
Interior Design: Lucy Jenkins
Cover Design: Salvatore Concialdi

Library of Congress Cataloging-in-Publication Data

Littauer, Stephen L.
    Grow rich with mutual funds—without a broker / Stephen Littauer.
        p. cm.
    Includes index.
    ISBN 0–7931–0950–7
    1. Mutual funds. I. Title.
HG4530.L57 1994
332.63′27—dc20   93–51507
                                                                      CIP

Dedication

To Susan, without whom there would be no book

Wealth hastily gotten will dwindle, but he who gathers little by little will increase it.

—Proverbs 13:11

Contents

Introduction

WHY INVEST IN MUTUAL FUNDS?

With mutual fund assets now totaling in the trillions of dollars in some 81.7 million shareholder accounts, the mutual fund industry has become a dominant force on the national financial scene. Much of the trading activity in the organized stock markets is done by the funds. Not counting reinvested dividends, investors poured $241.8 billion of new money into long-term mutual funds in 1993; $128.2 billion of that went into equity funds, according to the Investment Company Institute. Mutual funds fit well into every investor's overall financial program, and they deserve the careful attention of every investor.

Because of the uncertainties of today's securities markets, prudent investors in ever greater numbers have been moving their money into mutual funds. Unlike the investors in a new security who have been urged to "get in on the ground floor" but haven't been warned about the basement, these investors are seeking the same things investors have always sought in mutual funds: a better return on their assets coupled with reduced risk through professional management and diversification, plus excellent services and ease of use. Because mutual funds invest in a wide range of targeted stocks, you eliminate the risk of putting all your money in one stock.

Currently more than 4,000 mutual funds are operating in the United States with assets held totaling over $2 trillion. These funds range in size from such funds as the Boston Company Investment Series Contrarian Fund (begun in 1988) with $2.8 million in assets, to the Vanguard Group's Wellington Fund (begun in 1929) with $5.1 billion, the Franklin U.S. Government Securities Fund (begun in 1970) with $13.6 billion, to the Fidelity Magellan Fund (begun in 1962) with $21.0 billion.

One of the most important reasons why investors choose mutual funds is the availability of past performance records. No other investment management form can provide prospective clients with so complete and unquestionable a picture of what it has achieved in the past. With *Grow Rich with Mutual Funds* at your fingertips, you can easily see how well different mutual fund managers have handled the funds under their care and if those results are suitable to your own investment needs.

HOW TO USE THIS BOOK

Grow Rich with Mutual Funds—Without a Broker will demonstrate how you can successfully grow your mutual funds into a very substantial estate, investing your money confidently, conveniently and at very low cost. Then with patience, you can allow yourself to grow rich with mutual funds—without brokers!

This book is divided into three parts. Part One gives you the tools and tips you need to make your mutual fund investing decisions with confidence. These chapters describe how mutual funds operate, how indexes can be useful, how bonds are rated, how mutual funds are taxed and regulated, how to read a prospectus and where you can do your research inexpensively.

In Part Two, you will learn how to place your funds directly with top-performing funds without going through a broker and without paying any sales commissions. You will find out why most mutual funds develop less total return on money invested than do the market averages and how you can now beat most professional money managers. These chapters describe how to invest profitably without worrying about whether the market is too high or whether you should wait until it goes lower. You will learn how to speculate in mutual funds, how to buy funds at a discount from their actual value, how to invest for income and how to reduce taxes to an absolute minimum.

Part Three provides a wealth of information to guide you in selecting the types of investments that make the most sense for you. Individual chapters provide detailed information on how to invest for growth in the United States, how to invest for growth in international markets, how to take advantage of special opportunities, how to invest in specialized stock and bond funds, how to invest for income in corporate and government bond funds, and how to invest in tax-free municipal bond funds.

WHAT INDEX FUNDS CAN DO FOR YOU

Chapter 11, "Index Funds: The Answer to a Paradox," presents the solution to a problem facing mutual fund investors. It is a simple fact that the average mutual fund underperforms the market. According to Ibbotson Associates, the stock market has historically provided investors with an average return of 10 percent per year. Some investors, due to luck or skill, have earned more than 10 percent, while other have earned less. But the 10 percent average return is *gross*—before costs are deducted.

Investors who pay typical costs for investing in conventional mutual funds may expect to have a *net* return that has been reduced by these costs. Such costs include investment advisory fees, distribution charges, operating expenses and portfolio transaction costs. The average of these costs among all mutual funds runs around 2 percent, reducing the 10 percent average gross return to 8 percent. Investors who pay sales commissions when they purchase fund shares will come out with even less.

The result is this: *The average mutual fund, over time, will have a total return that is less than the market's total return.* Perhaps the first evidence of this phenomenon was a study of mutual funds conducted by the University of Pennsylvania's Wharton School of Finance and Commerce in 1950. That study concluded that mutual funds on average underperformed the stock market by approximately 1 percent. Recent data has corroborated this conclusion. For example, *Morningstar Mutual Funds* reported that over the ten years ending August 31, 1993, 453 domestic growth funds had an average total return of 12.30 percent.

This compared with a total return of 14.95 percent for the Standard & Poor's 500 Composite Stock Price Index for the same period.

By investing in low-cost and carefully managed index funds, mutual fund investors today have the opportunity to come very close to achieving the same total return as the market. As of the end of 1993, Lipper Analytical Services, Summit, New Jersey, reported that 40 index funds that replicate the S&P 500 Index were in operation. Other funds replicate such well-known market indexes as the Standard & Poor's Midcap 400 Index, the Wilshire 4500 Index, the Wilshire 5000 Index, the Russell 2000 Small Stock Index, the Morgan Stanley Capital International Europe Index and the Lehman Brothers Aggregate Bond Index.

WHICH FUNDS CAN MAKE YOU RICH?

In addition to providing an accurate picture of past performance, mutual funds clearly state their investment objectives (for example, current income or growth of capital), their policies (how they intend to achieve their objective) and their investment holdings. Mutual funds have a wide variety of different objectives and policies. Some funds pursue their investment strategies in specific geographic areas, such as Europe or the Far East. Still other funds invest in specific industries. For example, some funds invest only in public utility companies; others in technology, biotechnology, precious metals, health care, financial services or natural resources.

The number of categories goes on and on. For instance, at the end of 1993, according to Lipper Analytical Services, 38 funds restricted their investments to companies located in Asia and the Pacific Basin. In addition, 227 funds invested only in equity securities of relatively small companies with the potential for rapid growth. By far the largest group, some 493 funds are classified as *growth funds*. They seek an investment objective of long-term capital appreciation, with a large array of investment choices.

To show you a wide range of mutual fund categories, this book contains an extensive section with detailed information about 29 separate categories into which mutual funds may be classified. For each investment category, the investor is provided with the fund group's investment objective, plus a survey of the group with its average annual total returns. In each category, you will find recommendations for purchasing a specific fund, including a discussion of how the fund operates, historical financial data and a list of its top 25 security holdings. You will even be able to see how your own hypothetical $10,000 investment would have done if you had invested it in any of these recommended funds. You can obtain any of these recommended funds directly from the mutual fund company and without paying any sales commission! In addition, more than 150 high-performing funds are listed.

So let's get started on how to choose the best mutual funds that will work hardest for your goals and needs and help you build your wealth.

Part One

Tools To Help You Succeed

Chapter 1

The Mutual Fund Phenomenon

In recent years, mutual funds have enjoyed an astonishing growth. Investors in record numbers have been pouring billions of their dollars into an increasing number and variety of funds.

According to the Investment Company Institute, mutual fund assets totaled $1.60 trillion, held in over 72 million shareholder accounts by the end of 1992—almost equal to the $1.62 trillion, held by life insurance companies. Only commercial banks, with $2.4 trillion, were bigger. By September 1993, total mutual fund assets had leaped again to more than $1,913 trillion. In less than three years, net assets held by mutual funds more than tripled from the $570 billion they held at the end of 1990. The growth of mutual funds since their inception in the 1920s has been astounding. Figure 1.1 illustrates five-year increments of growth over the decades since 1940.

Modern-day mutual funds had their genesis in the early 19th century, when investment trusts—as they were then called—became popular in England and Scotland. The idea became a reality in the United States in 1924 with the organization of the Massachusetts Investment Trust. It was the first open-end mutual fund, meaning that shares were issued and redeemed on a continuing basis. During those early years, investment trusts were subject to various abuses and were brought into considerable disrepute.

FIGURE 1.1   Growth of Mutual Funds since 1940

Year	Total Net Assets	Year	Total Net Assets
1940	$ 448 million	1970	$ 47,618 million
1945	$ 1,284 million	1975	$ 42,179 million
1950	$ 2,531 million	1980	$ 58,400 million
1955	$ 7,838 million	1985	$251,695 million
1960	$17,025 million	1990	$570,744 million
1965	$35,220 million		

Source: CDA/Wiesenberger Investment Companies Service

Some of the great mutual funds of today were first organized in the 1930s. But the greatest growth of mutual funds occurred after World War II and has continued to this time with only occasional pauses. Declines in total mutual fund assets took place in some years—especially in 1969 and in 1973 to 1974—as a result of severe bear markets. From less than $2 billion in 1945, total fund assets jumped to $17 billion in 1960, $58 billion in 1980 and more than $1 trillion in 1991.

THE MUTUAL FUND IDEA

The basic idea of a mutual fund is simple. It is an organization whose only business is the proper investment of its shareholders' money, generally into stocks or bonds or a combination of the two (and in recent years into money market instruments), for the purpose of achieving specific investment goals. To do this, it attracts funds from many individual and institutional investors, and it undertakes to invest and manage those funds more effectively than the investors could on their own.

The ability of a mutual fund to accomplish its goals successfully depends primarily on how well it can invest a large amount of money into a diversified portfolio of securities that will meet its investment objective. In addition, it must manage its costs efficiently, provide continuous professional management over its extensive investment portfolio and, finally, provide the many services that mutual fund shareholders have come to expect.

Like other corporations, a mutual fund company issues shares of its own stock. Each share represents the same proportionate interest in the account (portfolio of securities) as every other share. After deduction of necessary expenses, income from the account is distributed to shareholders in the form of dividends. Investment profits and losses are reflected in the value of the shares. Realized profits are distributed to shareholders in the form of capital gains distributions.

BENEFITS OF MUTUAL FUNDS

Expertise from Professional Money Managers

One of the great benefits an investor enjoys by purchasing shares of a mutual fund is the services of the company's professional investment management and advisory services staff. Some of the best and most highly compensated investment managers in the world are employed by mutual fund companies. Not only must they produce good returns on the assets committed into their care, but the performance of the funds they manage must withstand continuous comparison to various market indexes as well as to other mutual funds.

With over 4,000 mutual funds operating in late 1993, the mutual fund industry is highly competitive. Like top-echelon performers in professional sports, mutual funds also have their superstars. They too are rewarded with very large compensation packages. Some have fleeting fame after showing excellent results for a short time and then fall into obscurity when their funds suddenly lag behind. Others who consistently deliver good performance over long periods of time see their funds continue to grow by attracting large numbers of new investors. The best mutual funds do whatever is necessary in an attempt to retain their top investment managers. With as little as $250 invested in an individual retirement account (IRA), the smallest mutual fund share owner benefits from the same top-quality investment management as does the endowment fund that has invested $10 million or more.

To invest more effectively, millions of Americans have, in effect, hired these professional money managers through mutual fund investing. Often called portfolio managers, these professionals perform extensive economic and financial research. Their purpose is to develop data so that intelligent decisions can be made about securities in the funds' portfolios. Investment analysts research basic economic trends, such as market conditions, interest rates and inflation, and then evaluate how particular companies and other security-issuing organizations will be affected. Managers study trade publications, research reports, surveys, balance sheets and other financial statements. They also talk directly with a cross-section of top company executives. Portfolio managers will often specialize in specific areas; for example, one may be responsible for utility companies, while a colleague concentrates on the computer industry and another follows overseas markets.

Investment managers make buy and sell decisions based on this research and the fund's investment objective, which is described in its prospectus.

Diversification

An important aspect of successful long-term investing is diversification, a proven method of reducing the risk inherent in all investing. Assets can be diversified among a variety of securities issuers, among types of securities and among a variety of industries. In other words, diversification fulfills the old adage, "Don't put all your eggs in one basket."

The mutual fund investor has an enormous advantage in the quest for diversification. It doesn't matter whether the amount available for investment is $10,000, $100,000 or $1 million. The multitude of mutual fund companies offer the individual investor a wide range of diversity. For example, by investing in mutual funds, a person can allocate 20 percent to U.S. government bonds, 20 percent to high-yielding corporate bonds, 20 percent to blue chip common stocks, 20 percent to the stocks of small emerging-growth companies and 20 percent to the stocks of companies located all over the world. And the investor knows that through these mutual funds, he or she is indirectly investing in literally hundreds of different companies.

Liquidity

When people consider different investment alternatives, often one of the first questions asked is "How quickly can I get to my money if I need it?" The ability to readily convert an asset to cash is called *liquidity*. For many investors, this may be an important characteristic for an asset to have.

Mutual fund share owners can convert their investment into cash quickly, conveniently and at an easily calculated value. In some cases, the owner can simply write a check for the amount of money needed. With other funds, the investor can call the mutual fund company and ask for a redemption of the amount desired. The appropriate number of shares will be redeemed at the current net asset value and a check mailed within a day or two. For faster action, the proceeds of the redeemed shares can be wired by the fund directly into the investor's bank account. The share value of every fund is calculated at the end of each business day, so the investor can always keep abreast of what his or her shares are worth.

Low Cost of Investing

All mutual fund companies are in business to make a profit. The cost to an investor for owning mutual fund shares can range from as little as 0.19 percent, in the Vanguard Index Trust 500 Portfolio, to as much as 2 percent or more. These costs are in the form of the fund's expense ratio (including advisory fees, distribution charges and operating expenses) and portfolio transaction costs (brokerage and other trading costs), which are deducted from the assets managed by the fund. The average general equity fund has an annual expense ratio of 1.3 percent of investor assets. Portfolio transaction costs typically run between 0.5 percent to 1 percent. Funds with a low expense ratio and low transaction costs can have an important positive impact on the returns investors receive on their investments.

In addition to liquidity, which was discussed earlier, an investor in *no-load mutual funds* (those that charge no sales or redemption fees) can get his or her money into and out of the market *at no cost*. There is no commission to buy and no cost to sell (in most cases), and no period of time that the investment must remain in effect. Investors have nearly complete flexibility in handling their money. Contrast this with the ownership of individual securities, where an investor must pay a commission to buy and then pay a commission to sell.

Performance and Policy

An important advantage of mutual funds to investors is the availability of past-performance records. No other investment management form can provide prospective clients with so complete and unquestionable a picture of what it has achieved in the past. The investor can easily see how well any fund manager has handled the funds under his or her care and if those results are suitable to the investor's own investment needs.

In addition to an accurate picture of past performance, mutual funds provide investors with a clearly stated picture related to their objectives, policies and investment holdings. For example, a growth fund would have an investment objective of long-term capital appreciation, while a bond fund might have an objective of current income. The investment policy of a mutual fund states in detail exactly how it intends to achieve its objective. For instance, one fund whose objective is a high rate of return from dividend and interest income provides that it "will invest at least 80 percent of its assets in common stock and securities convertible into, or exchangeable for, common stock." It then goes on to describe other types of investments it intends to make, as well as specific limitations on what it may do. And, at least once a year, each fund reports to its shareholders the securities the fund owns and the percentage held in each industry sector.

Convenience

The convenience of owning shares in one or several mutual funds is an important benefit. Contrast this with owning individual shares of stock in many companies, collecting dividends on each and having to keep records of each transaction. Recordkeeping alone is an important problem that is kept to a minimum by owning mutual funds.

Freedom from Care and Responsibility

Even experienced investors often reach the point where they no longer want the responsibility of managing their own investments. The financial world has become so diverse and complex that it is now virtually impossible for any individual to be competent in all its phases. Other investors simply want the peace of mind that comes from letting someone else do the worrying—and managers get paid for it. Often investors have bought a stock that seemed attractive, only to watch it immediately drop $5 or $10 dollars a share in value. Because of diversification, the volatility of such a stock in a mutual fund would hardly be noticed, and in any event would most likely be offset by another stock that is rising.

Account Statements

Mutual funds provide investors with a complete record of their investment activity in the form of *account statements,* which are provided at least annually and often on a quarterly or monthly basis depending on activity in the account. In addition to allowing you to monitor your investment, the account statement is essential for the preparation of future income tax returns.

A statement is generated whenever there is a purchase of additional shares, either through direct purchase by the investor or as a result of automatic dividend reinvestment; when shares are redeemed; or if there is an administrative change (e.g., a new name and address, distribution option, etc.). Some funds also send a statement with every cash distribution they mail.

Accumulation Plan

Perhaps the most popular service offered by most mutual funds is the *accumulation plan,* which allows an investor to conveniently make additional investments to an account after an initial purchase of shares. Such investments can be made on a regular or irregular basis.

This informal type of program has facilitated investing for many purposes. It has attracted companies that invest substantial amounts for their pension and profit-sharing plans, as well as millions of individuals who invest money for their retirement (such as in IRAs), their children's education, and so forth. The accumulation plan lasts just as long as the investor chooses to make additional purchases.

Bank draft investing increases the convenience of the accumulation plan and is offered by many mutual fund companies. Under this plan, a predetermined cash amount is invested monthly or quarterly directly from a shareholder's checking account via bank drafts. In addition, an increasing number of mutual funds allow organized groups, as well as individuals, to set up accumulation plans through salary deduction or other group method of payment.

Reinvestment Privilege

A most useful and financially effective service mutual funds offer is to permit investors to automatically reinvest their income dividends and capital gains distributions into additional shares of the fund. Many investors who own individual shares of stocks and bonds have found that it is difficult to efficiently invest the dividend and interest payments they receive. The amounts are generally small and arrive intermittently. That problem is solved with mutual funds.

Most funds reinvest distributions into additional shares at net asset value, although some *load funds* (those that charge a sales commission) reinvest at the offering price. Some fund groups permit the dividends from one fund to be reinvested into shares of another fund in the same group.

Exchange Privilege

Some fund groups also offer an *exchange privilege*. Under this arrangement, the share owner has the right to exchange the shares owned in one fund for the shares of another fund that is part of the same group, or "family." There are many families of funds. Some of the largest fund companies will have as many as 60 or more funds. An exchange can be made for a nominal charge (usually $5) or, in some cases, no charge at all.

While mutual funds are designed as long-term investments, sometimes investors want to move their money from one type of fund to another. For example, an investor may want additional diversification, or perhaps decide to pull out of stocks and move into bonds or a money market fund. The exchange privilege adds an important degree of flexibility and control that investors can have over their money.

Consider tax consequences carefully before making an exchange. The exchange of shares in one fund for shares in another is considered a sale and new purchase for tax purposes. If, at the time of transfer, the value of the shares being liquidated is greater than their original purchase cost, a capital gain is realized.

Automatic Withdrawal Plan

Most mutual funds permit investors to receive monthly (or less frequent) checks of a specified amount that are drawn against their fund accounts. Different funds have various limitations on the use of this plan. In many cases, the funds require a minimum balance of $10,000 in the account. Usually the withdrawal amount may not exceed a stated percentage of the market value of the account or be less than a certain dollar amount, such as $50.

Funds generally require that when a withdrawal plan is in effect, all income and capital gains distributions must be invested in additional shares. The amounts withdrawn under an automatic withdrawal plan may be more or less than the fund's income dividend amount. If it is more, the difference will have to come out of capital, creating the potential for the gradual erosion of an investor's principal.

Since a withdrawal plan is voluntary and flexible, it can be changed or terminated at any time by the share owner, who has complete control over the account. But this plan is a very attractive option for an individual who wants to receive a regular income of a specific amount over an extended period of time, or indefinitely.

Retirement Plans

Many mutual funds make available to their shareholders convenient vehicles for investing in different types of tax-favored retirement plans.

Prototype corporate retirement plans can be adopted with a minimum of cost and red tape. The model prototype plans have been preapproved as to form by the IRS and are easily set up and understood. They are available for both pension and profit-sharing plans.

Individual retirement accounts (IRAs), created by the Employee Retirement Income Security Act of 1974, allow certain individuals to set up tax-sheltered retirement plans of their own. Participants can make annual contributions and also roll over lump-sum distributions from corporate pension and profit-sharing plans into their IRAs.

Simplified employee pension plans (SEPs) were designed primarily for businesses that do not have employee retirement plans and also may be used by those companies that do have plans, but with some limitations.

Keogh custodial accounts are available for self-employed individuals who wish to have tax-sheltered retirement plans. These individuals may invest in mutual fund accounts and need only have an established plan and a bank custodial account.

SUMMARY

With nearly $2 trillion in assets, mutual funds have had an enormous impact on U.S. financial markets and on the financial lives of millions of individual investors. Investing in mutual funds is the only way that an individual investor with limited resources can hope to obtain all the benefits of professional management, diversification, liquidity, administration and reporting. And you can gain these benefits at minimal cost. The phenomenon of mutual funds has indeed been a miracle of capitalism.

Chapter 2

How Mutual Funds Operate

A mutual fund is an investment company that makes investments on behalf of individuals and institutions who share common financial objectives. The fund pools the money of many people. Professional money managers then use the pool to invest in a variety of stocks, bonds and money market instruments that are expected to help the fund's shareholders achieve their financial objectives.

When a mutual fund earns money, it distributes the earnings to its shareholders. If the money is received by the fund in the form of dividends from stocks, or in the form of interest from debt instruments, the proceeds are distributed to shareholders in the form of dividends. If securities are sold for a profit by the fund, the capital gains so realized are distributed to shareholders as capital gains distributions. Dividends and capital gains distributions may be taken by the shareholder in cash or reinvested in the fund. Because all distributions to shareholders are paid out in exact proportion to the number of shares owned, shareholders who have only a few hundred dollars invested receive the same rate of return as those who invest hundreds of thousands.

INVESTMENT OBJECTIVES AND POLICIES

Each mutual fund has a stated investment objective. Both the objective and specific investment policies on how the fund's manager attempts to achieve this objective are clearly described in the fund's prospectus. Investment objectives are generally stated in terms of one or more main goals, which may include

- growth—increasing the value of invested principal;
- income—generating a flow of current income through dividends; and
- stability—protecting the invested principal from loss.

Investment objectives are important to both the fund manager and investors. The fund manager uses the objective as a guide when selecting investments for the fund's portfolio. Potential investors use it to determine which funds are suitable for their own particular needs. Mutual funds' investment objectives cover a wide range. Some funds follow aggressive investment policies to achieve the greatest return possible, but at a higher degree of risk. Other funds seek more modest returns, attempting to maintain a minimal amount of risk.

An investment policy describes the means by which a fund will proceed to meet its objective(s) and is discussed at some length in the fund's prospectus. The policy will state the types of securities that the fund will hold and often the credit quality of those securities. For instance, some equity funds, in their quest for long-term capital growth, will invest only in the common stocks of large, well-established industrial companies. Other funds, seeking current income and some growth, will invest in the common and preferred stocks of utility companies. Still other funds will invest only in securities issued or guaranteed by the U.S. government, seeking current income with a high degree of safety. Funds seeking maximum capital appreciation might invest in the common stocks of small companies that seem to have the potential for rapid growth.

HOW THE FUNDS GET PAID

All mutual fund companies are in business to make a profit. Many started out as investment managers for clients such as pension funds, college endowments, charitable trusts and wealthy private individuals.

There is a constant drive to increase the cost-effectiveness of high-priced investment management talent. This has resulted in a proliferation of new mutual funds as a way to bring large sums of money under management. In fact, from 1983 to 1992, according to the Investment Company Institute, the number of mutual funds nearly quadrupled, from 1,026 to 3,848.

The manager of a fund has, in effect, one client with one investment objective and a single set of investment policies. The larger the fund, the more cost-effective it may become. While big funds often require more personnel to run them than do small funds, the number of people needed becomes proportionately much smaller as the size of the fund grows. The Fidelity Asset Manager fund, for example, with nearly $5.8 billion in assets on July 31, 1993, charges a management fee of 0.74 percent of average net assets. With other expenses of 0.43 percent, total fund operating expenses run to 1.17 percent of assets. This one fund provides annual revenue of nearly $68 million to Fidelity Investments (America's largest mutual fund manager). While providing a large source of income for Fidelity, the 1.17 percent cost to the investor is quite modest.

Other funds charge more or less, depending largely on the efficiency of their operations. Small funds, or those just getting started, will of necessity run higher total operating costs than their larger peers. For example, the Merger Fund, with just over $13 million in assets at the end of 1992, had total operating costs that were 2.78 percent of assets. At the low end is the Vanguard Index Trust 500 Portfolio. Its total operating expenses have been running at 0.19 percent of the $7.5 billion it has under management.

Every mutual fund must report its expense charges annually in its prospectus so investors can easily compare charges from one fund to another. Expense charges are just one factor to consider in the selection of a fund; but other things being equal (management ability, past performance, investment objectives and policies), a fund with low expenses will tend to produce a better return for the investor than will one with charges that are out of line with the competition.

The management fee is usually the largest part of total expenses. It covers the salaries of fund officers and other employees as well as expenses relating to office space and facilities, and the payment for investment management and advice. Other operating expenses borne by the fund include charges of the fund's custodian (the bank or other financial institution that keeps custody of stock certificates and other assets of the fund), accountants and attorneys; the cost of issuing share certificates and disbursing dividends; and expenses for printing, postage and mailing.

Many funds have also put into effect a distribution services agreement (Rule 12b-1) adopted by the Securities and Exchange Commission (SEC) under the Investment Company Act of 1940. This permits mutual funds to directly or indirectly pay expenses connected with the distribution and marketing of its shares. These *12b-1 fees* range anywhere from 0.05 percent in some funds to as much as 1.25 percent in other funds. Such fees can have an adverse impact on a fund's performance, especially when compared with similar funds that do not charge 12b-1 fees. The mutual fund listings in major daily newspapers indicate which funds charge these fees (see "The Value of Newspaper Mutual Fund Listings" later in this chapter).

Expenses are paid by a fund primarily out of investment income, which is more than sufficient in most cases. One exception would be funds that invest substantially in growth companies that pay few or no dividends. When investment income is not sufficient to cover expenses, the balance is paid out of invested capital.

SALES CHARGES

Many mutual funds, generally called *load funds,* are sold through stockbrokers and other salespeople working on commission. The offering price of these funds includes a sales commission or fee that can range from a high of 8.5 percent (the maximum permitted by law) to as low as 3 percent. With the increasing dominance of the mutual fund industry by such no-load fund companies as Fidelity Investments and the Vanguard Group, load funds have been forced to reduce their commissions, many of which are now in the 4–5 percent range.

The only reason for a mutual fund to levy a sales charge is to cover costs of distribution. Most of the charge (about 85 percent) goes to the broker-dealer who handles the sale. Of that amount, about one-third goes to the salesperson (registered representative) who handles the transaction for the customer. The other 15 percent stays with the mutual fund company's own sales arm.

Sales charges can be paid at the time of purchase (a *front-end load*) or when the shares are redeemed (a *back-end load*). In some cases there

FIGURE 2.1　Sample Schedule of Sales Charges

Amount of Purchase (in thousands)	Sales Charge as a Percentage of	
	Offering Price	Net Asset Value
Less than $100	4.50%	4.71%
$101 to $250	3.50	3.61
$251 to $500	2.60	2.67
$501 to $1,000	2.00	2.04
$1,001 to $3,000	1.00	1.01
$3,001 to $5,000	0.50	0.50
$5,001 and over	0.25	0.25

may be a small charge at the time of purchase (a *low-load*) and another charge at redemption.

Mutual fund shares with front-end loads are offered for sale at a price marked up from the *net asset value* or NAV (the value of all assets held in a fund divided by the total number of shares outstanding) by the amount of the sales charge. The result is called the *offering price*.

The sales charge on a front-end load fund is usually tiered, with break-points at different dollar purchase amounts. Figure 2.1 is an example of a typical schedule of sales charges for purchasing shares of a front-end load fund. These schedules appear in the fund's prospectus.

A fairly recent development in the marketing of mutual funds has been the *back-end load*. Under this arrangement, shares are purchased at the net asset value. The investor pays no sales charge at the time of purchase. However, the salesperson must be paid, so the investor will pay a deferred sales charge if he or she redeems the shares prior to the end of a stipulated holding period. The amount of the charge declines over time until it eventually disappears entirely. There are usually no break-points for large purchases in back-end load funds.

In typical back-end load funds, an investor is subject to a sales charge if the shares are redeemed within the first six years after purchase. For instance, early withdrawal charges might be assessed as follows:

Year after Purchase	*Withdrawal Charge*
First year	5%
Second year	4

Third year	3
Fourth year	2
Fifth year	2
Sixth year	1
After six years	0

It may seem that an investor who holds on to a back-end load fund for more than the stipulated holding period avoids any sales cost, but this is not the case. The money to pay sales commissions and other costs of distribution is charged against the fund's income in accordance with Rule 12b-1 under the Investment Company Act of 1940.

Rule 12b-1 fees are assessed by many mutual funds, both load and no-load, but they are especially high in the case of back-end load funds, because such funds must recoup the commissions paid to salespeople. The fee charged by back-end load funds is typically 1.25 percent each year. This directly reduces the fund's total annual return each year by the amount of the charge.

As an illustration of how 12b-1 fees can negatively affect a mutual fund's long-term total return, consider two funds that are each invested in a portfolio of corporate bonds with an average income yield of 8 percent. Both funds have an expense ratio of 1 percent, resulting in a net income of 7 percent. However, one fund pays out the full net income to its shareholders, providing them with a dividend distribution rate (yield) of 7 percent. The other fund, a back-end load fund with the same 1 percent expense ratio but charging an additional 1.25 percent annual 12b-1 fee, is able to provide its shareholders with a dividend distribution rate of only 5.75 percent. Thus the yield received by an investor in the back-end load fund in this illustration is 17.8 percent less than that of the fund charging no 12b-1 fee.

NO-LOADS: BUYING MUTUAL FUNDS WITHOUT A BROKER

One of the great opportunities available to investors today is the ability to buy into some of the best professionally managed portfolios of stocks and bonds without a broker and without paying any sales commissions. This is easily done by investing in *no-load* mutual funds. These funds sell their shares directly to the public, and in most cases, with no sales charges.

An increasing number of all mutual funds are no-load funds. More than 1,000 no-load funds are priced daily in the mutual funds section of *The New York Times, The Wall Street Journal* and other major newspapers. They can be purchased on a direct basis and at no cost to the investor. Of course, certain expenses and management fees are common to both load and no-load funds.

Generally, no-load mutual funds are not as widely known to the general investing public as the load funds, in which a sales commission is involved. This is because many people get their information from stockbrokers, who quite naturally are reluctant to provide information on mutual funds that pay no commissions. However, brokers do serve an important function: they give investment information to those people who either can't or won't take the time to become informed directly on their own.

All other things being equal (investment performance, operating expenses, various fees, investor services, etc.), you can save a great deal of money and increase your investment return significantly by investing in no-load funds. It is worth mentioning that in recent years the difference between load and no-load funds has become somewhat blurred. Some no-load funds now charge 12b-1 fees, purchase charges, redemption fees and account maintenance fees. If you are in any doubt about what charges may apply to the particular funds in which you have an interest, just call the funds. Nearly all have toll-free numbers, and they will be happy to answer your questions and mail you a prospectus.

Because no-load mutual funds are sold directly to the public without the use of investment brokers, it is up to the investor to take the initiative by contacting the mutual fund. Toll-free numbers are included in the appendix, which lists all the major mutual fund companies whose funds you can buy directly without a broker.

THE VALUE OF NEWSPAPER MUTUAL FUND LISTINGS

Many people who have owned mutual funds for years are still unsure about how to read the mutual fund listings in their daily newspapers. The information provided in these tables is important for both existing shareholders and potential investors. All the major mutual funds can be found in the daily listings of any major city newspaper. The extent of information provided will vary somewhat from one newspaper to another, with the most extensive coverage appearing in such publications as *The Wall Street Journal, The New York Times* and *Barron's*.

Typically, most newspapers will offer ranges for investment companies, with daily price data supplied by the National Association of Securities Dealers (NASD). The NASD requires a mutual fund to have at least 1,000 shareholders or net assets of $25 million before being listed. The following data are typically published on a daily or weekly basis:

- The individual mutual funds offered by each fund group
- The offering price or cost per share to purchase any mutual fund
- The net asset value or amount you will receive per share if a fund was sold on the trade date of the listing (less any applicable redemption charges or fees)
- Which funds are no-load (those that charge no commission when you buy shares)
- The actual amount of the sales commission charged to purchase shares of "load" funds
- Which funds have a redemption fee or contingent sales charge when shares are redeemed
- Which shares use share owners' assets to pay for distribution costs (12b-1 fee)
- Whether you will participate in the next income dividend or capital gains distribution
- Which funds are about to pay a stock dividend or if the shares are to be split
- The amount of any increase or decrease in the share price of each fund compared to the previous trading day

Some newspapers offer additional information.

The New York Times

Extra information, which varies by the day of the week, is provided as follows:

Tuesday—total maximum sales charge (including deferred charges) as a percentage of purchase price for each fund
Wednesday—each fund's one-year total return
Thursday—each fund's three-month total return
Friday—each fund's year-to-date total return

Saturday—return and risk ratings for each fund, as calculated by
Morningstar Mutual Funds

Sunday—the investment category and three-year total return, annualized, of each fund

The Wall Street Journal

Additional information published by *The Wall Street Journal* includes an investment objective for each mutual fund listed plus the following performance and cost calculations by Lipper Analytical Services, Inc.:

- *Total return*—Performance calculations as percentages, assuming reinvestment of all distributions but not reflecting sales charges. Percentages are annualized for periods greater than one year.
- *Maximum initial sales commission*—This is based on the prospectus.
- *Total expense ratio*—This is shown as a percentage and is based on the fund's annual report. The ratio is total operating expenses for the fiscal year divided by the fund's average net assets.
- *Ranking*—Funds are grouped by investment objectives, as defined by *The Wall Street Journal* and ranked on the longest time period listed each day. Here are the rankings: A = top 20 percent, B = next 20 percent, C = middle 20 percent, D = next 20 percent, and E = bottom 20 percent.

The particular information provided varies each day as follows:

Monday—Maximum initial sales commission
Tuesday—4-week and one-year total return, with ranking
Wednesday—13-week and three-year total return, with ranking
Thursday—26-week and four-year total return, with ranking
Friday—39-week and five-year total return, with ranking

Barron's

Barron's, a national business and financial weekly publication, provides the following additional information for each mutual fund listed:

- 52-week net asset value high and low
- Week's net asset value high, low, close and net change

- Total return data for one week, the year-to-date and rolling three-year time periods
- Latest income dividend and capital gains distribution with the record and payment dates for each
- 12-month income dividends and capital gains distributions paid

Included with this listing is a weekly summary report of mutual fund cumulative performance with dividends reinvested, broken down by investment categories. These summary reports, based on data supplied by Lipper Analytical Services, Inc., gives the performance of each category for the most recent week, year-to-date, 12-month and three-year periods. The equivalent returns of Lipper and other well-known indexes are also reported.

Barron's also provides three-month, one-year and five-year total returns in the *Barron's/Lipper Quarterly*. This special edition of *Barron's* is distributed in January, April, July and October.

SUMMARY

A mutual fund is an investment company that makes investments on behalf of individuals and institutions who share common financial objectives. Each mutual fund has a stated investment objective which is described in terms of growth, income and/or capital preservation. Each fund also has an investment policy which describes the means by which the portfolio manager will proceed to meet the objective.

One of the great opportunities available to investors today is to be able to invest in some of the best professionally managed portfolios of stocks and bonds without a broker and without paying any sales commissions.

Chapter 3

The Importance of Market Indexes

The securities market indexes of today are descended from illustrious forebears. Dow Jones & Company pioneered the field of U.S. stock averages on July 3, 1884. In the "Customer's Afternoon Letter," a two-page financial news bulletin and forerunner of *The Wall Street Journal,* a listing of the average closing prices of the following 11 active "representative" stocks was presented:

Chicago & North Western	Northern Pacific Preferred
D. L. & W.	Pacific Mail
Lake Shore	St. Paul
Louisville & Nashville	Union Pacific
Missouri Pacific	Western Union
New York Central	

These and subsequent Dow Jones & Company averages were not published regularly. While business historians cannot agree as to whether the Dow Jones 1884 average was the first true index of American stocks, it is generally accepted as the first *published* index. Charles Henry Dow, first editor of *The Wall Street Journal* and cofounder in 1882 of Dow Jones & Company, is generally assigned credit for the compilation.

The original average did not use a weighted mean or make adjustments of any kind. Dow simply added the closing prices of the stocks in his average and divided the total by the number of companies included in the list. He found charts and statistics useful, and in his editorials he advised traders to keep records on individual stocks as well as the full list. The evidence indicates that Dow did not look upon the averages as anything more than an indication of the statistical nature of the stock market as a whole.

The first average assembled in 1884 contained nine railroads, reflecting the importance of railroads to the market at that time, and two industrial companies. Dow sought to include actively traded stocks in his compilation, but they were not so easy to find. The average day's activity on the New York Stock Exchange (NYSE) was 250,000 shares, mostly in railroads.

Industrial stocks were new and speculative, with no past for comparative purposes. Still, Dow foresaw the role industrial companies would play in the future economic life of the country, and he worked on the goal of compiling an industrial average. After 12 years of adding, subtracting and substituting, on May 26, 1896, Dow came up with a list composed of 12 industrial stocks:

American Cotton Oil	Laclede Gas
American Sugar	National Lead
American Tobacco	North American
Chicago Gas	Tennessee Coal & Iron
Distilling & Cattle Feeding	United States Leather Preferred
General Electric	United States Rubber

After irregular publishing, continuous publication began on October 7, 1896. It is generally agreed that the present Dow Jones industrial and railroad averages had their inception on that date.

For nearly 100 years, industrial stocks have proliferated, and the industrial average has come a long way. It has become easily the best known and most often quoted of all the averages. It is also the most widely used stock market indicator, although Standard & Poor's 500 Stock Composite Index has become an important standard for many.

The Dow Jones Industrial Average is nothing more than a statistical compilation that reflects combined, not individual, performances. The two great advantages of the industrials are simplicity and continuity. The present high level of the average is a result of its continuity. Its base has never changed, since to do so would, in effect, start a new average.

A problem of the Dow Jones Industrials is that the average exaggerates market movements. This is because it is described in "points" and runs about 50 times the straight average price of industrial stocks. Over the years, stocks have been split, but the industrial average has not. It has been suggested that the publisher split the industrials one-for-ten or move the decimal one place to the left. However, the feeling is that the average has gone to its lofty height and moves up and down strictly according to arithmetic. If the arithmetic were changed, continuity would be lost—and continuity is the average's greatest advantage.

Something to keep in mind is that the market "averages" really are not averages any more. They were originally, and are still referred to as such. But although they are useful measures of the overall movement of the stock market, the numbers themselves should not be mistaken for dollars-per-share prices of stocks. This applies not only to the Dow Jones Industrials but to all stock averages, or *indexes,* as many are now called.

The reason for the disparity is *stock splits,* which occur when a company believes the per-share price of its stock is too high for broad investor appeal. The company then arbitrarily splits the high-priced shares, creating more lower-priced shares. For example, if a stock selling for $100 is split two-for-one, the new price will be $50, other factors remaining unchanged. Of course, each owner of each share of the old $100 stock must be given an additional share of stock so the value of his or her holding won't be reduced.

Stock splitting, which goes on continuously, year after year, would distort the averages unless statistical market value–weighted adjustments were not also made to compensate for them. Thus, the Dow Jones averages are not dollar averages of current market prices but movement indicators, kept essentially undistorted by stock splits over nearly 100 years.

The Dow Jones Industrial Average, originally consisting of 12 stocks, was increased to 20 in 1916 and then to 30 in 1928. Whenever any particular component stock for any reason becomes unrepresentative of the American industrial sector, a substitution is made and the average is adjusted, just as when a split occurs.

Critics sometimes charge that the Dow Jones Industrial Average includes only 30 companies and so fails to reflect the movement of hundreds of other stock prices. But these 30 securities are chosen as representative of the broad market and of American industry. The companies are major factors in their industries, and their stocks are widely held by both individuals and institutions. Changes in the components are made rarely, often as a result of mergers, but occasionally they may be made to effect a better representation.

Over time, especially in recent years, the number of market averages—now widely called indexes—has proliferated. Dow Jones & Company itself now publishes an average for 20 transportation stocks, one for 15 utility stocks, and a composite average of all 65 stocks. In addition, market indexes have been developed by investment services firms, an industry association and even mutual fund companies. Some of the more widely known indexes are presented below.

TODAY'S WIDELY USED MARKET INDEXES

American Gas Association (ASA) Stock Index. The AGA Stock Index contains approximately 107 publicly traded stocks of companies engaged in the natural gas distribution and transmission industry. The industry is composed of gas distribution companies, gas pipeline companies, diversified gas companies, and combination gas and electric companies.

AMEX Major Market Index. This indicator is a price-weighted average; i.e., high-priced issues have more influence than low-priced issues. It is composed of 20 blue chip industrial stocks and is designed to replicate the Dow Jones Industrial Average in measuring representative performance of the stocks of major industrial corporations. It is produced by the American Stock Exchange (AMEX) but consists of stocks listed on the NYSE, 15 of which are also components of the Dow Jones Industrial Average.

AMEX Market Value Index. This index was formerly known as the American Stock Exchange Index and was prepared on a different basis. It is now a capitalization or market value–weighted index. In other words, the impact of a component's price change is proportionate to the overall market value of the issue. It was introduced at a base level of 100.00 in September 1973 and adjusted to half that level in July 1983. It measures the collective performance of more than 800 issues that represent all major industry groups trading on the American Stock Exchange. American Depository Receipts (ADRs) and warrants, as well as common stocks, are included. Cash dividends paid by component stocks are assumed to be reinvested and are reflected in the index, a characteristic unique to the AMEX Market Value Index.

Benham North American Gold Equities Index. This index consists of stocks of North American companies engaged in exploring for, mining, processing, fabricating or otherwise dealing in gold. As of December 31, 1992, the aggregate market capitalization of the 28 companies included in the index was $18.3 billion.

Dow Jones Industrial Average (DJIA). The DJIA is the oldest and most widely quoted of all market indicators. Published by Dow Jones & Company, it is a price-weighted average of 30 actively traded blue chip stocks consisting primarily of industrial companies. The components, which change from time to time, represent between 15 percent and 20 percent of the market value of NYSE stocks.

The DJIA is calculated by adding the closing prices of the component stocks and using a divisor that is adjusted for stock splits and dividends equal to 10 percent or more of the market value of an issue, as well as for substitutions and mergers. The average is quoted in points, not dollars. The Dow Jones industrials consist of the following companies:

Allied-Signal Company
Aluminum Company of America
American Express Company
American Telephone &
   Telegraph (AT&T)
Bethlehem Steel
Boeing Company
Caterpillar, Inc.
Chevron Corporation
Coca-Cola Company
Disney (Walt) Company
DuPont de Nemours, E. I. & Co.
Eastman Kodak Company
Exxon Corporation
General Electric (GE) Company
General Motors (GM)
   Corporation
Goodyear Tire & Rubber
   Company

International Business Machines
   Corporation (IBM)
International Paper Company
McDonald's Corporation
Merck & Company
Minnesota Mining &
   Manufacturing (3M)
Morgan (J. P.) & Company
Philip Morris Company
Procter & Gamble Corporation
Sears, Roebuck & Company
Texaco Incorporated
Union Carbide Corporation
United Technologies Company
Westinghouse Electric
   Corporation
F. W. Woolworth & Company

Dow Jones Transportation Average (DJTA). This index is a price-weighted average of the stocks of 20 large companies in the transportation business, including airlines, railroads and trucking. From 1897 to 1969, this indicator was called the Dow Jones Railroad Average. The transportation average contains the following components:

Airborne Freight Corporation	Federal Express Company
Alaska Air Group, Inc.	Norfolk Southern Corporation
American President Companies	Roadway Services, Inc.
AMR Corporation	Ryder System Inc.
Burlington Northern Inc.	Santa Fe Southern Pacific Company
Carolina Freight Corporation	Southwest Airlines
Consolidated Freight Corporation	UAL Inc.
Consolidated Rail Corporation	Union Pacific Corporation
CSX Corporation	USAir Group
Delta Airlines	Xtra Corporation

Dow Jones Utility Average (DJUA). This is a price-weighted average composed of 15 geographically representative and well-established gas and electric utility companies. The utilities average consists of the following components:

American Electric Power Company	Niagara Mohawk Power Company
Arkla, Inc.	Pacific Gas & Electric Company
Centerior Energy	Panhandle Eastern Company
Commonwealth Edison Company	Peoples Energy Corporation
Consolidated Edison Company	Philadelphia Electric Company
Consolidated Natural Gas Company	Public Service Enterprise Group
Detroit Edison Company	SCE Corporation
Houston Industries	

Dow Jones 65 Composite Stock Average. This average consists of the 30 stocks in the Dow Jones Industrial Average, the 20 stocks in the Dow Jones Transportation Average and the 15 stocks in the Dow Jones Utility Average. This average is significant because it is a combination of the three blue chip averages and, therefore, gives a good indication of the overall direction of the largest, most established companies.

Lehman Brothers Aggregate Bond Index. This index measures total investment return (capital changes plus income) provided by a universe of fixed-income securities, weighted by the market value outstanding of each security. As of December 31, 1992, more than 6,000 issues (including bonds, notes, debentures and mortgage issues) were included in the index, representing more than $3.9 trillion in market value. The securities generally have an effective maturity of not less than one year, an outstanding market value of at least $25 million and investment-grade quality (rated a minimum of Baa by Moody's Investors Service, Inc., or BBB by Standard & Poor's Corporation).

Morgan Stanley Capital International Europe (Free) Index (MSCI-Europe (Free)). MSCI-Europe (Free) is a diversified, capitalization-weighted index comprising approximately 575 companies located in 13 European countries. Three countries—the United Kingdom, Germany and France—dominate MSCI-Europe (Free), with 40 percent, 14 percent and 14 percent of the market capitalization of the index, respectively, as of December 31, 1992. The "Free" index includes only shares that U.S. investors are "free to purchase." It excludes restricted shares in Finland, Norway, Sweden and Switzerland.

Morgan Stanley Capital International Pacific Index (MSCI-Pacific). This is a diversified, capitalization-weighted Pacific Basin index consisting of approximately 425 companies located in Australia, Japan, Hong Kong, New Zealand and Singapore. The MSCI-Pacific is dominated by the Japanese stock market, which represented 85 percent of its market capitalization as of December 31, 1992.

Morgan Stanley Capital International Europe, Australia and Far East (Free) Index (EAFE Free). EAFE Free is a broadly diversified international index consisting of more than 1,000 equity securities of companies located outside of the United States.

Nasdaq National Market System Composite Index. Nasdaq is a market value-weighted index composed of all the stocks traded on the National Market System (NMS) of the over-the-counter market, which is supervised by the National Association of Securities Dealers (NASD). The companies in this index are generally smaller growth companies.

New York Stock Exchange Composite Index. This index is market value–weighted and relates all NYSE stocks to an aggregate market value as of December 31, 1965, adjusted for capital changes. The base value of the index is $50, and point changes are expressed in dollars and cents.

Russell 2000 Small Stock Index.   This is a broadly diversified, small capitalization index consisting of approximately 2,000 common stocks. As of September 30, 1992, the average stock market capitalization of stocks in this index was $200 million.

The Schwab 1000 Index.   This index is composed of the common stocks of the 1,000 largest U.S. corporations (excluding investment companies) as measured by market capitalization. A particular stock's weighting in the index is based on its relative total market value, divided by the total market value of the index. As of December 31, 1992, the aggregate market capitalization of the stocks constituting the index was approximately $3.7 trillion.

Standard & Poor's 500 Composite Stock Price Index.   The S&P 500 Index measures the total investment return (capital change plus income) of 500 common stocks, which are chosen by Standard & Poor's Corporation on a statistical basis. The 500 securities, most of which trade on the NYSE, represented about 71 percent of the market value of all U.S. common stocks as of December 31, 1992. Each stock in the index is weighted by its market value. Because of its market-value weighting, the 50 largest companies in the S&P 500 Index currently account for about 50 percent of the index. Typically, companies included in the S&P 500 are the largest and most dominant firms in their industries.

Standard & Poor's 40 Stock Financial Index.   This is a market value–oriented index composed of 40 large financial institutions, such as banks and insurance companies.

Standard & Poor's 20 Transportation Stock Index.   This market value–oriented index is made up of 20 large transportation companies in the airline, trucking and railroad businesses.

Standard & Poor's 40 Utilities Stock Index.   This is a market value–oriented index consisting of 40 large and geographically representative electric and gas utilities.

Standard & Poor's 100 Composite Stock Index. This market value–oriented index is made up of the 40 stocks in the S&P Financial Index, the 20 stocks in the S&P Transportation Index and the 40 stocks in the S&P Utilities Index.

Standard & Poor's 400 Industrial Stock Index. This is a market value–weighted index comprising 400 large, well-established industrial companies, most of which are traded on the NYSE. The S&P 500 Index is made up of the S&P 400 Index plus the S&P 40 Utilities, the S&P 20 Transportation companies and the 40 financial institutions indexes.

Standard & Poor's/BARRA Value and Growth Indexes. To construct these indexes, Standard & Poor's Corporation semiannually ranks all common stocks included in the S&P 500 Index by their price-to-book ratios. The resulting list is then divided in half by market capitalization. Those companies representing half of the market capitalization of the S&P 500 Index and having lower price-to-book ratios are included in the S&P/BARRA Value Index; the remaining companies are incorporated into the S&P/BARRA Growth Index.

On December 31, 1992, the S&P/BARRA Value Index consisted of 320 common stocks in the S&P 500 Index, while the S&P/BARRA Growth Index consisted of the remaining 180. Each index represented half of the market capitalization of the S&P 500 Index. Typically, the stocks included in the S&P/BARRA Value Index exhibit above-average dividend yields and lower price-to-book ratios. By comparison, the stocks included in the S&P 500/BARRA Growth Index exhibit below-average dividend yields and higher price-to-book ratios.

Value Line Composite Index. This equally weighted geometric average is composed of the approximately 1,700 stocks traded on the NYSE, AMEX, and over the counter that are tracked by the *Value Line Investment Survey*. It is particularly broad in scope, since *Value Line* covers both large industrial companies and smaller growth firms.

Wilshire 4500 Index. This index consists of all U.S. stocks that are not in the S&P 500 Index and that trade regularly on the NYSE and AMEX as well as in the Nasdaq over-the-counter market. More than 5,000 stocks of midsize and small capitalization companies are included in the Wilshire 4500 Index.

Wilshire 5000 Index. This index consists of all regularly and publicly traded U.S. stocks; it provides a complete proxy for the U.S. stock market. More than 6,000 stocks, including large, medium-size and small capitalization companies, are included in the Wilshire 5000 Index. It represents the value, in billions of dollars, of all NYSE, AMEX and over-the-counter stocks for which quotes are available. This index is used to measure how all stocks are doing as a group, as opposed to a particular segment of the market.

Wilshire Small Cap Index. This index consists of common stock of 250 companies with an average market capitalization of $400 million, and it is designed to accurately reflect the general characteristics and performance profile of small capitalization companies. Stocks in the index were chosen on the basis of market capitalization, liquidity and industry group representation.

SUMMARY

The function of securities market indexes is to give a general rather than precise idea of fluctuations in the securities markets and to reflect the historical continuity of security price movements. So-called market "averages" are really not averages anymore. While they are useful measures of the overall movement of security markets, do not mistake the numbers themselves, usually called *points,* for dollars-per-share prices of stocks.

Chapter 4

How Bonds Are Rated for Safety

Mutual funds that include corporate or municipal bonds and other debt instruments in their portfolios specify the credit quality of bonds they are permitted to invest in. Fund managers utilize rating systems that have been developed by several widely recognized investment rating services. Many bonds, but not all, are evaluated by these services to determine the probability of default by the issuers.

Standard & Poor's Corporation, Moody's Investors Service, Inc., Duff & Phelps and Fitch's Investors Service are the major firms that analyze the financial strength of each bond's issuer, whether a corporation or a government body. Bonds are assigned ratings by these firms to assist in determining the suitability of a particular instrument for investment purposes. For example, investment-grade bonds are rated AAA, AA, A and BBB. Anything lower is speculative; institutions that invest other people's money may not, under most state laws, buy them.

Since an issuer pays a substantial cost to obtain a rating by one of these services, debt securities are often issued on an unrated basis. This is particularly true if the total value of the offering is deemed insufficient to justify the cost of obtaining a rating. The fact that a bond issue is unrated does not by itself necessarily indicate that it is an unsound investment.

CORPORATE BONDS

A description of the corporate bond rating systems used by Standard & Poor's and Moody's Investors Service follows (used with permission).

Standard & Poor's Corporation

Investment Grade

AAA—Debt rated AAA has the highest rating assigned by Standard & Poor's. Capacity to pay interest and repay principal is extremely strong.

AA—Debt rated AA has a very strong capacity to pay interest and repay principal and differs from the highest-rated issues only in small degree.

A—Debt rated A has a strong capacity to pay interest and repay principal, although it is somewhat more susceptible to the adverse effects of changes in circumstances and economic conditions than debt in higher rate categories.

BBB—Debt rated BBB is regarded as having an adequate capacity to pay interest and repay principal. Whereas it normally exhibits adequate protection parameters, adverse economic conditions or changing circumstances are more likely to lead to a weakened capacity to pay interest and repay principal for debt in this category than in higher-rated categories.

Speculative Grade

BB—Debt rated BB has less near-term vulnerability to default than other speculative issues. However, it faces major ongoing uncertainties or exposure to adverse business, financial or economic conditions that could lead to inadequate capacity to meet timely interest and principal payments. The BB rating category is also used for debt subordinated to senior debt that is assigned an actual or impled BBB rating.

B—Debt rated B has a greater vulnerability to default but currently has the capacity to meet interest payments and principal repayments. Adverse business, financial or economic conditions will likely impair capacity or willingness to pay interest and repay principal. The B rating category is also used for debt subordinated to senior debt that is assigned an actual or implied BB or BB– rating.

CCC—Debt rated CCC has a currently identifiable vulnerability to default and is dependent upon favorable business, financial and economic conditions to meet timely payment of interest and repayment of principal. In the event of adverse business, financial or economic conditions, it is not likely to have the capacity to pay interest and repay principal. The CCC rating category is also used for debt that is assigned an actual or implied B or B– rating.

CC—The rating CC is typically applied to debt subordinated to senior debt that is assigned an actual or implied CCC rating.

C—The C rating is typically applied to debt subordinated to senior debt that is assigned an actual or implied CCC– debt rating. The C rating may be used to cover a situation in which a bankruptcy petition has been filed but debt service payments are continued.

CI—The CI rating is reserved for income bonds on which no interest is being paid.

D—Debt rated D is in payment default. The D rating category is used when interest payments or principal repayments are not made on the date due even if the applicable grace period has not expired, unless S&P believes that such payments will be made during such grace period. The D rating will be used upon the filing of a bankruptcy petition if debt service payments are jeopardized.

The ratings from AA to CCC may be modified by the addition of a plus or minus sign to show relative standing within the major rating categories.

Moody's Investors Service, Inc.

Aaa—Bonds rated Aaa are judged to be of the best quality. They carry the smallest degree of investment risk and are generally referred to as "gilt-edge." Interest payments are protected by a large or exceptionally stable margin and principal is secure. While the various protective elements are likely to change, potential changes are most unlikely to impair the fundamentally strong position of such issues.

Aa—Bonds rated Aa are judged to be of high quality by all standards. Together with the Aaa group they constitute what are generally known as high-grade bonds. They are rated lower than the best bonds because margins of protection may not be as large as those for Aaa securities; there may be greater fluctuation of protective elements; or other elements may be present that make the long-term risks appear somewhat larger than those in Aaa securities.

A—Bonds rated A possess many favorable investment attributes and are considered upper-medium-grade obligations. Factors giving security to principal and interest are considered adequate, but elements may be present that suggest a susceptibility to impairment sometime in the future.

Baa—Bonds rated Baa are considered medium-grade obligations—i.e., they are neither highly protected nor poorly secured. Interest payments and principal security appear adequate for the present, but certain protective elements may be lacking or may be characteristically unreliable over any great length of time. Such bonds lack outstanding investment characteristics and, in fact, have speculative characteristics as well.

Ba—Bonds rated Ba are judged to have speculative elements. Their future cannot be considered well assured. Often the protection of interest and principal payments may be moderate and therefore not sufficiently secure during both good and bad times over the future. Uncertainty of position characterizes bonds in this class.

B—Bonds rated B generally lack characteristics of the desirable investment. Assurance of interest and principal payments or maintenance of other terms of the contract over any long period of time may be small.

Caa—Bonds rated Caa are of poor standing. Such issues may be in default, or elements of danger may exist with respect to principal or interest.

Ca—Bonds rated Ca represent obligations that are highly speculative. Such issues are often in default or have other marked shortcomings.

C—Bonds rated C are the lowest-rated class of bonds, and issues can be regarded as having extremely poor prospects of ever attaining any real investment standing.

Moody's applies the numerical modifiers 1, 2 and 3 in each generic rating classification from Aa through B in its corporate bond rating system. The modifier 1 indicates that the security ranks in the higher end of its generic rating category; 2 indicates a midrange ranking; and 3 indicates that the issue ranks in the lower end.

MUNICIPAL BONDS

As is the case with debt securities issued by corporations, credit risk should be considered in connection with bonds issued by states and municipalities. A mutual fund investor in tax-free shares should be concerned about the possibility that a bond issuer will fail to make timely payments of interest or principal to a portfolio. The credit risk of a portfolio depends on the credit quality of its underlying securities. In general, the lower the credit quality of a portfolio's municipal securities, the higher a portfolio's yield, all other factors (such as maturity) being equal.

A brief description of the municipal bond rating system used by Moody's Investors Service follows (used with permission).

Aaa—Bonds rated Aaa are judged to be the best quality, carrying the smallest degree of investment risk.

Aa—Bonds rated Aa are judged to be of high quality by all standards.

A—Bonds rated A possess many favorable investment attributes and are considered high medium-grade issues.

Baa—Bonds rated Baa are considered medium-grade issues.

Ba—Bonds rated Ba are judged to have speculative elements. Future payment of interest and principal cannot be well assured.

NR—Not rated.

MIG 1—Short-term tax-exempt debt instruments of the best quality with strong protection are given the rating MIG 1.

Prime 1—Prime 1 is the designation given to commercial paper of the highest quality.

SUMMARY

One of the risks that confront investors in fixed-income or bond funds is credit risk, which is the possibility that a bond issuer will fail to make timely payments of either interest or principal to a portfolio. Institutions that invest other people's money must include only investment-grade bonds in their portfolios in most states. These are bonds that carry credit ratings of A or better, as defined by such leading investment rating services as Standard & Poor's Corporation or Moody's Investors Services, Inc. Lower-rated debt securities are usually defined as those rated BB or lower by Standard & Poor's or Ba or lower by Moody's. Such instruments are considered speculative; they involve greater risk of loss than higher-rated securities and are more sensitive to changes in the issuer's capacity to pay.

Chapter 5

How Mutual Funds Are Regulated and Taxed

No one can prevent fools from being parted from their money. Nevertheless, over the years important laws have been enacted to prevent many possible abuses of trust. These laws are clear-cut and far-reaching. This chapter summarizes the key laws that affect mutual funds, as well as the way they are taxed.

The laws governing mutual funds require extensive disclosure to the Securities and Exchange Commission (SEC), state regulators and fund shareholders, and entail continuous regulation of fund operations. Mutual fund companies are perhaps the most strictly regulated business entities under the federal securities laws. A former chairman of the SEC said, "No issuer of securities is subject to more detailed regulation than mutual funds." The existing laws and regulations are a direct result of abuses that existed in the mutual fund industry, particularly in the 1930s.

It is interesting to note, however, that these laws do not include looking over the shoulders of each fund's managers to second-guess their investment judgment. That would occur only if it is determined that the fund is not being invested in accordance with the objectives and policy restrictions set forth in its prospectus and according to federal and state law. So the laws do not protect investors from bad management; instead, it is *caveat emptor*—let the buyer beware. An informed investor is a happy investor.

MAJOR FEDERAL STATUTES THAT REGULATE MUTUAL FUNDS

Securities Act of 1933

The Securities Act of 1933 requires filing with the SEC a registration statement containing extensive information about a mutual fund. In addition, the 1933 act requires each fund to provide potential investors with a current prospectus. The prospectus contains detailed disclosures about the fund's management, its investment policies and objectives, and other essential data. The 1933 act also limits the type and content of advertisements that may be used by a mutual fund.

This act is the most important of the laws governing the sale of mutual fund shares. Nearly all mutual fund companies of any size are subject to this act when they sell new shares to the public. The law basically provides that a fund company must furnish accurate and full information in connection with financial and other corporate matters, so that the investor has the necessary facts on which to base an intelligent judgment regarding the value of the securities being offered. This information must be filed by the fund company with the SEC in the form of a *registration statement*. The SEC then will review it for accuracy and completeness, allowing shares of the fund to be sold to the public only after it is satisfied as to its truthfulness and that no important matters have been omitted.

The fact that the SEC permits shares of a fund to be sold does not in any way imply its approval of the fund, nor does it imply that the fund is a good investment. When the SEC permits a registration statement to become effective, it merely indicates that the fund has apparently disclosed all the information that the law requires. If it turns out that the fund has falsified information in the registration statement, the law provides that the injured shareholder may sue those responsible.

The items in a registration statement of most interest to investors must be furnished in the form of a prospectus to the purchaser of any new security. Although an oral offer to sell may be made without a prospectus, any written offer must be accompanied by a prospectus. The prospectus should always be read carefully before anyone invests in a mutual fund (or any other newly issued security).

Securities Exchange Act of 1934

The purchase and sale of mutual fund shares, as with all securities, are subject to the antifraud provisions of the Securities Exchange Act of 1934. This act serves in various ways to protect investors in mutual fund shares. It enables the SEC to impose minimum financial and accounting standards on broker-dealers engaged in interstate commerce and subjects them to periodic inspections. In addition, this act requires the SEC to supervise the national stock exchanges to prevent unlawful manipulation of securities prices, which helps protect investors in closed-end investment funds. The act also makes it unlawful to purchase or sell securities by fraudulent means in interstate commerce.

Investment Company Act of 1940

Mutual funds must register with the SEC under the Investment Company Act of 1940, which is a highly regulatory statute. This act, which is administered by the SEC and supplements the other state and federal laws, provides a comprehensive system of regulation for the protection of investors. The act was adopted after the SEC had made a thorough study of investment companies and their practices.

The law specifically avoids any attempt to interfere with the exercise of management's judgment in the selection of investments, and in no way does it purport to guarantee an investor against loss. It is aimed at preventing certain abuses and eliminating conflicts of interest on the part of those involved in managing the business of an investment company.

The intent of the Investment Company Act of 1940 is to

- provide investors with complete and accurate information as to the nature of investment company securities and the policies, financial responsibility and circumstances of investment companies and their management;
- ensure that investment companies are organized and operated for the benefit of all shareholders rather than for the benefit of officers, directors, investment advisers or other special interest groups;
- prevent inequitable provisions in investment company securities and protect the preferences and privileges of outstanding securities;

- prevent undue concentration of control through pyramiding and other devices, and discourage management by irresponsible persons;
- ensure sound accounting methods;
- require adequate assets or reserves for the conduct of business; and
- prevent major changes in organization or business without the consent of shareholders.

Update: Recognizing that the 1940 act may need modernization to fit current market realities, the staff of the SEC released a comprehensive 500-page study on investment company regulation in 1992. In the study, the staff recommended certain changes to the 1940 act, as well as its regulations, its existing interpretations and provisions of other federal securities laws regulating mutual funds. Some of the changes would require SEC rulemaking to accomplish regulatory approval, while other changes would require an act of Congress. Some of the recommendations contained in the study have been officially proposed, and some have been adopted.

Investment Advisers Act of 1940

The Investment Advisers Act of 1940 regulates the activities of investment advisers to mutual funds.

Investment Company Amendments Act of 1970

The Investment Company Amendments Act of 1970 formalized the first major revision in 30 years of the Investment Company Act of 1940. The major changes established by this act included new standards for management fees and mutual fund sales charges.

It is now provided that the price at which mutual fund shares are sold to the public shall not include "an excessive sales load." The task of defining parameters was assigned to the National Association of Securities Dealers (NASD). The top sales charge in the mutual fund industry today is ordinarily 8.5 percent of the total payment or 9.3 percent of the amount invested.

Insider Trading and Securities Fraud Enforcement Act of 1988

The 1988 act requires investment advisers and broker-dealers to develop and enforce procedures to prevent insider trading. It also broadens the SEC's authority regarding insider trading violations.

Market Reform Act of 1990

The Market Reform Act of 1990 gives the SEC emergency authority to halt trading on a securities exchange and to restrict such practices as program trading during periods of extreme market volatility. This law was enacted in response to the October 1987 market crash.

STATE LAWS

In addition to these federal statutes, most states have enacted *blue-sky laws* to regulate the sale of securities, including mutual funds, within individual states. They cannot be summarized briefly because of the wide variety of their provisions. A few states go so far as to regulate sales commissions and investment policies.

Since mutual funds are incorporated under state general corporation law, they are also regulated as to the mechanics by which a fund company conducts its business. These laws, which vary widely, are not designed necessarily to protect mutual fund shareholders. Nonetheless, they are an essential part of the total legal protection afforded security holders of mutual funds domiciled in the United States.

WATCH OUT FOR HIDDEN TAXES: TAXATION OF MUTUAL FUND SHAREHOLDERS

Unwary investors in many mutual funds will find that taxes can take a huge bite out of investment returns. Most mutual fund managers pay little attention to shareholder taxation. One of the things mutual funds overlook is the advantage that comes from postponing taxes on capital gains. Ironically, unmanaged index funds, which are discussed in more detail in Chapter 11, "Index Funds," have very strong after-tax performance. They do very little stock trading and merely try to track the performance of a market benchmark, such as the S&P 500 Composite Stock Index. Thus, their capital gains remain unrealized and, hence, not yet taxable. For this reason alone, index funds make a lot of sense for the taxable portion of a high-income investor's portfolio.

Mutual funds themselves don't usually pay taxes. In general, mutual fund shareholders are taxed as if they were direct owners of a proportionate interest in the fund's portfolio of securities.

Most mutual funds elect to qualify under Subchapter M of the Internal Revenue Code as a *regulated investment company,* thus avoiding the tax bite. To qualify under Subchapter M, a fund must meet several requirements. This includes distributing at least 90 percent of its taxable income each year and following various rules of asset diversification. It must also satisfy a requirement about the source of its income and comply with a restriction on short-term capital gains.

By qualifying as a regulated investment company, taxes are permitted to "flow through" to the mutual fund's shareholders. Thus, fund income is taxed only once, when it is received by the shareholder. This "one-level" tax results from the deduction that funds receive for amounts distributed to shareholders. To avoid any income tax at the fund level, mutual funds generally distribute all their income and capital gains to shareholders. Also, to avoid the imposition of an excise tax, a fund must generally distribute 98 percent of its income in the calendar year in which the income is earned.

One aspect of the flow-through tax treatment relates to the character of distributions received by shareholders. Normally, income from interest and dividends received by mutual funds is taxed to their shareholders as ordinary income, and long-term capital gains received by funds are taxed to shareholders as long-term capital gains. In like manner, tax-exempt income received by funds passes through to shareholders as tax-exempt income.

In this way, fund income is taxed only once, to fund shareholders, and not to the fund itself. Under Subchapter M, a mutual fund deducts from its income the amount that is distributed to shareholders.

In addition, as a mutual fund shareholder, whenever you sell or exchange fund shares, you may have a capital gain or loss that must be reported to the IRS. A capital gain or loss may be realized when you sell shares of a fund, write a check on a fund or exchange from one fund into another.

To calculate your gains and losses, it is necessary to know your cost basis. *Cost basis* is the term used by the IRS for the amount of money

FIGURE 5.1   Results of $10,000 Invested in Two Funds for Ten Years for High-Tax-Bracket Investor

	Total Value Before Taxes	Total Value After Taxes	Taxes Paid
Windsor Fund	$45,370	$30,760	32.2%
Vanguard Index Trust 500 Portfolio	$43,070	$35,360	17.9%

you have invested in your mutual fund shares. If you sell for more than your cost basis, you have a gain; if you sell for less than your cost basis, you have a loss.

The Effect of Hidden Taxes on Shareholders

A study by John B. Shoven and Joel M. Dickson of Stanford University's Center for Economic Policy Research found that for investors in the 148 largest growth and growth-and-income stock funds in the United States, taxes ate, on average, 24.22 percent of the return that a high-tax investor would have earned through the ten years ending December 31, 1992. Furthermore, that tax loss was *before* sale of the funds' shares, which would trigger additional taxes.

An investment in two successful large mutual funds presents an interesting contrast. Assume that a high-tax-bracket investor placed $10,000 in both Vanguard's Windsor Fund and the Vanguard Index Trust 500 Portfolio on January 1, 1983, using federal tax rates in effect during that time. Figure 5.1 illustrates both the before-tax and after-tax results for the ten-year period ending December 31, 1992, and assumes reinvestment of all dividend and capital gains distributions.

Sales charges are not a factor in Figure 5.1, since neither of these funds charges a load or fee to purchase. If the funds were sold at the end of the ten-year period, the index fund would be subject to greater taxes. Still, a high-tax-bracket investor would be better off with the index fund than with Windsor, even though Windsor had a better pre-tax performance. Because an index fund is passively rather than actively managed, very little taxable gains distributions are made while the investor holds the investment. The result in this case is that taxes paid by an index fund shareholder are only slightly more than half the taxes paid by the Windsor Fund shareholder.

FIGURE 5.2   Results of $10,000 Invested in Two Other Funds for
Ten Years for High-Tax-Bracket Investor

	Total Value Before Taxes	Total Value After Taxes	Taxes Paid
CGM Capital Development	$64,826	$43,239	33.3%
Vanguard Index Trust 500 Portfolio	$43,070	$35,360	17.9%

Unrealized Capital Gains

One of the treasures to be enjoyed by investors in mutual funds is
unrealized capital gains. An unrealized gain occurs when a mutual fund
buys a security that appreciates in price, but the fund has not yet sold
the security. Until the fund realizes the gain by selling the security, fund
shareholders don't have to pay taxes on the gain. When a gain is
deferred, it means the shareholder enjoys the return on those deferred
taxes until the security is sold. A powerful compounding effect takes
place when taxes are postponed.

When investment managers trade stocks in their portfolios in an
effort to improve performance and beat the broad market indexes,
immediate tax liability is incurred for fund shareholders, making it
even more difficult for the managers to outperform tax-efficient index
funds. According to Robert Arnott, president of First Quadrant Corporation, a money management firm, a mutual fund's annual pretax return
must be 2–3 percent better than an index fund just to break even after
taxes.

The goal in considering taxes is not necessarily to pay the least but
rather to end up with the most. For an example of how this works, let's
take a look at CGM Capital Development Fund. It isn't very efficient
with taxes, because the manager's heavy trading activity has led to
large capital gains payouts. But it is among the very best funds on an
after-tax basis simply because its pretax returns are so strong. Many
less successful funds make smaller distributions but have poorer results, because they just haven't made much money. Figure 5.2 illustrates how the very successful CGM Capital Development Fund has
produced high after-tax results in spite of its heavy trading and big
capital gains payouts. The results are compared with the Vanguard
Index Trust 500 Portfolio. It is assumed that all income and capital

gains distributions are reinvested. Taxes are based on federal tax rates in effect during that period.

It's clear that outstanding performance can cover a lot of taxes, so there is no fast rule to follow. Keep in mind only that payment of taxes on realized capital gains distributed to you as a shareholder can have a big impact on the ultimate performance of your investment.

What To Do

It might be said that investors should buy into the *least* tax-efficient funds on a historical basis with the idea that, because those funds have already paid out their gains in the form of distributions, a new shareholder won't be buying into past liabilities. On the other hand, efficient funds that build up large unrealized capital gains in their portfolios can carry with them enormous potential tax burdens for their shareholders.

An example of what can befall an unwary investor is illustrated by what happened a few years ago with IDS Growth Fund. In mid-1986, IDS Growth appeared to be a very attractive fund to include in a taxable portfolio. The fund made hardly any income payouts, and its strategy of low portfolio turnover resulted in minimal capital gains distributions during the previous four years. During those years the fund had pretty good results, with a 32.7 percent return in 1982, 13.5 percent in 1983, −18.5 percent in 1984 and 36.2 percent in 1985. But from a tax standpoint, to have bought in 1986 would have been a terrible choice.

IDS Growth realized and paid out large gains in 1986, 1987 and 1989. The distributions were greater than 10 percent in each of those years. In 1990, new management came in and trimmed back big, successful positions in Wal-Mart and Philip Morris. Shareholders got stuck with a capital gains payout of $6.98 on shares with a net asset value of $21. Imagine the situation of the poor shareholder in a 31 percent tax bracket who bought shares the day before that payout was declared. He or she got hit with a 33 percent distribution and lost 10 percent of the investment to taxes the day after making his or her purchase.

One simple precaution you as an investor can take is to determine when capital gains distributions are normally paid on a fund being considered for purchase. Then make a judgment as to whether it might make sense to wait until after the distribution has been declared before buying into the fund.

Tax-Loss Carryforwards

Mutual fund investors can occasionally purchase shares in which some portion of future gains can be offset by past losses because of the potential for tax-loss carryforwards. This can occur after a sharp market retreat. Such a hidden advantage was offered by many funds following the 1987 stock market crash and was available in many European equity funds in late 1993. So, although mutual funds normally give an investor less control over the timing of distributions than would be available with direct ownership of securities, you can sometimes find hidden tax advantages in some funds.

SUMMARY

While there is no way to protect investors from losses due to poor management or market fluctuations, federal and state laws do provide for appropriate disclosure to investors of potential returns and risks associated with individual funds. These laws are designed to ensure that mutual funds are managed and operated in the interests of their shareholders and that investors receive information that will enable them to make appropriate investment decisions.

By qualifying as regulated investment companies under Subchapter M of the Internal Revenue Code, mutual fund income is generally taxed only once—when it is received by the shareholder. Mutual fund shareholders are taxed as if they were the direct owners of a proportionate interest in the fund's portfolio of securities.

Taxes are an issue that serious investors cannot ignore; they can take a large bite out of annual returns. Most mutual funds pay little or no attention to shareholder taxation, so the investor must. On the other hand, your investment strategy should not be dictated entirely by tax implications. Taken to an extreme, the only way to avoid taxes is to avoid investing and, therefore, all profits. Like risk, then, taxes should be managed within the context of your overall objectives.

Chapter 6

Using a Mutual Fund Prospectus

The most important source of information afforded mutual fund investors is the *prospectus*. The law stipulates that the offering of any mutual fund for sale to the public must be accompanied or preceded by a prospectus.

A prospectus sets forth concisely the information that a prospective investor should know about a specific mutual fund before investing. For more detailed information, a *statement of additional information* may be obtained without charge by writing or calling the mutual fund company on its toll-free line. The statement, which is incorporated by reference into the prospectus, has been filed with the Securities and Exchange Commission (SEC). Each prospectus also is required to display prominently the following statement: "These securities have not been approved or disapproved by the Securities and Exchange Commission or any state securities commission, nor has the Securities and Exchange Commission or any state securities commission passed upon the accuracy or adequacy of this prospectus. Any representation to the contrary is a criminal offense."

Before permitting a mutual fund company to offer a fund for sale to the public, the SEC examines the statement to be sure that it contains all the information that is required by law. When that requirement has been met, the fund company is notified that it may offer its fund for sale to the public.

WHAT THE PROSPECTUS CONTAINS: THE SCHWAB 1000 FUND

For illustration purposes, certain information contained in the April 30, 1993, prospectus of the Schwab 1000 Fund (distributed by Charles Schwab & Co., Inc.) is set forth in the following paragraphs. You will find this same type of data in the prospectuses of most mutual funds.

Investment Objectives and Policies

The first page of the 1993 prospectus of the Schwab 1000 Fund sets forth in typical fashion the information a typical investor wants to know about the investment objectives and policies of the fund. It states that the Schwab 1000 Fund "attempts to match the price and dividend performance (total return) of common stocks of United States companies as represented by the Schwab 1000 Index (the 'Index'), an index composed of the common stocks of the 1,000 largest United States corporations (excluding investment companies). The Fund is a diversified investment portfolio of Schwab Investments, a no-load, open-end, management investment company."

The Fund's investment *objective* is to provide a total return that matches that of the Schwab 1000 Index. The Fund's investment *policy*—how it intends to accomplish its objective—is described in detail further in the prospectus: "The Fund will follow an 'indexing' strategy under which stocks are purchased or sold in order to match the composition of the Index. Accordingly, the Sub-Adviser will not select securities for the Fund's investment portfolio based upon traditional economic financial and market analyses and/or forecasting."

The prospectus goes on to state that the fund will be managed to minimize costs and increase shareholders' total return. It expects to do that by adopting policies designed to keep its portfolio turnover rate as low as possible. Lower portfolio turnover acts to minimize associated transaction costs as well as the level of current realized capital gains. The purpose of this is to reduce shareholders' current tax liability for capital gains and increase their total return. The portfolio's turnover rate for the fiscal year ended December 31, 1992, was 1.05 percent. This contrasts significantly with the average mutual fund's turnover rate of 85 percent each year.

Additional policy information provided in the Schwab 1000 Fund prospectus covers the types of securities in which the fund will invest.

In this case, the fund intends to invest substantially all its assets in stocks that constitute the Schwab 1000 Index and, under normal market conditions, will invest at least 80 percent of its total assets in index stocks. It explains conditions under which the fund may omit or remove an index stock from its portfolio if the portfolio manager believes the stock to be insufficiently liquid or believes the merit of the investment has been substantially impaired by extraordinary events or financial conditions.

Other portfolio management considerations, such as the need to accommodate cash flows resulting from the purchase and sale of fund shares, are covered in the prospectus with an explanation of what type of action can be taken.

Fund Expenses

The prospectus of each fund includes a table illustrating all the expenses and fees you would incur as a shareholder of the fund.

Shareholder transaction expenses include any sales load imposed on purchases and those imposed on reinvested dividends, redemption fees and exchange fees. In the case of most no-load funds, there are no charges for any of these activities. Other funds will indicate their charges as a percentage of NAV or dollar amount.

The Schwab 1000 Fund prospectus lists the following charges:

Shareholder Transaction Expenses

Sales Load Imposed on Purchases	None
Sales Load Imposed on Reinvested Dividends	None
Deferred Sales Load	None
Early Withdrawal Fee	0.50%
Exchange Fee	None

Annual Fund Operating Expenses
(as a percentage of average net assets)

Management Fee	0.30%
12b-1 Fees	None
Other Expenses (after expense reimbursement)	0.25%
Total Fund Operating Expenses	0.55%
Annual Account Maintenance Fee	0.00%

Footnotes indicate that the early withdrawal fee applies only to redemption or exchange of shares held less than six months.

Selected Per-Share Data and Ratios

This prospectus provides a table with selected per-share data and ratios beginning on April 2, 1991, the date the fund was established, through August 31, 1993. Figure 6.1 reproduces this information from page 4 of the Schwab 1000 Fund prospectus. It permits an investor to see the fund's financial results for the period shown.

Explanation of the Schwab 1000 Index

Since it is the policy of the Schwab 1000 Index Fund to replicate the Schwab 1000 Index, attention is given in the prospectus to the nature of the index, how it is maintained and updated, and the reporting of its daily performance.

To be included in the index, a company must satisfy all of the following criteria:

1. It must be an "operating company" (not an investment company) incorporated in the United States, its territories or possessions.
2. A liquid market for its common stock shares must exist on the New York Stock Exchange (NYSE), American Stock Exchange (AMEX) or the Nasdaq National Market System (NMS).
3. Its market value must place it among the top 1,000 such companies as measured by market capitalization. A particular stock's weighting in the index is based on its relative total market value (market price per share multiplied by the number of shares outstanding) divided by the total market value of the index. As of December 31, 1992, the aggregate market capitalization of the stocks of those companies that constitute the index was approximately $3.7 trillion.

The prospectus states that the index represented approximately 86 percent of the total market value of all publicly traded U.S. companies as of December 31, 1992. The index was developed and will be maintained by Schwab to represent the total return of publicly traded common stocks of U.S. companies and serve as a standard of comparison for the fund's performance.

At least quarterly, Schwab reviews and occasionally revises, as appropriate, the list of companies whose securities are included in the index. The firm will also modify the index as necessary to account for corporate actions, such as new issues, repurchases, stock dividends

FIGURE 6.1 Selected Per-Share Data and Ratios from Schwab 1000 Fund's 1993 Prospectus Dated April 30, 1993

FINANCIAL HIGHLIGHTS

The following information with respect to per share data and ratios has been audited by Price Waterhouse, independent accountants, whose unqualified report covering each of the periods presented is incorporated by reference from the Statement of Additional Information. This information should be read in conjunction with the financial statements and accompanying notes which are also incorporated by reference to the Statement of Additional Information.

	Eight months ended 8/31/93[1]	Year ended 12/31/92	Period from 4/2/91 to 12/31/91
Net asset value at beginning of period	$ 11.96	11.26	10.00
Income from Investment Operations			
Net investment income	0.17	0.24	0.15
Net realized and unrealized gain on investments	0.79	0.71	1.26
Total from investment operations	0.96	0.95	1.41
Less Distributions			
Dividends from net investment income	(0.12)	(0.25)	(0.15)
Dividends from realized gain on investments	—	—	—
Total distributions	(0.12)	(0.25)	(0.15)
Net asset value at end of period	$ 12.80	$ 11.96	$ 11.26
Total return	8.06%	8.52%	14.25%
Ratios/Supplemental Data			
Net assets, end of period (thousands)	$515,272	$370,980	$192,206
Ratio of expenses to average net assets	0.45%[2]	0.35%	—[2]
Ratio of net investment income to average net assets	2.21%[2]	2.45%	3.21%[2]
Portfolio turnover rate	1%	1%	1%

Note: During the periods indicated above, the Investment Manager reduced its fee and absorbed certain expenses of the Fund. Had these fees and expenses not been reduced and absorbed, the ratio of expenses to average net assets for the periods ended August 31, 1993, December 31, 1992 and 1991 would have been 0.49%[2], 0.52% and 1.05%[2], respectively, and the ratio of net investment income to average net assets of the Fund would have been 2.17%[2], 2.28% and 2.16%[2], respectively.

[1] In 1993, the fiscal year end of Schwab Investments was changed from December 31 to August 31.
[2] Annualized.

Source: Charles Schwab & Co., Inc.

and/or splits, tenders, mergers, swaps, spinoffs or Chapter 11 bankruptcy filings.

Other Important Information

Mutual fund prospectuses contain a host of other information that is important to potential investors. The following information is typically found in most prospectuses:

Performance Record. Investment results for several periods throughout a fund's lifetime help an investor see how money invested in a fund has fared in the past. Some funds provide a complete history of their investment returns. In the case of relatively new funds, such as Schwab 1000 Fund, historical return data may be omitted.

Opening an Account. Each prospectus includes information on how to open an account and purchase shares in the fund, and will be accompanied by an Account Registration Form. Your purchase must be equal to or greater than the minimum initial investment. Depending on the fund, this may range from as little as $50 to more than $50,000. Most funds can be started in the $1,000–$3,000 range.

Fund shares may be purchased by mail, by wire, by exchange from another fund in the same family of funds, directly from your checking account, and through other means that are explained in the prospectus.

When opening a new account, you must select one of three distribution options:

1. *Automatic reinvestment option.* Both dividends and capital gains distributions will be reinvested in additional shares of the fund.
2. *Cash dividend option.* Your dividends will be paid in cash and capital gains will be reinvested in additional fund shares.
3. *All-cash option.* Dividend and capital gains distributions will be paid in cash.
4. Some funds permit distributions to be reinvested automatically in shares of another fund of the same family. Fidelity Investments calls this Directed Dividend Option®.

Important Tax Note: If you purchase shares shortly before a distribution of dividends or capital gains, a portion of your investment will be returned to you as a taxable distribution (regardless of whether you are reinvesting your distributions or taking them in cash).

Fund Management. This section explains who is responsible for overall management of the fund, as well as who provides the professional investment supervision. Information about the organizations and individuals providing management is given, including their background and professional credentials.

The fee structure to be paid for management services and how it is to be charged is set forth. In the case of the Schwab 1000 Fund, according to the prospectus, ". . . the Investment Manager receives from the Fund an annual fee, payable monthly, of 0.30% of the Fund's average daily net assets not in excess of $500 million and 0.22% of such assets over $500 million. For the foreseeable future, and, in any event, at least through December 31, 1994, the Investment Manager guarantees that the Fund's total fund operating expenses will not exceed 0.55%."

Share Price Calculation. In this section, the prospectus explains how and when share prices are calculated. The price of a fund's shares on any given day is their *net asset value* (NAV). This figure is computed by dividing the total market value of a fund's investments and other assets on that day, less any liabilities, by the number of shares outstanding. The NAV of the shares of a fund is determined on each day the New York Stock Exchange is open for trading at 4:00 PM Eastern time.

Tax-Advantaged Retirement Plans. Most mutual fund companies offer tax-advantaged retirement plans to their shareholders. The following plans are among the most popular:

- *Individual retirement plan*—A plan offering people with earned income the opportunity to compound earnings on a tax-deferred basis. This type of plan is fully covered in Chapter 14, "A Tax-Favored Retirement Plan for You."
- *Keogh plan*—A tax-advantaged plan for self-employed individuals and their employees that permits the employer to make annual tax-deductible contributions of up to $30,000.
- *Corporate retirement plans*—Retirement plans for large or small corporate entities that can help a company attract and retain valuable employees.

Purchase of Shares in the Fund. A prospectus will explain how shares may be purchased and whether you must go through a registered representative or may buy shares directly from the fund. Other information you may need to know is included, such as minimum investment requirements and methods of purchasing shares (i.e., by phone, by mail, in person, or by automatic investment).

Exchanges Between Funds. Shares can be sold by exchanging into another mutual fund in the same family of funds. It is important to remember that this constitutes a taxable event, and any gain or loss is reportable for income tax purposes. (Many funds charge a small fee—e.g., $5—for exchanges.)

Redeeming Shares. Mutual funds may be redeemed at the NAV per share that is next determined after receipt of proper redemption instructions. You may redeem your shares by telephone or by mail. Telephone redemption orders received prior to 4:00 PM (Eastern time) on any business day will be redeemed at the NAV determined for that day.

Automatic Reinvestment Plan. A fast, convenient way to make regular mutual fund investments to an account already established is the *automatic reinvestment plan*. Investments may be made by authorized transfers from a bank checking or savings account and by direct deposit of all or a portion of a payroll or government check. Depending on the requirements of the fund, such investments can be made twice monthly, monthly or quarterly. Minimum amounts are stipulated in the prospectus.

Miscellaneous Information. The prospectus also contains other information that you will find helpful in establishing and maintaining a mutual fund investment:

- *Signature guarantees*—For certain written transaction requests, most funds require that your signature be guaranteed by a bank, trust company or member of a domestic stock exchange. Having a document notarized does not qualify as a signature guarantee.
- *Certificates*—Most funds will issue share certificates on request.
- *Canceling trades*—A trade received by the fund in writing or by telephone, if believed to be authentic, may not normally be canceled. This would include purchases, exchanges or redemptions.

SUMMARY

The prospectus is a useful tool and should not be overlooked by the investor. The law requires that an offering of a mutual fund be preceded or accompanied by a prospectus. Most prospectuses today are easily understood and contain a wealth of information, including investment objectives, expenses and fees, historical performance data, a guide on how to open an account, and the various services furnished by the fund.

Chapter 7

Low-Cost Ways To Uncover More Information

W hether you plan to make just a single mutual fund investment or to maintain an ongoing investment program, it is important to have complete and accurate information. Only then is sound judgment even possible.

One way to obtain good information is to contact all the funds listed in our directory and ask them to send you prospectuses and other material (which they will gladly do), and then undertake your own analytical studies. But why reinvent the wheel? Hundreds of professional analysts spend all their working hours doing just that, and the results of their efforts are available to you, often at no cost!

Most public libraries subscribe to one or more mutual fund research services. The larger ones will have several. Each service takes its own approach, but they all strive for accuracy and completeness. Usually they are written in a style that is easy for the nonprofessional, part-time investor to understand. Look them over, and use the ones that suit you best. A little study will give you the confidence you need to trust in your own judgment. This will generally work out much better than investing on a tip, someone else's enthusiasm or the advice of a salesperson who will earn a commission from your decision.

It may be that you would like to have the convenience of a personal copy of one or more services. Some, such as the special editions of *Barron's* and *Forbes,* are inexpensive; others can be quite pricey. So you will probably want to make use of your public library, at least initially.

MAGAZINE PUBLICATIONS

Following are some of the leading publications and services that have gained the widest appeal.

Barron's

This national business and financial weekly is available by subscription and at newsstands.

Weekly: publishes annual and weekly price ranges and closing prices, weekly changes, latest income and capital gain distributions with record and payment dates, and last twelve months distributions. Includes Lipper mutual fund performance average for major fund types. Also lists taxable and tax-free money market funds, with asset size, average maturity of securities, and seven-day yields.

Quarterly: publishes special mutual fund sections in February, May, August and November featuring the Lipper Gauge of Mutual Fund Performance, with individual fund performance, list of averages, quarterly winners and losers, and industry news.

Forbes

The *Annual Mutual Fund Ratings,* published each year in September (available by subscription and at newsstands), features detailed review and performance evaluations of individual funds showing total return, yield, assets, sales charge and annual expenses. The annual ratings issue groups funds in categories: stock funds, balanced funds, foreign stock funds, foreign bond funds, bond and preferred stock funds, municipal bond funds and money market funds. A listing of fund distributors is also provided.

Research and Statistical Services

CDA/Wiesenberger Investment Companies Service
CDA Investment Technologies, Inc.
1355 Piccard Drive
Rockville, MD 20850
800-232-2285

Includes the annual volume *Investment Companies* and the monthly *Mutual Funds Update. Investment Companies* is a 1,200-page hardcover reference volume published each spring. The "bible" of the industry for over 50 years, *Investment Companies* is the most complete single source of information on investment companies. It covers more than 4,300 mutual funds, money market funds, unit investment trusts, variable annuity separate accounts and closed-end companies. *Mutual Funds Update* provides a performance review and analysis on mutual funds, money market funds and closed-end funds. It also includes *Panorama,* an annual directory and guide to mutual funds. *Panorama* features ten years of performance information and shareholder data, including fees and expenses, investment minimums, special services, addresses, telephone numbers and investment advisers.

Donoghue's Mutual Funds Almanac, Moneyletter, Money Fund Report
IBC/Donoghue
290 Eliot Street
Box 9104
Ashland, MA 01721-9104
800-343-5413

Designed for individual and corporate investors. Include a directory, toll-free numbers and ten-year performance on more than 1,100 funds. Have special section on betas and investment risk. Provide information on no-load funds, low-load funds and load funds. No closed-end funds are included.

Johnson's Charts
Johnson's Charts, Inc.
175 Bridle Path
Williamsville, NY 14221
716-626-0845

Publishes graphs and charts analyzing long-term performance of individual mutual funds. Included is information on historical income and capital gains payments, share price trends, and total returns with and without dividend reinvestments.

Lipper Analytical Services, Inc.
47 Maple Street
Suite 101
Summit, NJ 07901
908-273-2772

Provides statistical services on the mutual fund industry. Widely quoted and used by other financial publications.

Morningstar Mutual Funds
Morningstar, Inc.
225 W. Wacker Drive
Chicago, IL 60606
800-876-5005

Morningstar Mutual Funds is perhaps the most comprehensive, timely and useful source for mutual fund information. A comprehensive amount of vital information for tracking, analyzing, comparing and choosing mutual funds is condensed on a single page for each of over 1,200 mutual funds and is presented in one hard-cover binder. Every two weeks Morningstar provides subscribers with a 32-page report summarizing the current performance of all funds covered, plus a new issue of more than 120 updated full-page fund reports. *Morningstar Mutual Funds* is available for $55 for a three-month trial. The annual subscription price is $395.

Morningstar also publishes the *Mutual Fund Sourcebook,* the *Mutual Fund Performance Report,* the *Morningstar Mutual Fund 500,* the *5-Star Investor,* the *Morningstar Closed-End Funds,* the *Closed-End Fund Sourcebook,* the *Mutual Fund Styles of Investing Chart,* the *Variable Annuity/Life Sourcebook,* the *Variable Annuity/Life Performance Report,* *Morningstar Japan* and a variety of computer disk products.

The Mutual Fund Encyclopedia
Investment Information Services, Inc.
680 N. Lake Shore Drive
Tower Suite 2038
Chicago, IL 60611
800-326-6941

This annual publication profiles more than 3,000 no-load, low-load and load funds. Each profile gives a detailed statement of objectives and strategies and provides key financial statistics, including assets under management, current yield, portfolio turnover ratio, risk factors, and year-by-year and five-year total returns. To help decision making further, the minimum initial investment for each fund is noted, as well as the cost of investing in each fund and the company address and toll-free number.

Mutual Fund Profiles
Standard & Poor's Corporation
25 Broadway
New York, NY 10004
800-221-5277
212-208-8812

This publication is jointly produced with Lipper Analytical Services, Inc. Individual mutual fund profiles include statistical data; investment policy, performance and evaluation; and comparison with S&P 500 results and top holdings.

Investment Company Institute
1401 H Street NW
Suite 1200
Washington, DC 20005
202-326-5800

The Investment Company Institute is the national association of the American mutual fund industry. It produces a number of publications that an investor will find helpful. Following are two of the most useful.

Mutual Fund Fact Book.   A basic guide to the mutual fund industry. It provides annually updated facts and figures on the U.S. mutual fund industry, including trends in sales, assets and performance. It outlines the history and growth of the fund industry and its policies, operations, regulation, services and shareholders. It is priced at $15 and is available in bookstores or from the Institute.

Directory of Mutual Funds.   Published annually by the Institute. In addition to mutual fund names, addresses and telephone numbers (many are toll-free), the *Directory* lists each fund's assets, initial and subsequent investment requirements, fees charged, where to buy shares and other pertinent details. An extensive introductory text serves as a short course in mutual fund investing.

The Value Line Mutual Funds Survey
220 E. 42nd Street
New York, NY 10017
800-284-7607

The survey, produced in two binders, covers 2,000 funds encompassing a wide range of investment objectives, from aggressive growth to tax-free income. Full-page analyses are provided for 1,500 established mutual funds through biweekly ratings and reports, which include performance data, portfolio data, tax data and so on. Every fund is updated three times a year. The annual subscription cost is $295, while a three-month trial is available for $49.

SUMMARY

It may be an exaggeration to say that anyone can become an expert in anything in six months, but it is true that most investors will find it surprisingly easy to become competent in mutual funds by utilizing the information in this book, visiting a local library for research information (such as those sources listed above), and calling mutual fund companies for prospectuses and other material they gladly make available. Don't be afraid to take the step. You can do it!

Part Two

Building Your Wealth

Chapter 8

Growing Rich
Without a Broker

One of the wonders of mutual funds is their cost efficiency. The economies of scale enjoyed by large investment companies are passed on to the individual investor in the form of low expenses, which translates into higher investment returns (assuming able management). In addition, informed investors can now buy into many of these diversified, professionally managed portfolios of stocks and bonds at no cost. You can do this by investing directly in no-load mutual funds without going through a middleman. No-load mutual funds are offered for sale directly to the public and without a sales charge, thus avoiding fees and charges not relevant to investment performance.

NO-LOAD FUNDS

The first mutual funds to be offered without commission came out in the early 1920s. Now more than 500 no-load mutual funds are priced daily in the mutual fund sections of *The New York Times, The Wall Street Journal, Barron's* and other major newspapers.

More and more investors are buying mutual funds directly from fund companies and avoiding payment of any sales fees or commissions. Unlike opening an account at a bank, mutual fund investors can open an account and make investments without ever setting foot into their fund's offices or even knowing where they are located! This is done by dealing with no-load mutual fund companies. No-load funds are exactly like load funds in every respect except that shares of no-load funds are purchased directly and without the addition of a sales commission.

According to the *100% No-Load Mutual Fund Council,* total sales of mutual funds that are sold directly have increased steadily. They rose from 34.8 percent of all mutual fund sales in March 1991 to 37.3 percent in February 1992 and then to 42.4 percent in March 1992.

Today, the distinction between load and no-load funds has become somewhat blurred. Some funds considered to be no-load do, in fact, levy certain charges that are not related to the cost of investment management. These charges may include 12b-l sales distribution fees, low-loads, back-end loads, contingent deferred sales charges, and fixed redemption charges or exit fees. A recent study by *Morningstar, Inc.* in Chicago, Illinois, found that 28 percent of all mutual funds are pure no-loads, 8 percent are no-loads with 12b-1 fees, 10 percent have back-end loads and 12b-1 fees, 34 percent are front-end loads plus 12b-1 fees, and 20 percent are front-end load only.

Sales Charges

A sales commission, or *load,* does not compensate a fund's investment managers. Fund managers are compensated through a management fee that is charged against the fund. All funds, load and no-load, have management fees. In the case of a load fund, the sales charge is made in addition to the annual management fee, which generally runs between 0.5 and 1 percent of the fund's assets. Independent studies have consistently shown there is no difference in performance, on average, between the two types when the load is disregarded.

The maximum permitted sales charge (load) is 8.5 percent. However, since an 8.5 percent load is stated as a percentage of the total purchase price (net asset value + sales charge), the ratio of the load to the net amount invested in the fund is actually 9.3 percent. For example, if an investor purchases shares of a load fund for $10,000, $850 goes to the sales organization; the balance, $9,150, is actually invested in the fund and is the net asset value of the shares purchased. The $850 lost to the investor represents 9.3 percent of the value of the shares he has bought.

Many load funds have reduced sales charges to the 3–5 percent range, with the difference being made up through so-called back-end

FIGURE 8.1 $10,000 Invested at an Assumed Rate of 10 Percent

	Net Amount Invested	Value in Ten Years
Load Fund	$ 9,150	$23,735
No-Load Fund	$10,000	$25,939

loads, contingent deferred sales charges and/or 12b-1 fees. From an investment performance standpoint, the effect of a load is felt throughout the term of a shareholder's investment. This is because less money has been at work than would have been the case if the full amount of the purchase price were invested in a no-load fund.

The difference in growth of an investment of $10,000 in two comparable funds—one with an 8.5 percent load, the other no-load—can be dramatic. Over ten years, with an assumed 10 percent rate of return, the no-load fund earns $2,204 more. Figure 8.1 illustrates how this works.

The load fund investor was $850 behind at the beginning (8.5 percent of $10,000) and forever loses the 10 percent growth on that portion of his or her investment. Over an investing lifetime, the difference becomes greatly magnified.

Other Charges and Fees

Other charges made by mutual fund companies include contingent sales charges, exit fees, 12b-1 distribution fees and dividend reinvestment fees.

- *Contingent sales charges* (often called *back-end loads*) are paid to selling organizations and salespeople and can be as much as 5–6 percent for shareholders redeeming shares in the first year, declining by 1 percent per year for the next 5 to 6 years.
- *Exit fees* are the charges some management companies make either to withdraw or switch from one fund under its management to another such fund.
- *12b-1 distribution fees* permit a fund's management to use fund assets to pay for distribution costs, including advertising, distribution of fund literature such as prospectuses and annual reports, and sales commissions paid to brokers who distribute the fund.

FIGURE 8.2   The Relationship Between Performance and Expenses

	Five-Year Average Fund Performance
Annual expenses less than 0.5%	+42%
Annual expenses between 0.5% and 1.0%	+41%
Annual expenses between 1.0% and 2.0%	+37%
Annual expenses of 2.0% or more	+16%

Source: Reprinted by permission of *Mutual Fund Forecaster*, $49 per year, published by The Institute for Econometric Research, 3471 N. Federal, Fort Lauderdale, FL 33306; 800-442-9000.

The 12b-1 fees range from as low as 0.25 percent to as much as 1.00 percent per year and are deducted from a fund's assets.
- *Dividend reinvestment fees* are the charges imposed by a few fund managers for reinvesting the shareholder's dividend distributions.

Performance Results

In the end, able management is the best key to investment success. But given comparable managers, an investor is unquestionably better off investing in a fund with low costs and without sales commissions or fees.

An independent study of the impact of fees and charges on performance by *Mutual Fund Forecaster*, an investment advisory newsletter in Fort Lauderdale, Florida, analyzed the latest five-year track records of nearly 800 equity mutual funds. They found that the average pure no-load fund was up 38 percent, while the average load fund was up 35 percent. As might be expected, the higher the loads, the worse the performance. Another interesting aspect of the study involved expenses. One might think that the more shareholders pay for management, the better the performance would be. But the results indicated the opposite: The higher a fund's expense ratio, the lower its average performance, as shown in Figure 8.2.

Other studies bear out the fact that generally there is an inverse relationship between expenses and performance. Mutual funds with no 12b-1 fees have a higher performance than funds that charge such fees. Further, the higher the 12b-1 fee levied, the worse the performance. On average, you can't buy better performance by paying higher fees of any kind. There are certainly exceptions, but the burden of proof lies with the salesperson or organization asking you to pay a load or higher expenses.

BUILDING YOUR OWN PORTFOLIO

No investment is ideal for everyone, but mutual funds come close, as attested to by their popularity. The Investment Company Institute, an industry trade group, reports that 27 percent of U.S. households owned mutual funds in 1992, up from just 6 percent in 1980. Half of those households had an annual income of less than $50,000. Mutual fund shareholders have found that they can participate in an investment vehicle that provides professional management at relatively low cost, with diversification, compounding of income and liquidity.

After having decided that mutual funds have the characteristics that meet your particular needs, the next step is to select the ones best suited to you.

Chasing the High Flyers

A warning that every mutual fund investor should keep in mind is that past performance is no guarantee of future success. Studies conducted over many years have shown that today's winner may well become tomorrow's loser. The folly of making a habit of buying shares of mutual funds after they have had a banner year or two is illustrated in Figure 8.3, which identifies certain funds that had outstanding returns for one or two years, only to lag badly in the next.

In each case, except for INVESCO Strategic Health Sciences Portfolio, these top-performing funds did substantially better than the S&P 500 Index one year, then fell behind the index in the following year.

Do not infer from these examples, however, that funds invariably follow a good performance with a poor one. The purpose of Figure 8.3 is simply to raise a red flag of warning. Sometimes there are reasons that funds may do well in one year and falter the next. It may have more to do with luck or changing investment styles than inept management.

Market sectors come and go in terms of investment favor. Mutual funds that are heavily invested in a particular industry will be positively or adversely affected by events in that sector. A good example is the health-care industry, whose stocks soared in 1989 through 1991, then

FIGURE 8.3   Mutual Fund Total Returns in Successive Years

Fund	1988	1989
Babson Enterprise	32.47%	22.46%
Mutual Shares	30.92	14.93
Neuwirth	29.59	16.80
S&P 500 Index	**16.60**	**31.68**
	1989	**1990**
Lexington Strategic Investment	61.22%	–43.35%
Sherman, Dean	47.27	–44.14
Twentieth Century Vista	52.20	–15.73
S&P 500 Index	**31.68**	**– 3.12**
	1990	**1991**
INVESCO Strategic Health Sciences Portfolio	25.79%	91.80%
Fontaine Capital Appreciation	6.13	11.81
Mathers	10.43	9.45
S&P 500 Index	**– 3.12**	**30.48**
	1991	**1992**
INVESCO Strategic Health Sciences Portfolio	91.80%	–14.40%
Scudder Development	71.93	– 1.94
Twentieth Century Vista	73.69	– 2.13
S&P 500 Index	**30.48**	**7.62**

fell out of favor in 1992. This was reflected in the performance of Invesco Strategic Health Sciences Portfolio. During a period of market exuberance, it produced a total return for shareholders of 59.48 percent in 1989, 25.75 percent in 1990 and 91.80 percent in 1991. In 1992, however, it lost over 14 percent of its value, and by October of 1993 it had given up another 15.53 percent. For an investor buying shares of this fund, timing was of critical importance.

It is also helpful to understand the effect volatility can have on the value of your investment. The year-to-year movement of Lexington Strategic Investment Fund in 1989 and 1990 provides a good example of this effect, though an extreme one. A $10,000 investment in the beginning of 1989 would have had a value of $16,122 on December 31 as a result of the 61.22 percent total return in that year. In 1990, however, the 43.35 percent loss would have reduced the investment value to $9,133! While the percentage loss in 1990 was much less than the gain in 1989, it was applied against a larger invested value.

Nearly equal up-and-down performances come out even worse. In 1989, Sherman, Dean Fund was up 47.27 percent, increasing the value of a $10,000 investment to $14,727. But a loss of 44.14 percent in 1990 brought the value down to $8,226. Despite what you might think, a return of 50 percent in one year followed by a 50 percent decline in the next does not make you even. In fact, it leaves you with only 75 percent of your original investment.

Spreading the Risk

The prudent investor reduces risk through diversification. You can do this in two basic ways: (1) by investing money in different types of financial instruments, and (2) by diversifying within each type. A list of ten investment opportunities follows, beginning with the safest and continuing to the most speculative:

1. Federally insured certificates of deposit (CDs)
2. Life insurance company guaranteed annuities
3. U.S. Treasury securities (subject to fluctuation in market value)
4. Money market funds
5. Investment-grade bonds
6. Lower-grade bonds
7. Preferred and common stocks
8. Real estate
9. Limited partnerships
10. Commodities

Mutual funds provide access to most of these investments, and often within the same family of funds. The large mutual fund groups provide a nearly complete range of investment opportunities and risk profiles. Part III, "The Wide World of Mutual Funds," includes detailed information on 29 types of mutual funds, with a recommended fund in each category. Starting with the data provided in that section, you should have no trouble constructing a well-diversified portfolio suited to your own objectives.

Time Your Purchases To Avoid Unnecessary Taxes

Investors sometimes try to capture an extra income or capital gains distribution by purchasing mutual fund shares just before an expected payout is to be made. This should generally be avoided.

Mutual funds usually pay income and capital gains distributions at predetermined times—monthly, quarterly or annually. You may be tempted to buy shares before the distribution is made in order to increase investment return. However, in the case of capital gains and usually for income dividends, the net asset value (NAV) of a share will drop by the exact amount of the distribution on the day it is made. Thus, if shares are purchased in time to receive the distribution, the investor is even: There is no gain. What the investor does have, though, is a tax liability based on the amount of the distribution. Payment of an income or capital gains distribution is a taxable event and will cost the investor money. You can easily avoid this problem by waiting until the day after the distribution is effective to make a purchase.

The tax penalty for buying shares too soon can be most severe with equity funds, which often distribute large capital gains just before or just after December 31. In a strong stock market, where a fund has realized substantial capital gains on stocks it has sold, it may pay a capital gains distribution of as much as 20 percent of the share value. The share price will then drop by that amount. An investor who purchased shares shortly before the distribution will be faced with a substantial income tax bill on what has turned out to be a phantom gain.

Even in the case of bond funds, where income dividends ordinarily are paid monthly, find out when the next dividend is to be paid, and then decide whether it is better to invest now or wait until after the distribution is made.

Keep two factors in mind:

1. Other things being equal, share prices tend to move up as a dividend payment date approaches.
2. After a dividend is paid and the share price drops, you can buy more shares for the same dollar investment. You can then benefit from greater future dividends on the shares you own.

Develop a Plan

Mutual funds represent a unique way to grow rich. You can quite readily put together a portfolio of funds that represent a wide variety of investment alternatives. Your success depends on patience and common sense.

Safety Net.   First, develop a two-part financial safety net. *In allocating your assets among the various alternatives, consider your need for ready cash.* It has been said that one should keep about six months of income in cash or cash equivalents. A sudden illness, the loss of a job, an accident or some other unexpected need for cash might upset a long-term investment program that lacks sufficient cash reserves. Money market funds are an excellent vehicle for this purpose.

Next, consider the portion of your funds that you want to feel absolutely comfortable with from a safety standpoint, and to which you won't need immediate access. Such funds should earn a reasonable rate of return and should not be subject to severe market fluctuations. The percentage you allocate depends on your own individual needs, goals and personal attitudes. Mutual funds that invest in intermediate-term U.S. government securities or investment-grade corporate bonds might be appropriate for this purpose.

Balance Between Growth and Income.   After constructing the financial safety net part of your portfolio, you can turn to more aggressive mutual funds. The two main objectives that mutual funds meet best are growth and income. Think in terms of the balance you want to maintain between these two broad objectives and the amount of risk you are able to tolerate.

Trustees responsible for the investment of large pools of money, such as pension and profit-sharing plans, set specific percentages of their funds to be invested in stocks, bonds and cash equivalents. These are matters of investment policy and are subject to change over time as economic or market conditions warrant. A typical allocation among these broad classes of assets might be 50 percent in stocks, 35 percent in bonds and 15 percent in cash reserves. The prudent investor will also plan a strategy and develop a simple investment formula, then stick with it.

THE MAGIC OF DOLLAR COST AVERAGING

"Don't buy now. The market's too high." "Don't buy now. The market's going lower." If there's one piece of investment advice that everyone can agree on, it's "buy low and sell high." As old as the market itself, that advice is sound—but not always easy to follow. The securities markets are unpredictable, and picking the "best time" to buy in today's volatile environment is not just difficult, it's impossible (unless you are very lucky).

But here is an easy way to put time on your side: you can use time and the market's volatility to your advantage.

Dollar cost averaging is not new and, importantly, has been proven to work. It enables you to *use* time, instead of trying to *choose* time. This investment strategy is based on simple mathematics and the enduring principles of diligence and patience.

The patient and steady user of a dollar-cost-averaging program invests a *fixed amount of money* in regular installments, usually on a monthly basis, into a particular security. The system is well established as a strategy for buying stocks, but it is especially well suited for buying no-load mutual funds, as they can easily be purchased with a specific and unchanging number of dollars, and usually without transaction costs.

So what will it do for you? The "magic" of dollar cost averaging is that you make the market's natural volatility work for you by lowering the average price you pay for your shares. All you do is invest equal amounts of money in a given investment at regular intervals. Your cost per share will always be less than the average price of the shares you have purchased, with one caveat: the market must fluctuate.

Since each amount you invest remains constant, you will buy more shares when prices are low and fewer shares when prices are high. Thus, the average cost of the shares you purchase will always be lower than the average market price of the shares (at the times of your purchases). The "magic" is simple arithmetic.

How Does It Work?

An example how dollar-cost averaging works can be seen in Figure 8.4, which illustrates what can happen in a declining market.

The use of dollar cost averaging does not assure a profit or protect against a loss in a declining market. Nor does it protect against a loss if you stop the program when the value of your account is less than cost. But what it *can* do is significantly lower your cost per share, thereby increasing your profits when the price rises.

FIGURE 8.4   Effect of $1,000 Invested Periodically at Declining Prices

	Regular Investment	Share Price	Shares Acquired
	$1,000	$20	50.00
	1,000	15	66.67
	1,000	10	100.00
	1,000	5	200.00
Total	$4,000	$50	416.67

Average cost per share: $9.60 ($4,000/416.67)
Average price per share: $12.50 ($50/4)

Most cases involving the purchase of mutual fund shares will not see such dramatic price changes—at least not in the short term.

The prudent investor wants to maximize gains and minimize risk. A program of dollar cost averaging works best when followed consistently over an extended period of time.

Keeping in mind that the only prerequisite for a successful dollar-cost-averaging program to work is a fluctuating market, examine the following illustration. Figure 8.5 shows the cost/price differential that dollar cost averaging can provide in a fluctuating market.

Here we have an investment time horizon of one year. Twelve $100 purchases of mutual fund shares, made on the fifteenth day of each month beginning in January and ending in December, total $1,200. The initial price per share is $20 and the ending price is $20. During the year, purchases made at prices under $20 are exactly balanced by purchases made at prices over $20 per share. The result is that the average price of all purchases made is exactly $20 per share.

One might expect that the investor would end up with an account valuation of $1,200. But actually it is worth $1,238.80, for a net profit of 3.23 percent.

In this case, the annualized rate of return on money invested is 6.46 percent (any dividends earned would be additional). This is based on the fact that an average of $600 has been invested for 12 months: $100 was invested for 11.5 months, $200 for 10.5 months, $300 for 9.5 months, etc. With the last $100 investment being made on December 15, the full $1,200 was invested for just half a year.

Figure 8.6 illustrates the cost/price difference that dollar cost averaging provides in a rising market.

FIGURE 8.5   Effect of $100 Invested Monthly at Fluctuating Prices

	Regular Investment	Share Price	Shares Acquired
Jan 15	$ 100	$ 20	5.00
Feb 15	100	16	6.25
Mar 15	100	14	7.14
Apr 15	100	16	6.25
May 15	100	20	5.00
Jun 15	100	24	4.17
Jul 15	100	26	3.85
Aug 15	100	24	4.17
Sep 15	100	20	5.00
Oct 15	100	18	5.56
Nov 15	100	22	4.55
Dec 15	100	20	5.00
Total	$1,200	$240	61.94

Average cost per share: $19.37 ($1,200/61.94)
Average price per share: $20 ($240/12)
Total amount invested: $1,200.00
Final investment value: $1,238.80
Net profit: $38.80 = 3.23% (of amount invested)
Annualized rate of return on money invested: 6.46%

Many mutual fund investors have been building up their shareholder accounts through such systematic purchases over long periods of time. They may be adding as little as $25 a month to their accounts, or they may be corporate retirement plans investing millions of dollars each year. Both are taking advantage of dollar cost averaging. The combination of buying shares at a variety of price levels and acquiring more shares at low rather than high prices has proven to be an efficient and cost-effective method of accumulating securities.

As noted earlier in this chapter, fluctuating security prices are more important to successful dollar cost averaging than long-term growth alone. This surprising fact arises because during periods of declining *prices* the investor may actually get his or her best opportunity to acquire a large number of shares.

Most investors who pursue a dollar cost averaging program reinvest any income and capital gains distributions they receive. The effect in the beginning is minor, but as the program continues, the impact of compounding shares becomes more and more significant.

While you do not have to reinvest income dividends for dollar cost averaging to work, the reinvestment of capital gains distributions is

FIGURE 8.6   Effect of $100 Invested Monthly in a Period of
Rising Prices

	Regular Investment	Share Price	Shares Acquired
Jan 15	$ 100	$ 20	5.00
Feb 15	100	21	4.76
Mar 15	100	22	4.55
Apr 15	100	23	4.35
May 15	100	24	4.17
Jun 15	100	25	4.00
Jul 15	100	26	3.85
Aug 15	100	27	3.70
Sep 15	100	28	3.57
Oct 15	100	29	3.45
Nov 15	100	30	3.33
Dec 15	100	31	3.23
Total	$1,200	$306	47.96

Average cost per share: $25.02 ($1,200/47.96)
Average price per share: $25.50 ($306/12)
Total amount invested: $1,200.00
Final investment value: $1,486.76
Net profit: $286.76 = 23.9%
Annualized rate of return on money invested: 47.8%

very important. The reason is that capital gains distributions represent a return of principal. Thus, taking them in cash reduces your capital.

SUMMARY

Mutual funds provide a unique set of characteristics that make them nearly ideal long-term investments for most investors. They combine the benefits of diversification, professional management and low cost. An investor need have only patience and common sense to successfully achieve a secure financial future based on an investment portfolio of carefully selected mutual funds.

A consistently followed program of dollar cost averaging helps to assure favorable long-term investment results. Fluctuating market conditions actually enhance the performance of such a systematic investment program. Persistence in continuing to buy shares regularly throughout periods of declining, as well as rising, prices is essential in order to maximize your results.

Chapter 9

Funds You Can Buy at a Discount

Investment companies also sponsor closed-end funds, which, unlike open-end mutual funds, do not stand ready to issue and redeem shares on a continuous basis. Instead, closed-end funds have a fixed capitalization represented by shares that are publicly traded, often on major stock exchanges. One interesting, and potentially profitable, aspect of closed-end funds is that they are often available for purchase at a *discount* from their net asset value (NAV).

Like open-end funds, *closed-end mutual funds* operate by pooling the funds of shareholders and investing those funds in a diversified securities portfolio having a specified investment objective. The funds provide professional management, economies of scale and the liquidity available with public trading on a major exchange. While the NAV of closed-end funds is calculated the same way as for open-end funds, the price an investor will pay or receive for shares traded on an exchange may be above or below the NAV. This is because the price of shares is determined on an auction market basis, the same as for all other traded shares of stock. Thus, the investor in a closed-end fund has an additional tier of risk, and possible profit, that the open-end fund investor does not have. The value per share responds not only to the fluctuation in value of the underlying securities in the fund's portfolio, but also to supply and demand factors that influence the fund's share price as it trades on an exchange.

Closed-end funds frequently have specialized portfolios of securities and may be oriented toward current income, long-term growth of capital, or a combination of objectives. An example is the *Argentina Fund,* which invests in equity securities of companies that mainly do business in Argentina and trades on the New York Stock Exchange (NYSE). Another is *CIM High Yield Securities Fund,* which also trades on the NYSE and seeks a high level of income by investing in lower than investment-grade bonds.

Closed-end mutual funds hold two main attractions for investors:

1. Management of a closed-end fund is not concerned with continuous buying and selling of securities in its portfolio to accommodate new investors and redemptions, as is the responsibility of an open-end fund, and which may conflict with ideal market timing. Thus, a well-managed closed-end fund can often buy and sell on more favorable terms.
2. Shares of closed-end funds are frequently available for purchase at a discount from net asset value.

The resulting benefit of these two factors is that annual earnings of closed-end funds sometimes exceed the earnings of open-end funds with similar portfolios.

Shares of closed-end mutual funds are purchased and sold through securities broker-dealers. Commissions, which vary from broker to broker, are payable both when shares are purchased and again when they are sold. Typically, shares are traded in 100-share lots, but "odd lots" of fewer than 100 shares may also be transacted.

The price, or *market value,* of closed-end shares is determined by supply and demand factors affecting the market. Shares may trade at a premium or at a discount relative to the net asset value (NAV) of the fund. Factors at work in determining share price include the composition of the portfolio, yield, the general market and year-end tax selling. Some funds have buyback programs designed to support the market price, reduce the number of shares outstanding and increase earnings per share. When shares are first issued, they tend to sell at a premium for a time, then fall back when brokers stop aggressively promoting them and turn their attention to other products.

In addition to daily transactions of closed-end funds contained in the financial sections of major newspapers, *Barron's National Business and Financial Weekly* publishes a special section each week with a complete listing of closed-end funds. Closed-end funds selling at a premium or discount to NAV are also listed separately each Monday in *The New York Times* and *The Wall Street Journal.*

TYPES OF CLOSED-END FUNDS

Like open-end mutual funds, closed-end funds may be divided into various general classifications. In the section that follows, six closed-end funds are presented within each classification showing 52-week total returns of stock funds (for the period ending October 22, 1993) and 12-month yields for income-oriented funds (for the period ending September 30, 1993). These funds illustrate the variation in share prices to NAVs and the relationships of total return and yield to the premium or discount that a fund trades at relative to its NAV. No inference should be drawn from this listing that any particular fund should be purchased or avoided.

Each fund is shown with the exchange on which it trades: A = American, C = Chicago, N = NYSE, O = Over the counter, T = Toronto. Also listed, as of October 22, 1993, are its NAV, its market price, and the percentage premium or discount the market price bears to the NAV. A minus (–) indicates the fund trades at a discount, while a plus (+) indicates the fund trades at a premium.

General Equity Funds

General equity funds seek capital appreciation. They normally invest in the common stocks of well-established companies, with the aim of producing an increase in the value of their investments rather than a flow of dividends. Investors who buy shares of closed-end general equity funds are usually more interested in seeing share prices rise than in receiving income from dividends. The table below provides data on funds in the general equity group selling at a premium or discount to their NAVs on October 22, 1993.

General Equity Funds Selling at a Premium or Discount

Name of Fund	Stock Exchange	NAV	Market Price	Premium or Discount	52-Week Market Return
Funds Trading at a Discount:					
Adams Express	N	20.78	19¼	– 7.4%	11.3%
Baker Fentress	N	23.16	19	–18.0	18.9

Central Securities	A	18.12	17¼	− 4.8	66.5

Funds Trading at a Premium:

Blue Chip Value	N	7.85	7⅞	+ 0.3	11.0
Source Capital	N	41.81	47¼	+13.0	13.6
Zweig	N	11.83	13½	+14.1	20.2

Specialized Equity Funds

This group includes funds that primarily confine their investments to securities in certain sectors of the market, such as utilities, precious metals, emerging markets, natural resources, health care, and so on. Because of the diversity of their objectives, with some funds seeking income and others seeking growth of capital, total return comparisons are not always meaningful. The table below shows specialized equity funds selling at a premium or discount to their NAVs on October 22, 1993.

Specialized Equity Funds Selling at a Premium or Discount

Name of Fund	Stock Exchange	NAV	Market Price	Premium or Discount	52-Week Market Return
Funds Trading at a Discount:					
BGR Precious Metals	T	14.50	13½	− 6.9%	92.9%
Counsellors Tandem	N	18.40	16¾	− 9.0	32.0
Global Health Science	N	12.12	11¾	− 3.1	6.3
Funds Trading at a Premium:					
C&S Realty Income	A	9.23	9⅞	+ 7.0	36.2
Patriot Select Dividend	N	17.52	18⅝	+ 6.3	18.4
Templeton Global Utilities	A	15.60	16⅝	+ 6.6	28.4

World Equity Funds

Funds in this group generally confine their portfolios to the common stock of companies located in one country or region, although the investment objectives of some funds permit them to invest anywhere in the world. The table below shows world equity funds selling at a premium or discount to their NAVs on October 22, 1993.

World Equity Funds Selling at a Premium or Discount

Name of Fund	Stock Exchange	NAV	Market Price	Premium or Discount	52-Week Market Return
Funds Trading at a Discount:					
Americas All Seas	O	5.26	4⅛	– 21.6%	– 2.9%
Chile	N	35.87	33¾	– 5.9	27.9
Malaysia	N	24.78	22⅝	– 8.7	72.4
Funds Trading at a Premium:					
Asia Pacific	N	15.47	20⅞	+34.9	102.7
China	N	16.57	18½	+11.6	34.9
Germany	N	12.56	13⅝	+ 8.5	16.7

Convertible Securities Funds

Funds included in this group generally invest in bonds, notes, debentures and, to some extent, preferred stock that can be exchanged for a set number of shares of common stock in the issuing company at a prestated price or exchange ratio. As such, they have characteristics similar to both fixed-income and equity securities. Only seven funds are listed in this group, of which five traded at a discount to NAV and two traded at a premium on the date examined. The table below shows convertible securities funds selling at a premium or discount to their NAV on October 22, 1993.

Convertible Securities Funds Selling at a Premium or Discount

Name of Fund	Stock Exchange	NAV	Market Price	Premium or Discount	52-Week Market Return
Funds Trading at a Discount:					
American Capital Convertible	N	25.55	23¾	– 7.0%	27.5%
Bancroft Convertible	A	24.89	23	– 7.6	22.3
Castle Convertible	A	28.08	27½	– 2.1	34.0
Lincoln National Convertible	N	21.37	19⅝	– 8.2	28.7

Funds Trading at a Premium:					
Putnam High Income Convertible	N	9.72	9⅞	+ 1.6	28.2
TCW Convertible Securities	N	9.22	10	+ 8.5	23.9

Dual-Purpose Funds

A special form of closed-end fund is the *dual-purpose fund.* This type of fund contains two classes of stock. Common shareholders receive all capital gains realized on the sale of securities in the fund's portfolio. Preferred shareholders receive all the dividend and interest income from the portfolio. Dual-purpose funds have a specific expiration date, when preferred shares are redeemed at a predetermined price and common shareholders claim the remaining assets. They then vote to either liquidate or continue the fund on an open-end basis. The table below shows dual-purpose funds selling at a premium or discount to their net asset values on October 22, 1993.

Dual-Purpose Funds Selling at a Premium or Discount

Name of Fund	Stock Exchange	NAV	Market Price	Premium or Discount	52-Week Market Return
Funds Trading at a Discount:					
Gemini II Fund Capital	N	23.00	20	– 13.0%	51.5%
Hampton Utility Capital	A	18.70	18⅛	– 3.1	30.8
Quest for Value Capital	N	29.37	26	–11.5	20.0
Funds Trading at a Premium:					
Gemini II Fund Income	N	9.83	12⅞	+31.0	9.7
Hampton Utility Income	A	50.10	54	+ 7.8	13.4
Quest for Value Income	N	11.59	13⅜	+17.6	11.6

In each case, the common shareholders of the dual-purpose funds listed saw their shares trading at a discount to NAV, while the preferred shares traded at substantial (in two cases) premiums.

Bond Funds

Closed-end bond funds seek income for their shareholders. They do so by purchasing fixed-income securities issued by corporations and/or the U.S. government or its agencies, depending on the investment objectives spelled out in their charters. Funds in this group represent a wide range of risk categories, with some portfolios holding mainly high-yield "junk" bonds and others emphasizing investment-quality instruments. The table below illustrates bond funds selling at a premium or discount to their NAVs on October 22, 1993.

Bond Funds Selling at a Premium or Discount

Name of Fund	Stock Exchange	NAV	Market Price	Premium or Discount	52-Month Yield
Funds Trading at a Discount:					
ACM Government Income	N	11.80	11⅜	− 3.6%	8.4%
Franklin Multi-Income	N	11.62	10⅝	− 8.6	8.6
INA Investments	N	20.32	18¾	− 7.7	7.4
Funds Trading at a Premium:					
American Government Income	N	8.76	9½	+ 8.4	9.8
CIGNA High Income	N	7.56	8⅜	+10.8	11.2
Fortis Securities	N	10.17	11¼	+15.5	9.1

World Income Funds

World income funds invest in the debt securities of companies and countries worldwide, including the United States. They seek to provide current income for their shareholders. The table below shows world income funds selling at a premium or discount to their NAVs on October 22, 1993, with their 12-month yield for the period ending September 30, 1993.

World Income Funds Selling at a Premium or Discount

Name of Fund	Stock Exchange	NAV	Market Price	Premium or Discount	12-Month Yield
Funds Trading at a Discount:					
First Commonwealth	N	13.57	13	−4.2%	8.1%
Global Government	N	8.22	7⅝	−7.2	10.1
Templeton Global Income	N	8.60	8⅛	−5.5	8.6
Funds Trading at a Premium:					
Black Rock North American	N	12.36	12¾	+3.2	9.9
Dreyfus Strategic Government	N	11.09	11⅜	+2.6	8.4
Templeton Global Government	N	8.40	8¾	+4.2	7.8

National Municipal Bond Funds

Funds in this group invest in bonds issued by states and municipalities to finance schools, highways, airports, bridges, hospitals, water and sewer works, and other public projects. In most cases, income earned from these securities is exempt from federal income tax but may be subject to state and local taxes. The table below illustrates national municipal bond funds selling at a premium or discount to their NAVs on October 22, 1993, with their 12-month yield for the period ending September 30, 1993.

National Municipal Bond Funds Selling at a Premium or Discount

Name of Fund	Stock Exchange	NAV	Market Price	Premium or Discount	12-Month Yield
Funds Trading at a Discount:					
Black Rock Insured Municipal	N	11.29	10½	– 7.0%	5.9%
Kemper Municipal Income Trust	N	13.51	13	– 3.8	6.6
Municipal Yield Quality II	N	16.37	15¼	– 6.8	6.4
Funds Trading at a Premium:					
Colonial Municipal Income Trust	N	7.97	8⅝	+ 8.2	7.4
MFS Municipal Income Trust	N	9.06	10	+10.4	7.2
Nuveen Premium Income	N	16.36	17⅝	+ 7.7	7.8

Single-State Municipal Bond Funds

Single-state municipal bond funds seek income that is exempt from federal tax and also from tax by a particular state or municipalities within that state. Such funds invest primarily in bonds issued only by that state or its municipalities. The table below shows single-state municipal bond funds selling at a premium or discount to their NAVs on October 22, 1993, with their 12-month yield for the period ending September 30, 1993.

Single-State Municipal Bond Funds Selling at a Premium or Discount

Name of Fund	Stock Exchange	NAV	Market Price	Premium or Discount	12-Month Yield
Funds Trading at a Discount:					
Black Rock California Insured 2008	N	16.20	15½	−4.3%	4.7%
Municipal Yield New York Insured II	N	16.01	15¼	−4.7	5.9
Nuveen New York Quality Income	N	16.61	15⅝	−5.9	6.0
Funds Trading at a Premium:					
Dreyfus California Municipal Income	A	9.91	10½	+6.0	5.9
Dreyfus New York Municipal Income	A	10.65	11⅛	+9.2	5.3
New York Tax-Exempt Income	A	10.79	12⅝	+17.0	5.9

SUMMARY

Closed-end investment companies issue a limited number of shares and, unlike open-end mutual funds, do not stand ready to redeem them (buy them back). Instead, closed-end shares are traded in the securities markets, with price determined by supply and demand, making it possible for investors frequently to have the opportunity to buy shares at a discount from the net asset value.

Chapter 10

Low-Risk Investing with Zero and Growth Funds

Everyone is interested in a "sure thing"—a way to make money without risk. Most investors have also heard the big lie: "This stock is guaranteed to go up." Such a line is often used with penny stocks or other low-priced securities. The profits almost never materialize, except of course for the broker, who always makes money—when you buy and again when you sell. In today's environment, investors must be vigilant and use common sense to avoid the pitfalls waiting in the marketplace. But is there a way to make money without the risk of losing your investment? Surprisingly, yes.

Today you can easily put together yourself a simple investment package that will make you money while guaranteeing a return of your original investment. Only one stipulation is required to assure it will work: You must hold on to it for the time you originally decide upon.

THE ZERO-COUPON BOND FUND/GROWTH STOCK FUND COMBINATION

The concept is easy. Your investment is made in two parts, into two mutual funds. One portion of your assets goes into a zero-coupon U.S. government bond fund with a specific target date. The balance goes into a solid growth fund of your choice. You may select any growth fund you believe has potential for capital appreciation in the years ahead. To be sure the plan will work, you must hold the bond fund until the target date. At that time, you will get back your original investment from the zero-coupon fund, plus you will have the value of the growth fund. The growth fund would have to become worthless for you not to make some profit. Even then, you will still have your initial investment returned intact.

Unlike ordinary U.S. Treasury bonds that pay interest periodically, zero-coupon U.S. Treasury securities (zeros) are issued at deep discount and then redeemed for their full face value at maturity. Investment return comes from the difference between the price at which a zero is purchased and the price at which it matures (or is sold). Because a zero's maturity value is known at the time of purchase, investors have found these securities to be a dependable way to invest for the future.

My recommended fund, Benham Target Maturities Trust, offers six portfolios, each with a different target maturity year: 1995, 2000, 2005, 2010, 2015 and 2020. Because each portfolio is substantially invested in zero-coupon Treasury bonds, it is possible to calculate the anticipated growth rate and an anticipated value at maturity for each portfolio for each business day. This fund is a true no-load, meaning that you pay no sales commissions, back-end redemption charges or 12b-1 fees. Other zero-coupon funds that may be used in this concept, with their target dates, are listed at the end of this chapter.

How the Plan Works

Let's assume that you have $10,000 to invest and can leave it untouched for a certain period of years. You can set the plan up for any number of years, using a zero-coupon mutual fund with the target date you select. For the purpose of this illustration, we'll assume that you invested $10,000 on October 18, 1993, with maturity in October of the year 2010.

Step 1. Invest a portion of your money in a zero-coupon U.S. government bond fund. The Benham Target Maturities Trust has a portfolio with a target maturity year of 2010. The anticipated value at maturity of each share in the portfolio is $100. You can redeem your shares of the fund for $100 each in December 2010, or the trustees will liquidate the portfolio and pay a cash redemption on or before January 31 of the following year (2011).

On October 18, 1993, the net asset value (NAV) of the Benham Target Trust 2010 Portfolio was $39.55. Thus, in step 1 of the plan you simply purchased 100 shares of the fund on that date for a total of $3,955. This will grow to an anticipated value of $10,000 in December 2010, a period of 17 years.

Step 2. The balance of the $10,000 is then invested in a growth fund. This amounts to $6,045. For the sake of this example, let's invest it in the Berger 100 Growth Fund. Here we have no idea what it will do in the future. It could be worth more or less than the original investment.

However, we can look back and see how the fund performed in the past. For the 15-year period ending September 30, 1993, the Berger 100 Fund had an average annual total return of 16.43 percent. This is the approximate annual percentage change in net assets per share with capital gains and income dividends reinvested. Thus, if we had invested $6,045 in the Berger 100 Growth Fund on October 1, 1978, it would have been worth a total of $59,206 on September 30, 1993. Of course, as we have noted, past performance is not necessarily an indication of future results.

We do know that the U.S. government has always honored its obligations, and we can feel pretty confident that the zero-coupon bonds will be paid as promised at maturity. In December 2010, your zero-coupon bond fund will mature for $10,000. It must be stated that while the U.S. government stands behind the bonds it issues, it does not guarantee the shares of a mutual fund that holds them. To remove even that small element of risk, it would be necessary to buy the zero-coupon bond itself (which can be done through a stockbroker).

The Payoff

In summary then, here is how your investment would look.

$10,000 Assumed Investment

	Zero-Coupon U.S. Government Bond Fund[1]	Berger 100 Growth Fund[2]
Initial Investment	$ 3,955	$ 6,045
Ending Value	10,000	59,206

[1] Invested for 17 years and 2 months, from 10/18/93 to December 2010.
[2] A hypothetical 15-year investment ending on 9/30/08 with capital gains and income dividends reinvested. Not guaranteed.

This is my "sleep-well" investment. No matter what happens to the stock market, your original $10,000 will be safely returned to you at maturity. Remember, though, if you need your money early, the zero-coupon government bond fund may be worth more or less than $10,000. Due to market conditions, even government bonds fluctuate in value prior to maturity.

Tax Considerations

As we noted earlier, zero-coupon bonds do not make interest payments to the holder. Instead, they are purchased at a substantial discount and then mature for the face amount of the bond. However, for tax purposes, the holder is considered to receive the interest each year on an imputed basis. Simply stated, you will be taxed annually on the interest even though you don't receive it. For this reason, many taxpayers hold zero-coupon bonds in their IRAs, Keogh plans or other qualified retirement plans in which taxes are deferred.

ZERO-COUPON U.S. GOVERNMENT BOND FUNDS

The following are other U.S. government bond funds currently available, with their target maturity years. Funds with an asterisk are available for purchase directly from the company wth no initial sales charge.

AAL U.S. Government Zero Coupon Target Fund, Series 2001 (The)
AAL U.S. Government Zero Coupon Target Fund, Series 2006 (The)
*Benham Target Maturities Trust Series 1995
*Benham Target Maturities Trust Series 2000
*Benham Target Maturities Trust Series 2005
*Benham Target Maturities Trust Series 2010
*Benham Target Maturities Trust Series 2015
*Benham Target Maturities Trust Series 2020
*Dreyfus Variable Investment Fund Zero Coupon 2000 Portfolio
*Fidelity Zero Coupon Bond Fund 1993 Portfolio

*Fidelity Zero Coupon Bond Fund 1998 Portfolio
*Fidelity Zero Coupon Bond Fund 2003 Portfolio
*Scudder Zero Coupon 2000 Fund

SUMMARY

The zero-coupon bond/common stock combination enables cautious investors to set up a plan that ensures the return of their original investment while providing the opportunity for a substantial capital gain. The investor need only maintain the investment for the time originally stipulated. This approach is particularly attractive in a retirement plan that shields the investor from taxes until the program has been completed.

Chapter 11

Index Funds: The Answer to a Paradox

The basic idea of a mutual fund is to properly invest its shareholders' money, generally into stocks or bonds or a combination of the two (and more recently into money market instruments), for the purpose of achieving specific investment goals. To do this, it attracts funds from many individual and institutional investors, and it undertakes to invest and manage those funds more effectively than the investors could do on their own.

And yet, there is a paradox. Most mutual funds *underperform* the market averages, as measured by generally recognized stock market indexes.

As we saw in Chapter 3, *stock market index* is a value representation of a selected group of stocks, weighted according to the prices and number of shares outstanding of the various stocks. For example, the Standard & Poor's 500 Stock Index is one of the most widely followed. It is a broad-based measurement of changes in stock market conditions based on the average performance of widely held common stocks of 500 large U.S. companies. The index tracks industrial, transportation, financial and utility stocks. Many other indexes exist as well, such as the Dow Jones Industrials, the Wilshire 5000 and the S&P Midcap 400. Each index tracks a certain universe of stocks or bonds.

Over the ten years ending June 30, 1993, according to Morningstar Mutual Fund service, 928 U.S. domestic equity mutual funds had an

FIGURE 11.1 Average Annual Total Returns for Ten Years Ending
              June 30, 1993

Number of Funds	Investment Objective	Average Annual Total Return
53	Aggressive Growth	7.76%
57	Equity-Income	12.38
438	Growth	11.39
245	Growth and Income	11.69
135	Small Company	9.87
	S&P 500 Index	14.40

Source: *Morningstar Mutual Funds,* Morningstar, Inc., 225 W. Wacker Dr., Chicago, IL 60606; 312-696-6532

average annual return of 11.11 percent. The equivalent annual return for Standard & Poor's 500 Index during this same period was 14.4 percent. Figure 11.1 illustrates the average annual total returns for fund groups with different investment objectives, as well as that of the S&P 500 Index, for the ten years ending June 30, 1993.

According to the Vanguard Group, one of the nation's largest mutual fund managers, the Wilshire 5000 Index outperformed 75 percent of all general equity mutual funds over the ten-year period ending June 30, 1993.

The evidence is compelling. Over time, the broad stock market indexes have consistently outperformed the average general equity mutual fund. As can be seen in Figure 11.2, the average annual *total return* (capital change plus income) of the Wilshire 5000 was 249.13 percent over the ten-year period ending June 30, 1993. The Wilshire 5000 is a measure of the total U.S. stock market. During the same period, the average general equity fund had a total return of 179.43 percent.

The failure to match or exceed the performance of the major indexes extends to virtually all common stock fund groups, regardless of investment objective. Figure 11.3 illustrates the average annual total return of various stock groups and the S&P 500 Index for five- and ten-year periods ending August 31, 1993.

No fund group on average was able to match the record of the S&P 500 Index over the ten years ending August 31, 1993. And just two groups, aggressive growth and small company, beat the S&P over five years.

Why do most mutual funds underperform the market? After all, they are run by highly paid investment managers with access to comprehen-

FIGURE 11.2 Average Annual Total Returns for Ten Years Ending
June 30, 1993

	Cumulative	Annual Rate
Wilshire 5000 Index	249.13%	13.32%
Average General Equity Fund	179.43	10.82

Source: Vanguard Group—*Some Plain Talk About Indexing*, 1993

sive investment and economic data on which to base their decisions.
The major factor besides investment manager competence (some managers perform better than others) relates to the expense ratio and
transaction costs. Costs in the expense ratio include advisory fees,
distribution charges and operating expenses; transaction costs include
brokerage and other trading costs.

The average general equity fund has an annual expense ratio of 1.3
percent of investor assets. Traditionally, mutual fund managers have
high portfolio activity. According to data from Lipper Analytical Services, the average fund's portfolio turnover rate is 90 percent per year.
The trading costs implicit in this portfolio activity may be expected to
subtract another 0.5 percent to 1 percent annually from a fund's total
return. Thus, typical stock mutual funds have average costs from these
two sources of approximately 2 percent of investor assets. Funds that
charge sales commissions use up even more of the returns. So the total
returns of conventional mutual fund investors are reduced by the
expense ratio, transaction costs and, in many cases, sales charges.

Figure 11.4 indicates historical average annual total returns of
mutual funds in the growth fund group, which seek growth of capital
by investing mainly in well-known large capitalization stocks, and
comparative returns of the S&P 500 Index for years ending December
31. This is followed by total returns and the growth of $10,000 invested
for different periods ending April 30, 1993.

INVESTORS VERSUS
MANAGERS: INDEXING

What if it were possible for an investor to buy the entire market? If
an investor could buy and hold all the stocks in the S&P 500 Index, or
some other favored index, and if transaction and administration costs

FIGURE 11.3 Average Annual Total Returns for Periods Ending
August 31, 1993

		Average Annual Total Returns	
Number of Funds	**Fund Groups**	**Five Years**	**Ten Years**
54	Aggressive Growth	16.83%	9.93%
60	Equity Income	12.96	13.01
449	Growth	15.02	12.33
252	Growth and Income	13.34	12.28
137	Small Company	16.42	11.20
219	International Stock	9.77	13.75
172	Specialty Stock	13.33	8.38
	S&P 500 Index	15.85%	14.95%

Source: *Morningstar Mutual Funds,* Morningstar, Inc., 225 W. Wacker Dr., Chicago,
IL 60606; 312-696-6532

were low enough, theoretically it should be possible to obtain a total
return (capital change plus income) very close to that of the index.

Attempting to parallel the investment returns of a specified stock
market (or bond market) index is called *indexing,* which is a passive
approach emphasizing broad diversification and low portfolio-trading
activity. The investor attempts to duplicate the investment results of the
target index by holding all (or, in the case of very broad indexes, a
representative sample) of the securities in the index. Traditional active
money management, using market timing techniques or identifying hot
stocks or industry sectors to outpace the indexes, is not attempted.

The case for indexing was first introduced in the early 1970s by
academics who argued that securities markets were highly random and
so efficient that it is, in fact, very difficult for professional managers
to consistently outperform the broad market averages through individual stock selection. The problem is that the typical investor would find
indexing impossible to do. To duplicate the results of the S&P 500
Index, an investor would have to purchase and hold 500 individual
stocks. Even using a discount broker, the transaction costs would be
too much for the typical investor. The portfolio would have to be
adjusted for every stock dividend or split, or whenever a company was
added to or deleted from the index. If dividends were to be reinvested,
that would have to be done at once into the same stocks to keep the

FIGURE 11.4 Investment Returns of Growth Fund Group Compared
to S&P 500 Index

**Total Returns of Growth Fund Group and S&P 500
Index for Years Ending Dec. 31 from 1983 to 1992**

	Group Total Return	S&P 500		Group Total Return	S&P 500
1983	21.32%	22.47%	1988	14.90%	16.60%
1984	−1.71	6.27	1989	26.65	31.68
1985	29.00	31.83	1990	− 5.29	− 3.12
1986	15.19	18.68	1991	36.41	30.48
1987	2.60	5.26	1992	8.52	7.62

Total Returns for Different Periods Ending April 30, 1993

	Growth Fund Group		S&P 500 Index	
	Total Return	Growth of $10,000	Total Return	Growth of $10,000*
3 Months	−1.34%	$ 9,866	1.00%	$ 10,100
6 Months	6.90	10,690	6.59	10,659
1 Year	9.74	10,974	9.23	10,923
3-Year Average	13.48	14,614	13.57	14,648
5-Year Average	13.28	18,654	14.77	19,913
10-Year Average	11.76	30,399	14.40	38,394
15-Year Average	15.42	85,944	15.27	84,284

*Since it is not possible to invest directly in the S&P 500 Index, these amounts represent
a hypothetical investment of $10,000.
Source: *Morningstar Mutual Funds*, Morningstar, Inc., 225 W. Wacker Dr., Chicago,
IL 60606; 312-696-6532

portfolio in proper balance—all of which would be overwhelming for
the private investor.

THE PROBLEM OF COSTS

As a group, it is impossible for all stock investors to outperform the
overall stock market. According to data from Ibbotson Associates, the
stock market index on a long-term historical basis has provided a
compound total return of 10 percent per annum. But that figure is the
gross return, before costs. Investors who pay typical costs for buying
and holding individual securities may expect to have a net return

FIGURE 11.5 Percentage of General Equity Mutual Funds Outperformed
by Wilshire 5000 Index from 1983 to 1992*

Year	% of Funds	Year	% of Funds
1983	64	1988	68
1984	68	1989	73
1985	77	1990	41
1986	61	1991	56
1987	54	1992	53

*The returns of the index have been reduced by 0.30 percent per year to reflect
approximate costs of a well-run index mutual fund.
Source: Vanguard Group—*Some Plain Talk About Indexing*, 1993

significantly reduced by these costs and will earn significantly less than
the market return.

Mutual fund companies have the same problem. As indicated earlier,
conventional stock mutual funds have average costs of approximately
2 percent of invested assets. Assuming a gross return of 10 percent,
therefore, the investor in a conventional mutual fund might expect the
net return to be about 8 percent. To solve this problem, some mutual
fund companies have introduced *index funds*. With this approach, they
attempt to parallel the investment returns of specified market indexes.
One of the first to do this was the Vanguard Group, which established
the Vanguard Index Trust in 1976, seeking to mirror the Standard &
Poor's 500 Composite Stock Price Index (the S&P 500).

A key advantage of an index fund should be its low cost. An index
fund should pay no advisory fees (because no active investment management takes place), should reduce operating expenses to the lowest
possible level, and should keep portfolio transaction costs at a minimum. The total return of a properly run index fund should be very close
to the total return of the index it mirrors.

In any given year, hundreds of equity mutual funds will provide
returns in excess of market indexes. However, as shown in Figure 11.5,
in nine out of ten years since 1983, the Wilshire 5000 Index, which was
designed to represent the entire U.S. stock market, matched or surpassed the average performance of equity mutual funds. The index was
never a poor performer and was rarely in the bottom third. Largely as
a result of the broad diversification of the Index and the year-by-year

FIGURE 11.6 Percentage of Active Bond Managers Outperformed by Bond Market Index from 1983 to 1992

Year	Percent	Year	Percent
1983	51	1988	45
1984	69	1989	76
1985	54	1990	63
1986	51	1991	41
1987	38	1992	53

10-Year Average: 57%

Source: Vanguard Group (*Vanguard Bond Index Fund*—1993)

buildup of the cost advantage, the index surpassed 75 percent of general equity funds over the entire ten-year period.

Institutional investors with multimillion-dollar portfolios have also employed indexing as an investment strategy in the bond market, providing above-average diversification and performance at exceptionally low cost. As with stocks, indexed bond portfolios have performed better than the majority of nonindexed, or actively managed, accounts.

For the ten-year period ended December 31, 1992, the Lehman Brothers Aggregate Bond Index outperformed 57 percent of managed bond funds, according to The Vanguard Group. Figure 11.6 indicates the percentage of active bond managers outperformed by the bond market index.

PERFORMANCE OF INDEX FUNDS

An index fund by definition is designed to track as closely as possible the performance of the market index it replicates. If the portfolio is carefully managed, the major factor affecting how closely a fund comes to matching that index is cost. Some funds are able to control costs better than others. An investor should always seek out an index fund with low operation costs. Figure 11.7 lists several funds with their costs, as reported in their most recent prospectuses.

FIGURE 11.7   Annual Operating Expenses of Index Funds as a
Percentage of Net Assets

Index Fund	Index Replicated	Total Operating Expenses
American Gas Index Fund	Gas Companies	.85%
Benham Gold Equities Index Fund	Gold Equities	.75
Fidelity Market Index Fund	S&P 500 Index	.45
Fidelity U.S. Bond Index Portfolio	Lehman Brothers Aggregate Bond Index	.32
Fidelity U.S. Equity Index Portfolio	S&P 500 Index	.28
Helmsman Equity Index Portfolio	S&P 500 Index	.89
Peoples Index Fund	S&P 500 Index	.88
Peoples S&P Midcap Index Fund	S&P MidCap 400	1.17
Schwab 1000 Fund	Schwab 1000 Index	.45
Vanguard Balanced Index Fund	Wilshire 5000 and Lehman Brothers Aggregate Bond Index	.22
Vanguard Bond Index Fund	Lehman Brothers Aggregate Bond Index	.20
Vanguard Index Trust		
500 Portfolio	S&P 500 Index	.19
Extended Market Portfolio*	Wilshire 4500 Index	.20
Total Market Portfolio*	Wilshire 5000 Index	.21
Value Portfolio	S&P/BARRA Value Index	.20
Growth Portfolio	S&P/BARRA Growth Index	.20
Vanguard International Equity Index Fund		
European Portfolio	Morgan Stanley Capital Int'l Europe (Free) Index	.32
Pacific Portfolio	Morgan Stanley Capital Int'l Pacific Index	.32
Vanguard Quantitative Portfolios	S&P 500 Index	.40
Vanguard Small Capitalization Stock Fund	Russell 2000 Index	.18

*The Helmsman Fund has a 5.5 percent sales load. The Vanguard Extended Market
Portfolio assesses a 1 percent purchase fee and the Total Market Portfolio a 0.25 percent
purchase fee.

A Recommended Fund

Vanguard Index Trust 500 Portfolio
Vanguard Financial Center
P.O. Box 2600
Valley Forge, PA 19482
800-662-7447

Portfolio manager: George U. Sauter
Investment adviser: Vanguard Group
Sales Fee: No-load
Annual account maintenance fee: $10
Management fee: 0.10%
Other expenses: 0.09%
Total operating expenses: 0.19%
Annual brokerage cost: 0.01%
Minimum initial purchase: $3,000 (additional amount $100)
Minimum IRA purchase: $500
Date of inception: August 31, 1976
Net assets of the fund as of June 30, 1993: $7.528 billion

Investment Objective

Vanguard Index Trust 500 Portfolio seeks to match the investment performance of the Standard & Poor's 500 Composite Stock Price Index, an index emphasizing large-capitalization stocks. It attempts to do this by holding all 500 stocks in approximately the same proportions as they are represented in the index, a technique known as *complete replication*.

The S&P 500 Index is composed of 500 common stocks, which are chosen by Standard & Poor's Corporation on a statistical basis to be included in the index. The inclusion of a stock in the S&P 500 Index in no way implies that Standard & Poor's Corporation believes the stock to be an attractive investment. The 500 securities, most of which trade on the NYSE, represented, as of December 31, 1992, approximately 71 percent of the market value of all U.S. common stocks. Each stock in the S&P 500 Index is weighted by its market value.

Because of the market-value weighting, the 50 largest companies in the S&P 500 Index currently account for approximately 50 percent of the Index. Typically, companies included in the S&P Index are the largest and most dominant firms in their respective industries.

Performance

The table below indicates annual total returns of Vanguard Index Trust 500 Portfolio for each year ending December 31 and comparative results for the S&P 500 Index. This is followed by total returns and the growth of $10,000 invested for different periods ending June 30, 1993.

Total Returns of Vanguard Index Trust 500 Portfolio and S&P 500 Index from 1983 to 1992

	Fund Total Return	S&P 500 Index		Fund Total Return	S&P 500 Index
1983	21.29%	22.47%	1988	16.22%	16.60%
1984	6.21	6.27	1989	31.37	31.68
1985	31.23	31.83	1990	−3.33	−3.12
1986	18.06	18.68	1991	30.22	30.48
1987	4.71	5.26	1992	7.42	7.62

	Fund Total Return	Growth of $10,000
3 Months	0.43%	$10,043
6 Months	4.78	10,478
1 Year	13.41	11,341
3 Year Average	11.22	13,759
5 Year Average	13.98	19,233
10 Year Average	14.05	37,248
15 Year Average	15.18	83,353

Source: *Morningstar Mutual Funds,* Morningstar, Inc., 225 W. Wacker Dr., Chicago, IL 60606; 312-696-6532

Financial History

Figure 11.8 provides information on selected per-share data and ratios for a share of Vanguard Index Trust 500 Portfolio outstanding during each year ended December 31 from 1983 to 1992.

Comments

For investors who want to invest in large capitalization companies, Vanguard Index Trust 500 Portfolio seems the most profitable way to go. Very few active investment managers are able to add value in the efficient large capitalization group. Over the past three-, five- and ten-year periods, the S&P 500 Index has outperformed the total returns of the average mutual fund investing in large capitalization stocks.

This fund stands out as one of the best vehicles available for indexing the market. Its annual expenses are only 19 basis points, the lowest available to retail investors. This permits Vanguard to mirror its target

FIGURE 11.8 Selected Per-Share Data and Ratios for Vanguard Index Trust 500 Portfolio

500 Portfolio

Year Ended December 31,

	1992	1991	1990	1989	1988	1987	1986	1985	1984	1983
Net Asset Value, Beginning of Year	$39.32	$31.24	$33.64	$27.18	$24.65	$24.27	$22.99	$19.52	$19.70	$17.56
Investment Activities										
Income	1.20	1.22	1.24	1.27	1.14	.95	.96	.97	.93	.93
Expenses	(.08)	(.07)	(.07)	(.07)	(.06)	(.07)	(.07)	(.06)	(.05)	(.06)
Net Investment Income	1.12	1.15	1.17	1.20	1.08	.88	.89	.91	.88	.87
Net Realized and Unrealized Gain (Loss) on Investments	1.75	8.20	(2.30)	7.21	2.87	.36	3.30	5.08	.30	2.85
Total from Investment Activities	2.87	9.35	(1.13)	8.41	3.95	1.24	4.19	5.99	1.18	3.72
Distributions										
Net Investment Income	(1.12)	(1.15)	(1.17)	(1.20)	(1.10)	(.69)	(.89)	(.91)	(.88)	(.87)
Realized Net Gain	(.10)	(.12)	(.10)	(.75)	(.32)	(.17)	(2.02)	(1.61)	(.48)	(.71)
Total Distributions	(1.22)	(1.27)	(1.27)	(1.95)	(1.42)	(.86)	(2.91)	(2.52)	(1.36)	(1.58)
Net Asset Value, End of Year	$40.97	$39.32	$31.24	$33.64	$27.18	$24.65	$24.27	$22.99	$19.52	$19.70
Ratio of Expenses to Average Net Assets	.19%	.20%	.22%	.21%	.22%	.26%	.28%	.28%	.27%	.28%
Ratio of Net Investment Income to Average Net Assets	2.81%	3.07%	3.60%	3.62%	4.08%	3.15%	3.40%	4.09%	4.53%	4.22%
Portfolio Turnover Rate	4%	5%	23%	8%	10%	15%	29%	36%	14%	35%
Shares Outstanding, End of Year (thousands)	159,811	110,526	69,555	53,626	38,815	33,527	19,984	17,148	14,841	11,861

Source: Vanguard Index Trust prospectus dated May 1, 1993

almost perfectly. In 1992, for instance, the fund came only 19 basis points short of matching the S&P 500's gain.

While no single mutual fund is necessarily appropriate for all investors, the feeling of safety that comes with an investment in a 500-stock portfolio of the market's best-known companies has drawn many investors into this fund. In 1982 it had total net assets of $110 million. By 1987 this grew to $826 million, then to over $2 billion in 1990 and to over $7.5 billion by mid-1993.

Vanguard Index Trust 500 Portfolio appears to be an ideal investment for investors seeking to replicate the return of the S&P 500 Index.

Portfolio

Total stocks: 500 as of March 31, 1993
25 Largest Holdings

American International Group
Amoco
AT&T
Bell Atlantic
BellSouth
Bristol-Myers Squibb
Chevron
Coca-Cola
EI DuPont de Nemours
Exxon
Ford Motor
General Electric (GE)
General Motors (GM)
GTE
Intel
International Business Machines (IBM)
Johnson & Johnson
Merck
Minnesota Mining & Manufacturing (3M)
Mobil
PepsiCo
Philip Morris
Procter & Gamble
Royal Dutch Petroleum
Wal-Mart Stores

Composition of Portfolio
As of March 31, 1993

Cash	1.0%
Stocks	99.0

Stock Sector Weightings
As of March 31, 1993

Consumer Durables	7.1%
Consumer Staples	12.4
Energy	10.3
Financials	10.9
Health	8.0
Industrial Cyclicals	11.3
Retail	7.4
Services	7.8
Technology	9.8
Utilities	15.0

FIGURE 11.9 Total Annual Returns of S&P 500 Index and Russell 2000 Index from 1979 to 1992

Year	S&P 500	Russell 2000	Year	S&P 500	Russell 2000
1979	18.5%	43.1%	1986	18.6%	5.7%
1980	32.4	38.6	1987	5.2	−8.8
1981	−4.9	2.0	1988	16.5	24.9
1982	21.5	25.0	1989	31.6	16.2
1983	22.5	29.1	1990	−3.1	−19.5
1984	6.2	−7.3	1991	30.3	46.1
1985	31.6	31.1	1992	7.6	18.4

Source: Vanguard Small Capitalization Stock Fund prospectus dated June 14, 1993

CREATING A PORTFOLIO OF INDEX FUNDS

It is possible to construct a portfolio of mutual funds that is entirely made up of index funds, thus sparing an investor from attempting to pick the "best-performing" funds. As more index funds become available, the investor can diversify among various segments of the U.S. and world economies, as well as different investment goals. Even now, a fairly wide range of choices is available.

Keep in mind that different investment universes carry different risk and reward parameters. For example, small capitalization stocks that constitute the Russell 2000 Index have been more volatile in price than the larger capitalization stocks included in the S&P 500 Index. Among the reasons for the greater price volatility of small-company stocks are the less-certain growth prospects of smaller firms, the lower degree of liquidity in the markets for such stocks, and the greater sensitivity of small companies to changing economic conditions.

Besides exhibiting greater volatility, small-company stocks may fluctuate independently of larger-company stocks. Figure 11.9 illustrates the greater risks associated with small capitalization stocks by comparing annual investment returns for the S&P 500 and Russell 2000 Indexes since 1979.

Figure 11.10 presents a listing of various investment objectives, together with index funds designed to meet those objectives and market indexes that the funds seek to replicate.

FIGURE 11.10 Investment Objectives with Matching Index Funds

Investment Objective	Market Index	Index Fund
Stocks paying above-average dividends	S&P/BARRA Value Index	Vanguard Value Index Portfolio
Stocks with a higher potential for growth	S&P/BARRA Growth Index	Vanguard Growth Index Portfolio
Large capitalization companies	S&P 500 Index	Dreyfus Peoples Index Fund
		Fidelity Market Index Fund
		Helmsman Equity Index Portfolio
		Vanguard 500 Portfolio
Medium-size companies	S&P Midcap 400	Dreyfus Peoples S&P Midcap Index Fund
Small- and medium-size companies	Wilshire 4500 Index	Vanguard Extended Market Portfolio
Small companies	Russell 2000 Small Stock Index	Vanguard Small Capitalization Stock Fund
Entire U.S. equity stock market	Wilshire 5000 Index	Vanguard Total Market Portfolio
European companies	MSCI EAFE	Vanguard International Equity—European Portfolio
Pacific Basin companies	MSCI EAFE	Vanguard International Equity—Pacific Portfolio
High-Grade Bonds	Lehman Brothers Aggregate Bond Index	Vanguard Bond Index Fund

There will always be actively managed mutual funds that outperform index funds over long periods. It may be luck. Pure chance would say that some investment managers will provide exceptional returns over long "winning streaks." Or it may be skill. There may be some investment managers with exceptional abilities who can earn superior returns over time. The problem is to identify, in advance, those who will be superior with any consistency.

OPERATING INDEX FUNDS

The following index funds, which are not intended to be a complete list, were in operation at the end of 1992:

American Gas Index Fund
American General Series Portfolio Company
Benham Gold Equities Index Fund
Colonial International Equity Index Trust
Colonial U.S. Equity Index Trust
Dreyfus Edison Electric Index Fund
Dreyfus Life and Annuity Index Fund
Dreyfus People and Index Fund
Drefus People S&P Midcap Index Fund, Inc.
Federated Index Trust Max-Cap Fund
Fidelity Commonwealth Trust
   Fidelity Market Index Fund
Fidelity Institutional Trust
    Fidelity U.S. Bond Index Portfolio
    Fidelity U.S. Equity Index
Gateway Index Plus Fund
Hartford Index Fund
Helmsman Equity Index Portfolio
IDS Blue Chip Advantage Fund
Mainstay Equity Index Fund
Monitrend Mutual Fund
   Summation Index Series
New England Zenith Fund
   Stock Index Series
New York Life Institutional Funds
   EAFE Index Fund
   Indexed Bond Fund
   Indexed Equity Fund
Peoples Index Fund
Peoples S&P Midcap Index Fund
PNC Family of Funds
   Index Equity Portfolio
Principal Preservation Portfolios
   S&P 100 Plus Portfolio
Schwab 1000 Fund

SEI Index Funds
  Bond Index Portfolio
  S&P 500 Index Portfolio
SMA Investment Trust
  Equity Index Fund
T. Rowe Price Index Trust
  Equity Index Fund
United Services Funds
  U.S. All American Equity Fund
Vanguard Balanced Index Fund
Vanguard Bond Index Fund
Vanguard Index Trust
  500 Portfolio
  Extended Market Portfolio
  Total Market Portfolio
  Value Portfolio
  Growth Portfolio
Vanguard International Equity Index Fund
  European Portfolio
  Pacific Portfolio
Vanguard Quantitative Portfolios
Vanguard Small Capitalization Stock Fund
Van Kampen Merritt Series Trust
  Stock Index Portfolio

SUMMARY

For the investor who does not want to depend on a specific actively managed mutual fund, an index fund with low operating costs makes it possible to buy and hold an entire segment of the securities market and come very close to matching its total return.

Index funds provide an investor with four important advantages:

1. The *relative predictability* of close correlation with the returns of their respective target indexes over time.
2. The reduction of individual stock risk through *broad diversification*. Diversification, of course, does not protect share prices from losses that occur in a sharp market downturn.

3. The *cost savings* of operating without an investment adviser, minimal portfolio turnover and reduced administration expenses.
4. *Deferred taxation* of capital gains, since minimal portfolio turnover results in virtually no capital gains distributions.

Chapter 12

Investing for Income

In the middle of 1990, short-term interest rates began a substantial and continuing decline. As shown in Figure 12.1, the yield on three-month U.S. Treasury bills hovered around 8 percent for the first six months of 1990, then dropped rapidly. For most of 1991 Treasury bill yields were under 6 percent, and by June 30, 1993, they moved down to just over 3 percent. Consequently, many money market fund and certificate of deposit investors have suffered "interest rate shock."

Investors in longer-term bonds were not spared, as they also watched yields fall from their mid-1990 highs, but less steeply; they are now well above money market rates. While the spread between the three-month Treasury bill and the 30-year Treasury bond was only about 50 basis points (one-half of 1 percent) in early 1990, it had widened to over 350 basis points by mid-1993. On June 30, 1993, the 30-year U.S. Treasury bond yielded 6.7 percent, or 3.6 percent above the three-month bill yield.

Investors have not ignored these changes. With the disappearance of the high yields afforded by money market funds in 1990, money began flowing out of that safe haven and into bond funds. For those concerned about the drop in yield from their money market funds and certificates of deposit (CDs), caution is in order. The temptation to pursue higher rates less carefully can be dangerous, but prudent investors might indeed review their portfolios and consider longer-term investments that can deliver greater returns.

FIGURE 12.1 U.S. Treasury Yields: 3-Month Bill Versus 30-Year Bond,
1990–1993

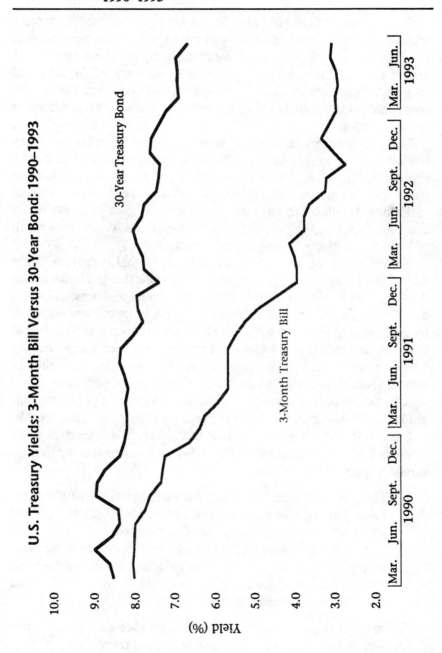

INVESTMENT CHOICES

A wide range of mutual fund choices are available for the investor seeking the right combination of yield and safety. Money market funds offer money market rates and have historically provided stability of principal. In addition, a variety of short-term, intermediate-term and long-term funds are available for higher yield and more durable income, but with the trade-off of progressively greater fluctuations in principal value.

The additional yield available when moving from CDs or money market funds to longer-term and higher-yielding mutual funds can be significant. However, the age-old warning of *caveat emptor* is more applicable. An investor who selects an investment only on the basis of yield may be subject to an unhappy surprise. Higher yield is usually associated with higher risk, although in some cases it can be the result of lower costs by the issuing organization.

Higher risks generally arise from lower credit quality or from longer maturities. Lower credit quality involves the risk that the issuer of the debt obligation will not be able to pay off interest and principal when due. The degree of risk can be indicated by the types of investments or by credit ratings assigned by major rating services, such as Standard & Poor's Corporation and Moody's Investors Service. Credit quality concerns can be reduced by investing in the diversified portfolios of mutual funds. Even with mutual funds, the quality of portfolios varies widely, from funds that invest in U.S. Treasury bonds or investment-grade corporate bonds to those that purchase high-yield "junk" bonds.

For a full understanding of yield and safety, it is important to be aware of how longer maturities affect risk. An investor seeking income should consider two basic rules:

1. The principal values of bonds fluctuate inversely with interest rates. That is, when interest rates go up, bond prices fall, and when interest rates go down, bond prices rise.
2. The longer the maturity, the more volatile the value of the bond (both up and down). Of course, any rise in the value of the bond enhances the investor's "total return," while any decline in the value of the bond reduces it.

Figure 12.2 illustrates how the principal value of a bond varies depending on its maturity and changes in interest rates.

FIGURE 12.2 Percentage Change in the Price of a Par Bond Yielding 8 Percent

	Increase in Interest Rates		Decrease in Interest Rates	
Stated Maturity	+1%	+2%	−1%	−2%
Short-Term (2.5 years)	−2%	−4%	+2%	+5%
Intermediate-Term (10 years)	−7	−13	+7	+15
Long-Term (20 years)	−9	−17	+11	+23

Since interest rates are rarely stable for very long, one cannot simply take the approach of selecting the highest-yielding investment of acceptable credit quality. In fact, during the last 15 years, interest rates have swung wildly.

During the late 1970s and first part of the 1980s, while inflation rates increased, interest rates soared. Money market fund investors benefited from the high yields, but bond prices were depressed sharply. Then when the Federal Reserve Board won its battle to reduce inflation in the early 1980s, interest rates steadily declined. It was a bonanza for long-term bondholders who had high yields locked in and watched the value of their bonds appreciate. Providing both high yields and price appreciation, bonds were excellent investments in the 1980s and early 1990s.

If an investor knew where interest rates were headed, selecting the right investment would be easy. One would simply invest in money market funds before rates rose and in long-term bonds before rates fell. Unfortunately, as is the case in attempting to predict the direction of stocks, there is no evidence whatsoever that anyone can predict the course of interest rates with the remotest sort of consistency or accuracy.

RULES FOR FIXED-INCOME INVESTING

Inflation is apparently under control—at least for now—but we can expect interest rates to continue to fluctuate. Here are some basic considerations to help you earn the optimum level of income consistent with the degree of safety you seek.

Match Maturities with Your Needs.   One way to avoid trouble is to make sure that the maturity of your fixed-income investment coincides with the time when you will need your money. When putting money aside temporarily to pay for a large purchase in a few months or for emergency purposes, consider only a short-term investment, such as a money market fund. Don't be lured to long-term bonds, even for much higher yields.

On the other hand, a retired person needing a high level of continuing income should probably not overload with money market funds because the income from the fluctuates with interest rates. The retiree might be wiser to consider long-term bonds, which generally provide higher starting yields and more durable income. Investors with long-term goals can also benefit from the higher yields associated with long-term bonds and can tolerate the short-term volatility that accompanies them.

Some investors with short-term or intermediate-term investment objectives (such as putting a child through college, saving for a house, and so on) and some long-term investors may feel uncomfortable with the volatility of long-term bonds. To meet these needs, the most suitable investments may be short (one- to three-year) or intermediate (five- to ten-year) bonds. Providing a yield higher than money market funds, they also limit principal fluctuations to a reasonable degree.

Diversify.   Most individuals have multiple needs. We need temporary cash reserves for emergencies, and many of us are saving for a house and/or putting children through college, planning for retirement, and so on. So it makes sense to hold a combination of funds: a money market fund for stability, a short-term or intermediate-term fund for higher yield with low to moderate risk, and a long-term bond fund for highest yield and a high degree of volatility. Your personal portfolio of funds should reflect your own unique needs. One benefit of this approach is that part of your portfolio will do well in any interest-rate environment.

Invest in Quality.   Most people looking for income-producing investments are interested in safety. If you are among them, it usually doesn't pay to go with lower quality. Having made your decision on the appropriate maturity, stick with high-quality investments. For the highest degree of safety, invest in funds that hold principally U.S. Treasury obligations. Next down the scale would be funds investing in

U.S. government agency obligations, then investment-quality corporate bonds, and finally lower-quality corporate bonds and so-called "junk bonds." The lower-grade issues should be avoided unless you understand and are willing to accept the risks in return for the higher yields they offer.

Remember Taxes.   In the end, investors care not about the nominal yield, but about the *after-tax* return on their investments—that is, the income that remains after deducting federal, state and local taxes. High-tax-bracket investors will often benefit by investing in municipal bond funds of appropriate quality and maturity, rather than in comparable U.S. government and corporate bond funds that are fully subject to federal taxes. Tax-free municipal bond funds are available in money market, short-term, intermediate-term and long-term varieties.

In addition, single-state municipal bond funds are available that invest only in the bonds of a particular state, the interest of which is exempt from income taxes levied by that state as well as from federal income tax. Further, income from U.S. Treasury bond portfolios may be exempt from state income tax.

Look for Low-Cost Bond Funds.   Other factors being equal, the lower the costs associated with an investment, the higher will be the yield. For instance, two money market funds with similar investment portfolios are likely to have identical *gross* yields from their investments. The *net* yields paid to investors may vary substantially, however. The difference arises from expenses, and the higher yield will be paid by the lower-cost fund.

Costs can vary widely. Figure 12.3 illustrates the differences in the mutual fund industry.

Obviously, a high-quality bond fund that has a gross yield of 7.5 percent will pay a net yield of 7.22 percent if its expenses are 0.28 percent, but will be able to pay only 6.44 percent if its expenses are 1.06 percent.

Avoid Paying Sales Charges.   The characteristics of bond funds and money market funds are such that it is hard to find justification for an investor to pay a sales charge. Returns are relatively predictable when compared to the quality and maturity of the universe from which bonds are selected; income is a very high component of total return; and it is difficult for portfolio managers to achieve performance superiority.

FIGURE 12.3   Operating Costs of Mutual Funds as a Percentage of Total Assets

	Industry Average	Low-Cost Funds
Money Market Funds	0.61%	0.28%
Taxable Bond Funds	1.06	0.28
Tax-Free Bond Funds	0.77	0.23

Source: Vanguard Group

Beyond these factors, the impact of sales charges is especially large over short-term periods and so reduces investors' flexibility to make changes as objectives change.

SUMMARY

The low money market rates confronting investors today create a dilemma. Tempting higher yields available from long-term bonds may entice investors to leave the safe haven of money market accounts. Long-term bonds will indeed prove advantageous if interest rates hold steady or decline even further. However, interest rate movements are unpredictable, so the risk associated with a rate increase must be considered carefully and understood.

Chapter 13

IRAs: A Tax-Favored Retirement Plan for You

Saving for your future is important, but just as important is *how* you invest your savings. First, your savings should benefit from tax advantages, and second, your funds should be consistently invested for maximum effectiveness.

Section 408(a) of the Internal Revenue Code of 1986 describes the individual retirement account (IRA), which makes it possible for you to establish a long-term retirement program with two important tax advantages:

1. All your earnings accumulate tax-free in your IRA until you begin making withdrawals. Over time, this tax-deferred accumulation will have a major effect on your IRA, causing your assets to grow at a more rapid rate.
2. Because your IRA contributions may be tax-deductible, you may be able to reduce your federal income taxes now.

Under a voluntary IRA program, you may make investment contributions on a regular monthly, quarterly or annual basis and thereby take advantage of the powerful effect of *dollar cost averaging,* an investment strategy of investing equal amounts of money at regular intervals regardless whether securities markets are moving up or down. (See the section, "The Magic of Dollar Cost Averaging" in Chapter 8.) This practice reduces average share costs to the investor, who acquires more shares in periods of lower securities prices and fewer shares in periods of higher prices. Being able to invest specific dollar amounts, together with the elements of diversification, professional management and low cost, makes mutual funds an ideal IRA investment vehicle.

WHAT TO LOOK FOR IN AN IRA MUTUAL FUND INVESTMENT PROGRAM

In selecting a mutual fund company for your retirement planning needs, pay particular attention to the following criteria.

Investment Choice.   Select a mutual fund company that offers IRA investors a selection of different investment portfolios to choose from. These might include aggressive common stock funds, income-oriented bond funds, money market funds, balanced funds that combine stocks and bonds, passively managed index funds and funds that invest in international markets.

Flexibility.   An IRA is a long-term investment. Market conditions and your investment objectives can change. So it is important that your mutual fund company offers a range of funds with different investment objectives into which you can exchange your shares.

Investment Performance.   Look for a fund with consistent long-term past results. While no investment manager can promise top performance every year, seek an above-average long-term history rather than concentrating on short-term results. Keep in mind the caveat that appears in every mutual fund prospectus: "Past performance is no guarantee of future results." It should be memorized by every investor.

Commission-Free Investing.   Whether a mutual fund charges a commission (load) or fee to purchase its shares is irrelevant to the performance of its portfolio managers, but such a charge will certainly cause you to start off with an immediate loss of capital. So other things being equal (e.g., investment performance and objectives), focus first on investing in a no-load fund.

Low Cost.   Operating a mutual fund involves significant costs, but you have to pay close attention to the important differences in how the

FIGURE 13.1 $4,000 Invested Each Year at 10 Percent

Number of Years Invested	Accumulated Value of the Account
5	$ 26,862
10	70,125
15	139,799
20	252,010
25	432,727
30	723,774
35	1,192,507
40	1,947,407

funds control these costs. First look for a fund with a low expense ratio, which is the proportion that annual expenses, including all cost of operation, bear to average net assets for the year. Some funds charge a number of costs that others completely avoid. These costs include 12b-1 fees, contingent deferred sales charges, long-term redemption charges or exit fees, and dividend reinvestment charges.

High-Quality Service.   Easy-to-read account statements and comprehensive fund reports are important to keep you informed about the progress of your retirement account.

INVESTING FOR PROFIT

For most people, an IRA is a long-term retirement program, and the investments you select should be made with that thought in mind. According to Ibbotson Associates, the stock market has historically provided investors with an average return of 10 percent per year. In recent years the returns have been higher. For example, in the ten years ending June 30, 1993, Standard & Poor's 500 Composite Stock Price Index had an average annual total return of 14.35 percent.

As noted above, past performance is no guarantee of future results. But as an example, Figure 13.1 shows the potential results of investing $4,000 per year in an IRA investment program for two working spouses over different time frames with an average annual return of 10 percent.

The important benefit that all earnings accumulate tax-free in your IRA until you begin making withdrawals contrasts with one of the least attractive features of mutual funds: the problem that all income dividends and capital gains distributions (whether paid out or reinvested) are taxable in the year they are paid. The "mountain chart" reproduced in Figure 13.2 appears in the Stratton Monthly Dividend Shares, Inc. annual report of January 31, 1993. It illustrates the impact of dividend income and capital gains distribution on the growth of a $10,000 investment in Stratton Monthly Dividend Shares on May 31, 1980, left to accumulate through January 31, 1993—a period just four months short of 13 years. At the end of that time, the fund was worth a total of $48,761. In this case, *more than 85 percent of the appreciation in value resulted from reinvested dividends and capital gains.*

In the nearly 13 years that this fund was in operation, the total value of the original shares grew to $15,701. Shares acquired through reinvestment of income dividends were valued at $31,818, and shares acquired through reinvestment of capital gains distributions had a value of $1,242, for a total of $48,761. In addition, the accumulating income dividends and capital gains distributions are not subject to tax until withdrawn.

Here's What You Need To Know

Eligibility.   Generally, anyone under age 70½ who earns income from employment, including self-employment, may make annual contributions to an IRA.

Amount You May Contribute.   A maximum of $2,000 or 100 percent of your compensation, whichever is less, may be contributed to your IRA each year.

Your Spouse.   Since each employed spouse may open a separate IRA and contribute 100 percent of compensation up to $2,000 a year, a working couple can make total contributions of up to $4,000 annually to their IRAs.

Nonworking Spouse.   If your spouse earns no compensation (or earns less than $250) for the year, you may be eligible to increase your total IRA contribution by having an additional but separate *Spousal IRA* established for your spouse. With a Spousal IRA, your maximum annual IRA contribution may be increased to $2,250, which may be split between the separate IRA accounts of you and your nonworking spouse in any manner you wish, so long as not more than $2,000 is contributed to either account for any one year.

Tax-Deductibility.   Your IRA contributions will be deductible for federal income tax purposes if neither you nor your spouse is an active participant in an employer-maintained retirement plan. If one of you is an active participant in an employer-maintained retirement plan, the deductibility of your IRA contributions will be determined by your adjusted gross income as follows:

- *Adjusted gross income of $40,000 or less ($25,000 on single returns)*—Your IRA contributions will be fully deductible.
- *Adjusted gross income above $40,000 ($25,000 on single returns*—The deduction for your IRA contributions will be reduced proportionately as your adjusted gross income increases above these limits. Deductibility will be phased out completely when your adjusted gross income reaches $50,000 ($35,000 on single returns).

Definition of "Active Participant in an Employer Retirement Plan." You are generally considered to be an active participant for a tax year if you participate in any employer-maintained retirement plan (including pension, profit-sharing, 401(k), 403(b), SEP or Keogh plan) during any part of the year. The Form W-2 you receive from your employer each year should indicate whether you are an active participant in the employer's retirement plan.

If neither you nor your spouse is an active participant in an employer-maintained retirement plan, your IRA contributions will be fully deductible regardless of your income level.

Nondeductible IRA Contributions.   You are permitted to make nondeductible contributions to your IRA to the extent you are not eligible to make deductible IRA contributions. Earnings on such nondeductible contributions are not subject to federal income tax until you withdraw them. In the meantime, you will enjoy one of the most important benefits associated with IRAs: compounded, tax-deferred earnings.

When IRA Contributions May Be Made.   For each tax year, you can make deductible or nondeductible contributions to your IRA at any time up to the due date for filing your income tax return (not including

FIGURE 13.2 Mountain Chart Showing Sample $10,000 Invested in
Stratton Monthly Dividend Shares from May 31, 1980
to January 31, 1993 (All Dividend Income and Capital
Gains Distribution Reinvested)

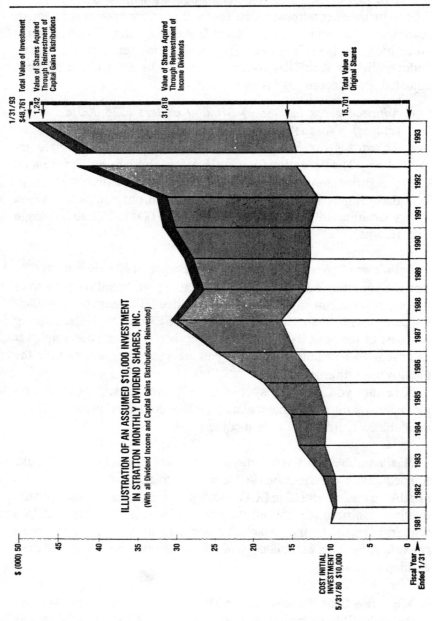

FIGURE 13.2 (continued)

Initial Investment	$9,113	9,354	10,808	10,667	11,795	14,604	16,320	13,181	12,824	12,861	12,084	14,609	15,701	
Reinvested Inc. Divs.	$ 583	1,641	3,107	4,379	6,627	10,328	13,744	13,041	15,044	17,513	19,388	26,570	31,818	
Reinvested Cap. Gains Distributions	$ —	—	—	—	—	—	503	1,043	1,015	1,018	956	1,156	1,242	
Total Value	$9,696	10,996	13,915	15,045	18,422	24,932	30,567	27,265	28,883	31,392	32,428	42,335	48,761	
If Divs. and Distribs. Were Taken in Cash:														
$ Amt. Div. Inc.	$ 593	924	882	1,013	1,076	1,139	1,197	1,081	1,092	1,076	1,155	1,024	1,018	= 13,270 TOTAL DIV. INC.
$ Amt. Cap. Gains Distrib.	$ —	—	—	—	—	—	263	341	—	—	—	—	—	= 604 TOTAL CAP. GAIN

NOTE: If dividend income and capital gains distributions were taken in cash, the results would be as shown above under "value of original shares."

Performance quotations represent past performance, and should not be considered as representative of future results. The investment return and principal value of an investment in the Fund will fluctuate so that an investor's shares, when redeemed, may be worth more or less than their original cost.

extensions). For most taxpayers, the latest date for any year is April 15 of the following year. But remember, the *sooner* you contribute to your IRA, the sooner tax-sheltered earnings will accrue.

Contributions Are Voluntary.   You do not need to make contributions to your IRA every year, nor are you required to make the maximum contribution in any year. You may contribute any amount you wish, provided you don't exceed the limits. However, if you decide in any year not to make the maximum IRA contribution, you may not make up the missed contribution amount in later years.

Age Limitation on Continuing Contributions.   You may make contributions to your IRA for each year you earn compensation up to the year you attain age 70½.

Withdrawals from Your IRA.   Generally, you may start withdrawals from your IRA as early as age 59½. Withdrawals must begin by April 1 following the year you attain age 70½.

Taxation of Withdrawals.   Withdrawals from your IRA will be taxed as ordinary income, with the exception that if you make any nondeductible contributions to your IRA, your IRA withdrawals will be treated partly as a nontaxable return of your nondeductible IRA contributions, and partly as a taxable distribution of your IRA earnings and any deductible IRA contributions.

Withdrawals before Age 59½.   Because an IRA is intended to provide for your retirement, the law imposes an additional tax of 10 percent if you withdraw prior to age 59½ for reasons other than your disability. This 10 percent tax is applied to the taxable amount of your withdrawal and is in addition to the ordinary income tax you pay on your withdrawal. The 10 percent additional tax will not apply to distributions made to your beneficiary in the event of your death. Also, the 10 percent tax will not apply to certain installment or annuity payments made for your life or life expectancy, or for the joint lives or life expectancies of you and your beneficiary, regardless of when these payments begin.

Methods of Distribution.   Withdrawals from your IRA may be made in the form of one or more lump-sum payments, or in regular monthly, quarterly or annual installments. Installment payments may be paid over a period that does not exceed your life expectancy or the joint life expectancies of you and your beneficiary.

In Event of Your Death.   Any amount in your IRA at the time of your death will be distributed to your designated beneficiary(ies). If you do not designate a beneficiary or your designated beneficiary(ies) predeceases you, your beneficiary will be your estate.

Transfers and Rollovers.   You are permitted to transfer your existing IRA assets from one custodian to another without paying taxes. Such a direct transfer may be made as often as you wish. If you receive a distribution of assets from an existing IRA, you may make a tax-free rollover contribution of all or part of the assets you receive to another IRA. The rollover must be completed within 60 days after you receive the distribution from your existing IRA in order to avoid paying income or penalty taxes. You may make only one such tax-free rollover every 12 months. Remember, a transfer is when IRA assets are transferred directly from one custodian to another. A rollover occurs when you receive IRA assets from one custodian and then make a rollover contribution to another custodian.

SUMMARY

The individual retirement account (IRA) makes it possible for individuals to establish a meaningful long-term retirement program with important tax advantages: All earnings accumulate tax-free in your IRA until you begin making withdrawals, and because your IRA contributions may be tax-deductible, you may be able to reduce your federal income taxes today.

Chapter 14

How To Defer Taxes with Variable Annuities

It is possible today to take advantage of a plan that permits you to defer income taxes on the earnings from mutual fund investments. This plan is called a *variable annuity*. An investor begins participating in a variable annuity with a lump-sum purchase, much like an investment in a mutual fund.

A variable annuity consists of (1) an insurance contract that provides the tax deferral on your investment earnings, as well as the death benefit and guaranteed payout, and (2) the underlying mutual fund investments provided by a mutual fund company.

A variable annuity has two distinct phases in its life span: an accumulation phase and a distribution phase.

During the *accumulation* phase, your money is invested in mutual funds that have been specially created for the annuity program. You may allocate assets among several mutual fund portfolios over a long-term period—say 10, 15, 20 years or even longer. All capital gains, interest earnings and dividends are credited to your account on a tax-deferred basis. In this respect, a variable annuity resembles a nondeductible IRA (See Chapter 13, "A Tax-Favored Retirement Plan for You"). However, unlike an IRA, *the Internal Revenue Service (IRS) imposes no legal restrictions on the amount you can invest* in a variable annuity. Subject to insurance company limitations, you may invest as much and as often as you wish.

The *distribution* (or annuitization) phase comes after the accumulation phase, at which time you actually receive payments from your variable annuity. You may choose to receive your distribution either as a lump sum or in periodic payments for a specified time, such as 10 years, 20 years, or for life. If you have not taken a full distribution by the time of your death, your assets pass directly to your beneficiaries (if you have so instructed), thereby avoiding the costs and inconvenience of probate.

As with other tax-deferred plans, if you withdraw your money before you reach age 59½, you may be liable for a 10 percent penalty tax imposed on your accumulated earnings by the IRS, in addition to ordinary income taxes.

An important feature of a variable annuity is the *death benefit*. In the event of your death during the accumulation phase, the insurance company guarantees that your beneficiary will receive at least the amount of your investment (less any withdrawals you may have made and premium taxes) or the value of the account, whichever is higher.

WHO SHOULD INVEST?

A variable annuity generally makes sense for a specific type of investor. If you are in a high federal tax bracket and also pay state or local taxes, a variable annuity may be suitable for you as a long-term investment. The tax shelter during the accumulation phase will have a dramatic effect on your assets over time, permitting them to grow at a more rapid rate, as illustrated in Figure 14.1

The chart in Figure 14.1 assumes a $25,000 investment and a hypothetical 10 percent rate of return. It illustrates what happens to this amount with tax deferral over a number of years compared to the same amount in an investment taxed each year at 33 percent. The results do not reflect the actual performance of any particular fund, nor do they include annuity charges.

The top line illustrates how your money grows with tax deferral and no withdrawal before taxes. The middle line shows how your money grows with tax deferral and if you take a lump-sum withdrawal and pay all your taxes immediately. The bottom line shows how your money grows without tax deferral.

As indicated in the top line, if you have not made any withdrawals from your variable annuity, at the end of the 20 years your account

FIGURE 14.1 The Tax-Deferred Compounding Advantage of a Variable
Annuity ($25,000 Invested, 10% Rate of Return)

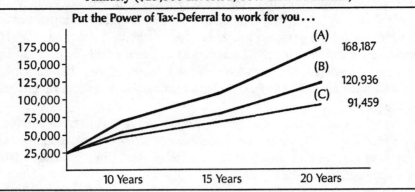

(A) Your money grows tax-deferred, no withdrawal before taxes.
(B) Your money grows tax-deferred, and you withdraw your money in a lump sum and pay taxes immediately.
(C) Your money grows in an investment that is taxed annually at 33 percent.
Source: Reprinted by permission of Fidelity Investments (Fidelity Retirement Reserves—1993)

would have a pretax value of $168,187. If you then take a lump sum withdrawal of the entire amount, your account would be taxed $47,251 (assuming a 33 percent combined federal and state tax bracket), leaving you with net proceeds of $120,936, as shown in the middle line. Thus, compared with the bottom-line 20-year accumulation of $91,459, the variable annuity has produced "value added" for you of $29,477.

This lump-sum distribution example is just one of the distribution options available in a variable annuity at the end of the accumulation phase, and it is the least tax-efficient. You could elect to take your distribution under any of several different available options. For instance, by electing to receive periodic payments, you could potentially reduce the taxes on your distribution. Or you could simply continue the accumulation phase, allowing your assets to compound tax-deferred until you reach age 85.

A variable annuity plan is not a financial and tax panacea. Because a variable annuity generally carries higher costs, primarily due to the insurance feature, it may not be appropriate until you have exhausted other tax-advantaged investment programs. These would include a deductible or nondeductible IRA, an employer-sponsored retirement plan or a Keogh plan for the self-employed. Most large mutual fund companies have such plans available at little or no cost to implement.

A variable annuity plan is designed for long-term investing. It should not be used as a short-term investment vehicle simply to benefit from the tax-deferral feature. Looking again at Figure 14.1, you'll notice that it takes longer for the advantages of tax deferral to offset the higher costs of the variable annuity as compared to the average mutual fund. Generally, it is best to think of a variable annuity plan as a suitable investment for periods of at least ten years.

SELECTING A VARIABLE ANNUITY PLAN

Since first arriving on the investment scene in the early 1960s, variable annuity plans have proliferated. They are now offered by more than 80 life insurance companies, often in concert with mutual fund companies. Information on more than 150 variable annuity plans is published in *Barron's National Business and Financial Weekly*. In addition to the names of insurance companies offering the variable annuity together with mutual company affiliates (if any), the data presented include each contract's accumulated unit value and its 4-week and 52-week total returns. The performance data do not, however, include the potential effects of any sales or redemption charges or additional fees. These can be significant.

Here are a number of factors to consider in determining which variable annuity might be suitable for you.

Pricing. As you would do in evaluating mutual funds for purchase, it is also important in the case of variable annuities to determine what costs are involved. Because of the insurance feature, a variable annuity's expenses are inherently higher than those of a mutual fund alone.

According to Variable Annuity Research and Data Service, the total annual expenses of the average variable annuity is 2.24 percent, which includes an average of 1.15 percent for the death benefit. Look for a plan that offers a below-average cost structure. For example, the Vanguard Variable Annuity Plan's total expenses are 1.08 percent, which includes a death benefit charge of only 0.45 percent.

As with mutual funds alone, variable annuities are sold on both a load and no-load basis. Other things being equal (especially investment performance), choose a no-load plan—one that is available without any commissions, sales charges, exchange fees or surrender charges. Among mutual fund companies offering no-load variable annuities are

FIGURE 14.2   Fee Table of the Vanguard Variable Annuity Plan Contract

The following table illustrates all expenses that you would incur as a Contract Owner, except for premium taxes that may be assessed by your state (see "Charges and Deductions"). The expenses and fees shown are for the 1991 fiscal year. The purpose of this table is to assist you in understanding the various costs and expenses that you would bear directly or indirectly as a purchaser of the Contract. The fee table reflects all expenses for both the Separate Account and the Fund. For a complete discussion of contract costs and expenses, see "Charges and Deductions."

Owner Transaction Expenses	Separate Account
Sales Load Imposed on Purchases	None
Redemption Fees	None
Exchange Fees	None

Annual Account Maintenance Fee	$25.00

Annual Separate Account Expenses	Separate Account
Mortality and Expense Risk Charge*	.45%
Administrative Expense Charge	.10%
Total Annual Separate Account Expenses	.55%

* This charge is reduced in various increments to 0.30% for average daily net assets in excess of $1.5 billion.

Annual Fund Operating Expenses	Money Market Portfolio	High-Grade Bond portfolio	Balanced Portfolio	Equity Index Portfolio
Management Expenses	.32%	.37%	.31%	.38%
Investment Advisory Fees	.00*	.00*	.10	.00*
Distribution Costs*	.00	.00	.00	.00
Other Expenses	.02	.03	.10	.07
Total Fund Operating Expenses	.34%	.40%	.51%	.45%

TOTAL EXPENSES	Money Market Portfolio	High-Grade Bond portfolio	Balanced Portfolio	Equity Index Portfolio
Total Separate Account Expenses	.55%	.55%	.55%	.55%
Total Fund Operating Expenses	.34	.40	.51	.45
Grand Total, Separate Account and Fund Operating Expenses	.89%	.95%	1.06%	1.00%

Distribution Costs and Investment Advisory Fees for the Fund's 1991 fiscal year were less than .01% of the Fund's average net assets for that period.

Source: Vanguard Variable Annuity Plan Contract prospectus dated May 1, 1992

the Vanguard Group, The Scudder Family of Funds and Fidelity Investments.

Low expenses are particularly important in a variable annuity, as they are with any investment plan. Over time, generally, the lower the costs, the higher the returns.

Each variable annuity plan is offered with a prospectus, as are conventional mutual funds. Among other important information included in the prospectus is a table of fees, which sets forth all expenses that an investor would incur as owner of a variable annuity contract. Figure 14.2 is a reproduction of the fee table that appears in the 1992 prospectus of the Vanguard Variable Annuity Plan Contract.

Investment Alternatives.   A variable annuity's investment alternatives should have fundamentally sound objectives that seek long-term superior investment returns commensurate with the market risks assumed by an investor. For example, consider the investment choices offered by the Vanguard Group:

- The Money Market Portfolio invests in high-quality certificates of deposit, bankers acceptances, commercial paper and U.S. government securities.
- The High-Grade Bond Portfolio, an "indexed" portfolio, invests in high-quality government and corporate bonds and seeks to parallel the total return of the Salomon Brothers Investment-Grade Bond Index.
- The Balanced Portfolio invests 60 percent to 70 percent of its assets in common stocks and 30 percent to 40 percent in high-quality corporate bonds.
- The Equity Index Portfolio attempts to match the performance of the unmanaged Standard & Poor's 500 Composite Stock Price Index.

A variety of investment alternatives gives you the flexibility to tailor your investment portfolio to meet your particular needs.

Performance.   Past performance is no guarantee of future results. But it is useful when examining how adept management has been at increasing the assets of its variable annuity holders during the accumulation phase. Some funds have quite clearly done better than others. Figure 14.3 shows 52-week total returns in investment subaccounts of three variable annuity plans from three well-known insurance

FIGURE 14.3 Total Returns from Three Variable Annuity Plans

Charter National Life Insurance Company
Scudder Horizon Plan

Portfolio	52-Week Total Return*
Balanced	15.07%
Bond	15.97
Capital Growth	29.26
International	28.52
Money Market	1.86

*For the 52-week period ending October 20, 1993.

National Home Life Assurance Company
of New York
Vanguard Variable Annuity Plan

Portfolio	52-Week Total Return*
Balanced	14.81%
Equity Income	12.81
High-Grade Bond	10.85
Money Market	2.45

*For the 52-week period ending October 27, 1993.

Fidelity Investors
Fidelity Retirement Reserves

Portfolio	52-Week Total Return*
VIP Equity Income	25.32%
VIP Growth	30.60
VIP High-Income	18.14
VIP Money Market	2.25
VIP Overseas	34.52
VIP2 Asset	19.42
VIP2 Investment Grade	11.58

*For the 52-week period ending October 20, 1993.

FIGURE 14.4 52-Week Total Returns of Other Variable Annuity Plans
(Subaccounts: Growth, Income, or Growth and Income)

Life Insurance Company	Subaccounts	52-Week Total Return
AIG		
AIG Variable Account I	Growth	20.16%**
Anchor National		
American Pathway II	Growth and Income	15.65*
Bankers Security		
The USA Plan	Growth and Income	14.58*
Connecticut Mutual		
Panorama	Growth	28.88*
	Income	15.35*
Jefferson-Pilot		
Separate Account A	Growth	10.61*
	Income	12.93*
Lincoln National		
American Legacy	Growth and Income	14.54*
Metropolitan		
Preference Plus	Growth	22.37*
	Income	11.99*
North American Security		
Venture	Growth and Income	13.37*
Northwestern National		
Select Annuity II	Growth	30.21*
United Investors		
Advantage II	Growth	19.43*
	Income	19.98*

*For the 52-week period ending October 20, 1993
**For the 52-week period ending October 27, 1993

companies that you can purchase directly without a broker or insurance agent. For each plan, the name of the insurance company sponsor appears first, with the name of the variable annuity plan.

Figure 14.4 is a representative sample of the more than 80 insurance companies that offer variable annuity plans, with 52-week total returns reported for their growth, income, or growth and income subaccounts.

Premium Taxes. The state where you live is important, because variable annuity contract owners will pay premium taxes in the 13 states where state law imposes such taxes. Premium taxes range from as little as 1 percent to as much as 3.5 percent.

The following states assess a premium tax on *all* initial and subsequent purchase payments:

	Qualified Plan	Nonqualified Plan
Pennsylvania	0.0%	2.00%
South Dakota	0.0	1.25

The following states assess a premium tax against the accumulated value of the plan if the owner chooses an annuity payment option instead of receiving a lump-sum distribution:

	Qualified Plan	Nonqualified Plan
Alabama	1.00%	1.00%
California	0.50	2.35
District of Columbia	2.25	2.25
Kansas	0.00	2.00
Kentucky	2.00	2.00
Maine	0.00	2.00
Mississippi	0.00	2.00
Nevada	0.00	3.50
North Carolina	0.00	1.90
West Virginia	1.00	1.00
Wyoming	0.00	1.00

ANNUITY PAYMENT OPTIONS

If you decide in the distribution phase to opt for periodic payments instead of a lump sum, you will have to choose either a *fixed annuity option* or a *variable annuity option*. Under a fixed annuity option, the amount of each payment will be set on the annuity date (the date on which annuity payments begin) and will not change. If you choose a variable annuity option, annuity payments (after the initial payment) will reflect the investment experience of the investment portfolio(s) you have selected.

The following annuity payment options are generally available:

- *Life annuity*—Monthly annuity payments are continued for life.
- *Joint and last survivor annuity*—Monthly annuity payments are continued for the life of two people and thereafter for the life of the survivor. This is typically used in a husband-and-wife situation.
- *Life annuity with period certain*—Monthly annuity payments are continued for the life of an annuitant, with a period certain of not less than 10 years, 15 years or 20 years, as elected.
- *Installment or unit refund life annuity*—Monthly annuity payments are continued for the life of an annuitant, with a period certain determined by dividing the accumulated value of the account by the first annuity payment.
- *Designated period annuity*—Available *only* as a fixed annuity option. Monthly annuity payments are continued for a period certain, as elected, which may be from 10 to 30 years.

For annuity payment options involving life income, the age of the annuitant or of a joint annuitant will affect the amount of each payment. Since payments to older annuitants are expected to be fewer in number, the amount of each annuity payment will be greater. The value of all payments, both fixed and variable, will be greater for shorter guaranteed periods than for longer guaranteed periods, and greater for life annuities than for joint and survivor annuities, because they are expected to be made for a shorter period.

VARIABLE ANNUITY PAYMENTS REFLECT INVESTMENT RESULTS

The value of variable annuity payments will reflect the investment results of the chosen investment portfolio. On or after the date annuity payments begin, the payment option is irrevocable. You may choose just one annuity option from among those made available by the company per each portfolio.

Annuity tables calculate the value of your variable annuity payments and are based on an assumed interest rate. If the actual investment results exactly equal the assumed interest rate (highly unlikely), then the variable annuity payments will remain the same—equal to the first payment. However, if actual investment experience exceeds the assumed interest rate, the variable annuity payments will increase; conversely, they will decrease if the actual experience is lower.

HOW VARIABLE ANNUITIES ARE TAXED

Section 72 of the Internal Revenue Code governs the taxation of annuities. As a variable annuity contract owner, you are not taxed on increases in value under a contract until some form of withdrawal or distribution is made. Proceeds of a full or partial withdrawal from a variable annuity prior to the annuity date is treated as taxable income to the extent that the amounts held in the contract exceed the "investment in the contract," which generally constitutes all purchase payments paid for the contract less any amounts received under the contract that are excluded from your gross income. The taxable portion is taxed at ordinary income tax rates.

For fixed annuity payments, the taxable portion of each payment is determined by using a formula known as the *exclusion ratio,* which establishes the ratio that the investment in the variable annuity contract bears to the total expected amount of annuity payments for the contract's term. That ratio is then applied to each payment to determine the nontaxable portion of the payment. The remaining portion of each payment is taxed at ordinary income rates.

For variable annuity payments, the taxable portion is determined by a formula that establishes a specific dollar amount of each payment that is not taxed. The dollar amount is determined by dividing the investment in the contract by the total number of expected periodic payments. The remaining portion of each payment is taxed at ordinary income tax rates. Once the excludable portion of annuity payments to date equals the investment in the contracts, the balance of the annuity payments will be fully taxable.

Penalties.   If you withdraw amounts or receive distributions from your variable annuity before age 59½, a penalty tax is imposed equal to 10 percent of the taxable portion of amounts withdrawn or distributed.

Exemptions from Penalties.   However, the penalty tax does not apply if withdrawals or distributions are made

- in the event of your death or total disability,

- as part of a series of substantially equal payments made at least annually under a life or joint life annuity,
- from a qualified plan,
- under an immediate annuity contract, or
- that are purchased by an employer on termination of certain types of qualified plans and that are held by the employer until the employee separates from service.

SUMMARY

A variable annuity is a contract with an insurance company using mutual funds as a tax-deferred investment vehicle. The insurance contract gives an annuity its tax-deferral and guaranteed-payout advantages, while the underlying mutual funds provide the return on your investment. An investor begins participating in a variable annuity plan with a lump-sum purchase, much like an investment in a mutual fund. A variable annuity makes sense for a high-income investor who wants to defer taxes and has exhausted other methods of federally created tax-deferred investing, such as IRAs, SEP-IRAs, Keoghs and other retirement programs.

Chapter 15

Speculating in Mutual Funds

Is it possible to speculate in mutual funds? You bet it is, and you can do it profitably.

Mutual funds are considered the conservative investor's friend. And so they are, combining the desirable characteristics of risk reduction through diversification, low cost of investing, ease of use, wide selection of investment opportunities, published performance records, prompt and complete shareholder reports, and strict governmental regulation. Some of the same characteristics that appeal to conservative investors are also valuable to the speculator.

Diversification of securities held in a mutual fund portfolio means that a speculator can concentrate on market, industry or geographic trends or events. You don't have to be concerned that the financial officer of a particular company has doctored the books to boost profits, or that a few of the top executives have embezzled hundreds of millions of dollars. Events like these, specific to individual companies, have happened and will happen in the future. But when they do, it won't have a significant impact on the diversified portfolio of a well-run mutual fund.

Low cost of investing enables a speculator to buy into and sell out of a fund at little or no cost. Buying a no-load mutual fund that charges no fee or commission to purchase and has no redemption fee or back-end load when you want to jump out can have an important bearing on whether you make money on a "round-trip" transaction.

Contrast this with the high costs involved in buying and selling stocks or commodities. Historically, transaction costs have been the main reason most speculators lose money.

Ease of use is important to a speculator. With a no-load mutual fund, you can purchase shares directly from the investment company. A toll-free telephone call permits you to buy or sell at the fund's same-day closing net asset value; of course, you must call prior to the 4:00 PM close of the NYSE.

The *wide selection of investment opportunities* available in the mutual fund universe gives you ample room to operate in. Large mutual fund groups, like Dreyfus, Fidelity, T. Rowe Price, Scudder and Vanguard operate many types of mutual funds, including those that tend to be very volatile.

Shareholder reports following each trade provide you with a complete and easily understood record of transactions, important for tracking your performance and for tax reporting.

Strict government regulation protects you from the abuse of trust that is too often present without the disclosure and regulation that federal and state laws require. Mutual funds are among the most highly regulated business entities under the federal securities laws—one less problem for a speculator to have to worry about.

SPECULATING IN INDEX FUNDS

Index funds have been organized that track many of the most widely followed market indexes. The following securities market indexes, or industry groups, have index fund counterparts:

American Gas Association companies
Lehman Brothers Aggregate Bond Index
Morgan Stanley Capital International Europe (Free) Index
Morgan Stanley Capital International Pacific Index
North American gold-producing companies
Russell 2000 Index
Schwab 1000 Index
S&P/BARRA Growth Index
S&P/BARRA Income Index
S&P 500 Composite Stock Index
S&P Midcap 400 Index
Wilshire 4500 Index
Wilshire 5000 Index

FIGURE 15.1   Total Returns of Vanguard Index Trust 500 Portfolio 1983 to 1992

	Vanguard Fund	S&P 500		Vanguard Fund	S&P 500
1983	21.29%	22.47%	1988	16.22%	16.60%
1984	6.21	6.27	1989	31.37	31.68
1985	31.23	31.83	1990	-3.33	-3.12
1986	18.06	18.68	1991	30.22	30.48
1987	4.71	5.26	1992	7.42	7.62

Vanguard Index Trust 500 Portfolio replicates the S&P 500 Composite Stock Price Index. The fund seeks investment results that correspond to the price and yield performance of the S&P 500. Because its annual expenses are only 19 basis points, the fund has been able to mirror the S&P 500 almost exactly. And since it is a no-load fund, it works very well for someone who wants to place bets on the index. The fund does charge an annual account maintenance fee of $10. The fund's annual total returns, as well as those of the S&P 500, are illustrated in Figure 15.1.

A low-cost, well-run index fund provides a straightforward, low-cost vehicle for betting on what a particular segment of the market will do. For a complete discussion of index funds and the market indexes they replicate and seek to track, read Chapter 11, "Index Funds: The Answer to a Paradox."

SPECULATING IN SPECIALTY FUNDS

Quite a few funds tend to be very volatile because of their investment policy. The types of securities held in their portfolios can have wide price swings under certain market conditions.

Benham Target Maturities Trust 2015 Portfolio presents an opportunity for a play in long-term interest rates. This fund invests only in zero-coupon U.S. Treasury securities scheduled to mature in the year 2015, giving it a habitually long-term duration. Its extreme stance makes the fund highly interest rate–sensitive. Since the price of its shares reacts inversely to interest rate movements, they will rise when interest rates fall and decline when interest rates rise. The total annual returns for Benham Target Maturities Trust 2015 Portfolio since 1986

FIGURE 15.2 Total Returns of Benham Target Maturities Trust 2015 Portfolio 1986* to 1992

1986	13.20%	1990	−1.22%
1987	−18.49	1991	16.39
1988	42.09	1992	7.29
1989	34.70		

*The fund commenced operation on September 1, 1986.

are illustrated in Figure 15.2. Through August 31, 1993, the fund's total return was up 36.23 percent.

An interesting aspect of speculating in the Benham Target Maturities Trust 2015 Portfolio is that while the fund's share price will fluctuate in accordance with interest rate movements, an investor *can be guaranteed a profit* (that is, if he or she has patience). This is because the fund has a target net asset value of $100 in the year 2015. As long as the net asset value of shares purchased is below $100, an investor is assured a profit. The net asset value on August 31, 1993, was $29.29.

INVESCO Strategic Portfolios Health Sciences is another example of a specialty fund that has been subject to wide price swings, though not as extreme as some of the precious metal funds.

This fund normally invests at least 80 percent of its assets in the equity securities of companies engaged in the development, production or distribution of products or services related to the health sciences. It invests heavily in biotechnology stocks. The total annual returns for INVESCO Strategic Portfolios Health Sciences since 1984 are shown in Figure 15.3. Through June 30, 1993, the fund's total return was down another 17.54 percent.

Lexington Strategic Investments has been a pure South African gold play and, as such, subject to that country's political and currency

FIGURE 15.3 Total Returns of INVESCO Strategic Portfolios Health Sciences 1984* to 1992

1984	1.62%	1989	59.48%
1985	30.50	1990	25.79
1986	31.03	1991	91.80
1987	7.06	1992	−14.40
1988	16.05		

*The fund commenced operations on January 19, 1984.

FIGURE 15.4 Total Returns of Lexington Strategic Investments
1982 to 1992

1982	70.19%	1986	28.53	1990	−43.35%
1983	−1.93	1987	23.62%	1991	−18.93
1984	−34.12	1988	−43.00	1992	−60.71
1985	−29.45	1989	61.22		

instability. The fund normally invests in the securities of companies that explore for and mine, process, fabricate and distribute natural resources such as hydrocarbons, minerals, gold, silver, uranium, platinum and copper. Its objective is to seek capital appreciation.

Over the ten years ended June 30, 1993, the fund had a *negative* total return of over 10 percent. Since 1982, the fund's annual total returns have experienced wide swings, as illustrated in Figure 15.4.

In the first six months of 1993, the funds was up an astounding *190.70 percent!* Clearly, a prescient (or lucky) speculator could have cashed in on these swings. The only problem with this fund for an in-and-out investor is the load. The fund has a 5.75 percent load and must be purchased through a broker.

Nomura Pacific Basin Fund invests in equity securities of corporations domiciled in Pacific Basin countries, including Japan, Australia, Hong Kong, Singapore, Malaysia, New Zealand and the Philippines. Japanese holdings are predominant. There is no load or fee to purchase or sell shares, so the fund works well as a cost-efficient way to play the Pacific Basin market. The total annual returns for Nomura Pacific Basin Fund since 1986, its first full year of operation, are illustrated in Figure 15.5.

The fund had a total return of 27.69 percent for the first six months of 1993.

United Services Gold Shares is a no-load fund, which eliminates the cost when buying shares. However, there is a redemption fee of

FIGURE 15.5 Total Returns of Nomura Pacific Basin Fund 1986 to 1992

1986	74.27%	1990	−15.51%
1987	34.90	1991	11.93
1988	15.18	1992	−12.74
1989	22.91		

FIGURE 15.6 Total Returns of United Services Gold Shares 1982 to 1992

1982	72.34%	1986	37.87%	1990	−34.22%
1983	1.17	1987	31.59	1991	−15.65
1984	−29.65	1988	−35.74	1992	−50.83
1985	−26.84	1989	64.73		

0.10 percent when shares are sold within one month of purchase. This shouldn't cause too much of a problem.

This fund normally invests at least 65 percent of its assets in securities of companies involved in gold operations. But since the fund invests worldwide, it doesn't have price swings quite as wide as Lexington Strategic Investments. Its total ten-year return through 1992 was also negative, at −7.38 percent. Figure 15.6 shows the total annual returns for United Services Gold Shares since 1982.

Following the loss of half its value in 1992, the fund *gained 91.60 percent* in 1993 through June 30.

SUMMARY

Some of the same characteristics that make mutual funds ideal for conservative investors are also very helpful to a person who wants to "play the market." Investors who want to speculate in the market as a whole, or in special segments of it, can find ready vehicles to use in the form of index funds or specialized objective funds.

Part Three

The Wide World of Mutual Funds

Chapter 16

Understanding Types of Mutual Funds

Mutual funds are generally classified into broad categories according to their investment objectives. An objective defines what the fund is striving to do. These objectives vary from speculative, such as precious metals or gold funds, to conservative, high-quality corporate bond funds. Investors interested in investing in mutual funds should first set for themselves clear and reasonable investment objectives. A careful reading of the following list of mutual fund categories will help shape your understanding of what investment objective alternatives are available and which ones most nearly match your own needs and tolerance for risk.

Andrew Carnegie, the Scottish-born industrialist who built a great steel company a century ago, said, "Put all your eggs in one basket, and watch that basket." Your own investment portfolio is the basket, and carefully selected mutual funds can be the eggs. A prudent investor reduces risk through diversification, and investing in a diversified basket of various types of mutual funds is an excellent way to accomplish this. No definitive list of investment objectives exists, but the categories presented in this book are generally accepted as covering the mutual fund universe.

INVESTMENT CATEGORIES

This section of the book is devoted to describing each mutual fund category, including the investment objective, a survey of the group with historical investment returns, a recommended fund that you can purchase directly from the mutual fund company, and a list of other mutual funds in the same category with five-year investment results. You will find a considerable amount of detailed information about the recommended fund, including its investment objective, investment policy, operating expenses, historical investment performance, 25 largest security holdings, composition and weightings of its portfolio, plus a commentary.

Domestic Equity Funds

Aggressive growth funds seek maximum capital gains as their investment objective. Current income is not a factor in selecting securities. Some may invest in companies that are somewhat out of the mainstream, such as fledgling businesses, new industries, companies that have fallen on hard times, or industries that are temporarily out of favor. Some funds may use specialized investment techniques, such as short-term trading or option writing.

Equity-income funds seek a high level of current income for their shareholders by investing primarily in the equity securities of companies with good dividend-paying records.

Growth funds invest in the common stock of well-established companies. Their primary goal is to produce an increase in the value of their investments through capital gains rather than through a flow of dividends. Investors who purchase growth funds are more interested in seeing the value of their shares rise than in receiving income from dividends.

Growth and income funds invest primarily in the common stock of companies that have had increasing share value and also a solid record of paying dividends. This type of fund attempts to combine long-term capital growth with a steady stream of dividend income.

Small-company growth funds seek capital appreciation by investing primarily in stocks of small companies, as determined by either market capitalization or assets.

International Stock Funds

Europe stock funds seek long-term capital growth by investing primarily in equity securities of companies located in Europe, normally maintaining at least 65 percent of their assets in that market. Current income is normally not a consideration in the selection of securities.

Foreign stock funds invest mostly in the securities of companies that have their principal business activities outside of the United States. Long-term growth of capital is their primary objective, although some funds also seek current income and growth of income.

Pacific stock funds seek capital appreciation through investments in companies that have their principal business activities in the Pacific Basin. Such countries include Japan, Australia, Hong Kong, Singapore, Malaysia, New Zealand and the Philippines. Current income is normally not an important consideration.

World stock funds seek long-term capital growth by investing in equity securities of issuers located throughout the world, maintaining a percentage of their assets (usually 25–50 percent) in the United States. Some funds also seek current income and growth of income.

Specialty Stock Funds

Financial services funds seek capital appreciation by investing primarily in equity securities of financial service companies, including banks, brokerage firms and insurance companies. Current income is a secondary consideration for some funds.

Health-care funds seek growth of capital by investing mainly in equity securities of health-care companies, including drug manufacturers, hospitals and biotechnology companies. Current income is generally not a consideration in selecting securities.

Natural resources funds seek capital appreciation by investing at least 65 percent of their assets in the common stock of companies that explore, develop, produce and/or distribute natural resources. Natural resource companies include those in precious metals, minerals, water, timber, oil, natural gas, coal, uranium and similar industries.

Precious metals funds seek capital appreciation by normally investing at least two-thirds of their assets in equity securities of companies engaged in the mining, distribution or processing of precious metals—especially gold and silver.

Technology funds seek growth of capital by investing primarily in companies engaged in the development, distribution or servicing of technology-related equipment, processes or products. These companies will often be small growth companies or companies investing heavily in research and development where untried technologies hold great promise, but whose commercial success is not yet established.

Utilities funds primarily seek current income by investing in the equity securities of public utility companies that provide electricity, natural gas, water, sanitary services, telephone or telegraph service, or other communications services. Capital appreciation is a secondary objective.

Hybrid Funds

Asset allocation funds seek total return by putting highest priority on the decision as to which types of securities will be held, often based on an analysis of trends in the business cycle. Often, separate managers will be responsible for each class of security (e.g., stocks, bonds, convertibles, real estate, etc.), and an allocator will supervise the process of determining the percentage of assets going into each sector.

Balanced funds generally have a three-part objective: (1) to conserve the investor's principal, (2) to pay current income, and (3) to promote long-term growth of both principal and income. A portfolio mix of bonds, preferred stocks and common stocks is used to accomplish this objective.

Income funds invest in both equity and debt securities primarily for the purpose of providing current income. These funds will generally invest no more than 50 percent of their assets in equities.

Specialty Bond Funds

Convertible bond funds invest primarily in bonds, notes, debentures and preferred stocks that can be converted into a set number of shares of common stock in the issuing company at a pre-stated price or exchange ratio. As such, they have characteristics similar to both fixed-income and equity securities.

High-yield corporate bond funds seek income usually by investing at least 65 percent of their assets in bonds rated below BBB (by Standard & Poor's rating service), or Baa (by Moody's rating service). In return for a generally higher yield, investors must bear a greater degree of risk than they would for higher-rated bonds.

World bond funds seek current income. Capital appreciation is usually a secondary objective. These funds invest primarily in bonds not denominated in U.S. currency, which are frequently offerings of foreign governments. Assets are allocated among countries, geographic regions and currency denominations in an attempt to achieve a high total investment return.

Corporate Bond Funds

General corporate bond funds seek income by investing in fixed-income securities, primarily corporate bonds with an average rating of AA (Standard & Poor's rating service) or Aa (Moody's rating service). Some funds will hold as much as 35 percent of their portfolio in high-yield "junk bonds," while others invest more than 60 percent of their assets in U.S. government backed issues. Still other funds maintain nearly 35 percent in foreign-backed instruments.

High-quality corporate bond funds seek income by investing in fixed-income securities, of which at least 65 percent are rated A or higher. Many funds in this group will also invest a significant portion of their assets in lower-tier investment-grade or speculative high-yield bonds.

Short-term world income funds seek income and a stable net asset value by investing primarily in a portfolio of various non–U.S.- currency-denominated bonds. These instruments usually have an average maturity of three years or less. Funds in this group may engage in substantial hedging strategies to reduce fluctuation of net asset value.

Government Bond Funds

Government bond—adjustable-rate mortgage funds seek current income with minimum fluctuation of share price by investing at least 65 percent of their assets in U.S. government-backed adjustable-rate mortgages (ARMs) or other adjustable-rate securities collateralized by mortgage securities.

General government bond funds seek current income by investing primarily in securities issued or guaranteed by the U.S. government and its agencies or instrumentalities. These issues will range from short-term U.S. Treasury bills to longer-term notes and bonds. The high quality of the securities held in these portfolios is designed to protect shareholders against credit risk.

Government bond—mortgage funds seek current income as well as preservation of capital by investing primarily in mortgage-backed securities guaranteed as to timely payment of interest and principal by the U.S. government and issued by its agencies or instrumentalities. Many of these funds invest in other securities, such as intermediate and long-term government bonds, privately issued mortgage-related securities and repurchase agreements collateralized by mortgage securities.

Government bond—Treasury funds generally have a preponderance of their assets invested in U.S. Treasury bills, notes and bonds, and other "full faith and credit" obligations of the U.S. government. Most funds seek current income and protection of capital.

Municipal Bond Funds

Municipal bond funds seek income by investing primarily in tax-free bonds issued by states or municipalities to finance schools, highways, bridges, hospitals, airports, water and sewer works, and other public projects. The main appeal of municipal bonds is the fact that they provide income that is exempt from federal income taxes and, in some cases, from state and local taxes.

Single-state municipal bond funds are just like other municipal bond funds except that their portfolios contain the issues of only one state. A resident of that state has the advantage of receiving income that is exempt from both federal *and* state taxes.

SUMMARY

Mutual funds are generally classified into broad categories according to their investment strategies. Potential investors will find an extensive universe of mutual fund categories to choose from, ranging from very speculative to ultraconservative. After setting your own clear and reasonable objectives, you now have an opportunity to put together a diversified portfolio of funds from among the types that meet your own particular needs.

Chapter 17

Domestic Stock Funds: Investing for Growth in the United States

Aggressive Growth Funds

Usual Investment Objective of the Group

Mutual funds included in the aggressive growth fund group seek maximum capital gains as their investment objective. Current income is not a significant factor. Some may invest in stocks of companies that are somewhat out of the mainstream, such as fledgling firms, new industries, companies that have fallen on hard times, or industries temporarily out of favor. Some may also use specialized investment techniques, such as option writing or short-term trading.

Survey of the Group

Aggressive growth funds constantly look for stocks that may be overlooked and will produce top-drawer returns in the future. In the last year or so, funds that concentrated on value plays and were heavily weighted in cheaper cyclical stocks outperformed their peers that held large stakes in biotechnology and other health-related companies.

Funds that showed large gains in early 1993 include Fidelity Capital Appreciation Fund, Third Avenue Value Fund and American Heritage Fund. The first two funds are heavily weighted in cyclicals, distressed utilities and financial stocks, while American Heritage is known for choosing from a wide horizon of choices and for extremely high turnover. Fidelity also did well from its silver-mining stocks. The performance of one fund, Fontaine Capital Appreciation, was near the top of the group early in 1993 as a result of its 17 percent exposure to gold-mining stocks. Indicative of the volatility of this group, however, is the fading of Fontaine when the price of gold dropped drastically later in the year.

The big losers in early 1993 were those funds that were heavily weighted in health care. The stocks of nearly all companies in this sector were hit hard, but the stocks of medical device and biotechnology companies were especially affected. Pharmaceutical and health maintenance organization stocks were barely scathed, though. The end result was that funds that kept large portions of their portfolios in health-care stocks suffered big losses.

Aggressive growth funds as a group performed pretty well over most historical periods. An exception was the ten-year period ending April 30, 1993, during which they had an average return of 7.22 percent versus the S&P 500 average return of 14.4 percent. Volatility has been exceptional, even considering the group's investment objective of maximum growth.

The table below indicates the historical average total return of the aggressive growth group and the S&P 500 Index for years ending December 31.

Aggressive Growth Group versus S&P 500 Index

	Group Total Return	S&P 500		Group Total Return	S&P 500
1983	19.14%	22.47%	1988	15.59%	16.60%
1984	−15.68	6.27	1989	27.49	31.68
1985	25.92	31.83	1990	−8.96	−3.12
1986	10.53	18.68	1991	48.61	30.48
1987	−3.57	5.26	1992	8.42	7.62

Source: *Morningstar Mutual Funds,* Morningstar, Inc., 225 W. Wacker Dr., Chicago, IL 60606; 312-696-6532

Recommended Fund

Strong Discovery Fund
P.O. Box 2936
Milwaukee, WI 53201-2936
800-368-1030

Portfolio manager: Richard S. Strong
Investment adviser: Strong/Cornelison Capital Management
Sales fees: No-load
Management fee: 1.0%
Total operating expense: 1.51%
Minimum initial purchase: $1,000 (additional: $50)
Minimum IRA purchase: $250 (additional: $50)
Date of inception: December 31, 1987
Net assets of fund as of April 30, 1993: $198.5 million

Investment Objective
Strong Discovery Fund seeks maximum capital appreciation through a diversified portfolio of securities. Current income is not a factor in selecting investments.

Investment Policy
The fund may invest up to 100 percent of its assets in common stocks, convertible securities and warrants. It may also invest up to 100 percent of its assets in nonconvertible corporate debt and intermediate-to long-term government debt securities, if the adviser believes these securities offer the opportunity for capital appreciation.

The fund intends to engage in short-term trading, and it may invest a substantial portion of its assets in small, unseasoned companies. It may invest up to 15 percent of its assets directly in foreign securities and may invest without limit in American Depositary Receipts.

Performance
The tables below indicate the annual total returns of the Strong Discovery Fund for each full year of operation ending December 31 and comparative results for the S&P 500 Index, followed by total returns and the growth of $10,000 invested for different periods ending April 30, 1993.

FIGURE 17.1 Strong Discovery Fund Selected Per-Share Data and Ratios

SELECTED PER SHARE DATA AND RATIOS
(For each share of a Fund outstanding throughout each period)

The following Selected Per Share Data and Ratios for each of the Equity Funds has been audited by Coopers & Lybrand, independent certified public accountants.

	Investment Income	Expenses	Net Investment Income	Dividends from Net Investment Income	Net Asset Value at Beginning of Period
Strong Discovery Fund					
Year Ended December 31,					
1988	$1.11	$0.16	$0.95	$0.97	$10.00
1989	0.54	0.24	0.30	0.28	11.44
1990	0.51	0.24	0.27	0.31	13.18
1991	0.27	0.27	0.00	–	12.51
1992	0.15	0.21	(0.06)	–	17.49

* In thousands.
(1) Represents return of capital distribution.
(2) For years prior to 1985, pursuant to the Securities and Exchange Commission's rules amendment,

the portfolio turnover rates exclude long-term U.S. government securities.
(3) Includes $0.83 treated as ordinary income distribution for tax purposes.

Source: Strong Discovery Fund prospectus dated May 1, 1993

Strong Discovery Fund versus S&P 500 Index

	Fund Total Return	S&P 500		Fund Total Return	S&P 500
1988	24.45%	16.60%	1991	67.61%	30.48%
1989	24.01	31.68	1992	2.52	7.62
1990	–2.75	–3.12			

Total Returns for Different Periods Ending April 30, 1993

	Fund Total Return	Growth of $10,000
3 Months	1.92%	$10,192
6 Months	16.97	11,697
1 Year	9.60	10,960
3-Year Average	21.31	17,852
5-Year Average	17.08	21,999

Source: *Morningstar Mutual Funds*

Financial History

Figure 17.1 illustrates per-share data for a share outstanding throughout each period and selected ratio information for each year ended December 31.

FIGURE 17.1 *(continued)*

Their report is included in the Annual Report of the Equity Funds for the fiscal year ended December 31, 1992. The Selected Per Share Data and Ratios should be read in conjunction with the Financial Statements and related notes included in the Funds' Annual Report.

Net Realized and Unrealized Gains or (Losses) on Investments	Distributions from Net Realized Gains and Other Capital Sources	Net Asset Value at End of Period	Ratio of Expenses to Average Net Assets	Ratio of Net Investment Income to Average Net Assets	Portfolio Turnover Rate*	Shares Outstanding at End of Period*
$1.49	$0.03	$11.44	2.0%	11.9%	441.6%	1,193
2.43	0.71	13.18	1.9	2.4	549.6	4,395
(0.63)	–	12.51	1.9	2.1	493.9	4,496
8.41	3.43[3]	17.49	1.6	0.0	1,059.9	9,291
0.23	1.65[4]	16.01	1.5	(0.4)	1,258.6	12,073

(4) Includes $1.50 treated as ordinary income distribution for tax purposes.
(5) Ordinary income distribution for tax purposes.

(6) Includes $0.22 treated as ordinary income distribution for tax purposes.

Comments

Strong Discovery Fund investments tend to consist of securities in small capitalization companies with smaller trading volumes. From time to time, the fund seeks capital appreciation by investing a substantial portion of its assets in small, unseasoned companies that the manager believes have favorable prospects for earnings growth.

In early 1993, the fund moved into a defensive mode. Rather than increasing the fund's cash position as had been done in the past, Mr. Strong employed several other strategies in an effort to protect the fund from a market decline. For example, 12 percent of the fund's assets were invested in the Hong Kong stock market. He believes that, in addition to providing decent yields, the Hong Kong market will move independently of the U.S. market. This is contrary to the thinking of some analysts, who believe the Hong Kong market is due for a correction.

In another, more common, defensive measure, the fund's position in value-oriented, large capitalization companies such as Kodak and Sears has been increased. Real estate trusts have also been purchased to take advantage of their steady income and low volatility.

Some of the large capitalization stocks were a productive addition to the fund in early 1993, with both Kodak and Sears helping the fund's performance; each had price increases of more than 15 percent through April. Hong Kong's bull market was also a benefit to the fund in 1993. Overall, by the end of April the fund outperformed nearly three-fourths of its peers.

Strong Discovery Fund has done very well in the first five years of its existence, with a total return averaging over 17 percent. But total return performances of 24 percent in 1988 and 1989, followed by 2.75 percent in 1990, 67.6 percent in 1991 and back to 2.5 percent in 1992, will remind an investor of the roller-coaster ride that may lie ahead.

Portfolio

Total stocks: 181 as of March 31, 1993

25 Largest Holdings

Magnetek	Ethan Allen
Walt Disney	Intel
Eastman Kodak	US Banknote
Megafoods Stores	Payless Cashways
Canandaigua Wine Class A	Apache
Sears Roebuck	Showboat
Harley-Davidson	Kendall International
USX-Delhi Group	Jan Bell Marketing
Longhorn Steaks	Seagull Energy
Georgia-Pacific	Bankers Life Holdings
Technology Solutions	Family Dollar Stores
Tide West	United Retail Group
McDonald's	

Composition of Portfolio

As of March 31, 1993

Cash	2.7%
Stocks	97.2
Convertibles	0.1

Sector Weightings

As of April 30, 1993

Natural resources	7.4%
Industrial products	13.5
Consumer durables	15.8
Nondurables	9.6
Retail trade	17.3

Services	20.6
Utilities	2.5
Transportation	0.4
Finance	9.2
Multi industry	3.7

Other High-Performing Aggressive Growth Funds

	Five-Year Growth of $10,000*
Enterprise Group Capital Appreciation Portfolio	$22,407
Kaufmann Fund	34,819
Keystone America Omega Fund—Class A	22,627
Merger Fund	**N/A**
Nicholas-Applegate Growth Equity Fund—Class A	23,984
Thomson Opportunity Fund—Class B**	27,104

*For the period ending April 30, 1993
**This fund is closed to new purchases

Funds listed in **bold type** are available by direct purchase.

N/A indicates that the fund has not completed five full years of operation.

Summary

Investors who enjoy roller-coaster rides can anticipate the possibility of big profits from the aggressive growth group. But be prepared for sharp reactions when the market goes against these funds. The prudent investor will risk only a small portion of his or her assets in this group.

Equity Income Funds

Usual Investment Objective of the Group

Equity income funds seek a high level of current income for their shareholders by investing in equity securities. Since common stocks have historically been the best financial asset for combating inflation and providing real growth of capital, funds in this group attempt to deliver maximum income coupled with long-term capital growth by investing primarily in equity securities of companies with good dividend-paying records. The high dividend yield of their portfolios helps to reduce volatility and limit capital losses.

Survey of the Group

In 1993, equity income funds were responsible for a lot of happiness among their shareholders. Through April, these funds enjoyed better returns than any other equity group. While funds with many other investment objectives were losing money, the equity income group managed a gain of 5.1 percent. This outperforming of other groups is unusual, since in general equity income funds tend to emphasize income and not growth of capital.

In 1993, this group's focus on income was its saving grace, with high-yielding financial, utility and energy stocks being heavily weighted in the portfolios. These sectors significantly benefited the equity-income group. Fidelity Equity Income Fund was helped by the extended run of financial stocks, while declining interest rates boosted Utilities, a favorite of Stratton Monthly Dividend Shares. Merrill Lynch Strategic Dividend Fund was helped by the long-awaited upside swing of its large holding of energy stocks.

When interest rates turn around, as they did briefly in April of 1993, the equity income group can be hurt. During that month, these rate-sensitive funds were hit hard, losing nearly 1 percent, as both utility and financial stocks suffered. Even so, the group outperformed the S&P 500, which lost 2 percent in April.

One thing to keep in mind when looking for an income fund in the equity area is that those funds that stick to their basic mandate of income can perform well over the long pull, while keeping their risk low. An example of this is Stratton Monthly Dividend Shares, which is our recommended fund.

The table below indicates the historical average total return of the Equity Income Group and the S&P 500 Index for years ending December 31.

Equity Income versus S&P 500 Index

	Group Total Return	S&P 500		Group Total Return	S&P 500
1983	22.68%	22.47%	1988	17.11%	16.60%

1984	8.10	6.27	1989	21.36	31.68
1985	26.37	31.83	1990	-6.23	-3.12
1986	17.04	18.68	1991	27.22	30.48
1987	-1.99	5.26	1992	9.30	7.62

Source: *Morningstar Mutual Funds*

Recommended Fund

Stratton Monthly Dividend Shares
610 West Germantown Pike, Suite 361
Plymouth Meeting, PA 19462-1050
800-634-5726

Portfolio manager: James W. Stratton
Investment adviser: Stratton Management
Sales fees: No-load
Management fee: 0.63%
Other expenses: 0.47%
Total operating expense: 1.10%
Minimum initial purchase: $2,000 (additional: $100)
Minimum IRA purchase: None
Date of inception: April 1, 1972
Net assets of fund as of April 30, 1993: $142.1 million

Investment Objective
Stratton Monthly Dividend Shares seeks a high rate of return from dividend and interest income on its investments in common stock and securities convertible into common stock.

Investment Policy
The fund invests 80 percent of its assets in common stock and securities convertible into, or exchangeable for, common stock. It may invest in real estate investment trusts. The fund intends to invest at least 25 percent of its assets in securities of public utility companies engaged in the production, transmission or distribution of electric, energy, gas, water or telephone service. But it reserves the right also to hold cash and cash equivalents for temporary defensive purposes. Cash reserves may be invested in short-term debt securities, securities of the U.S. government, bankers' acceptances and certificates of deposit.

Performance

The tables below indicate the annual total returns of Stratton
Monthly Dividend Shares and the comparative results of the S&P 500
Index for years ending December 31, followed by total returns and the
growth of $10,000 invested for different periods ending April 30, 1993.

Stratton Monthly Dividend Shares versus S&P 500 Index

	Fund Total Return	S&P 500		Fund Total Return	S&P 500
1983	20.71%	22.47%	1988	9.76%	16.60%
1984	21.19	6.27	1989	18.77	31.68
1985	29.90	31.83	1990	−3.83	−3.12
1986	20.46	18.68	1991	35.10	30.48
1987	−11.40	5.26	1992	10.33	7.62

Total Returns for Different Periods Ending April 30, 1993

	Fund Total Return	Growth of $10,000
3 Months	5.79%	$10,579
6 Months	13.42	11,342
1 Year	21.47	12,147
3-Year Average	18.76	16,750
5-Year Average	13.41	18,761
10-Year Average	13.29	34,827

Source: *Morningstar Mutual Funds*

Financial History

Figure 17.2 illustrates selected per-share data and ratios for a share
of Stratton Monthly Dividend Shares outstanding throughout each year
ended January 31.

Comments

Stratton Monthly Dividend Shares has had a continuing influx of
new money as a result of investor appreciation of its excellent performance in terms of both monthly dividend payments and total return.
Assets under management grew from $30.6 million at the end of 1990
to $43.2 million in 1991, $88.5 million in 1992 and $142.1 million by
the end of April 1993. The fund's fine returns can be attributed to the
manager's huge emphasis on electric-utility companies, which make
up more than 70 percent of its portfolio. They performed extraordinar-
ily well as interest rates continued their secular downtrend over the last
few years.

FIGURE 17.2 Selected Per-Share Data and Ratios for Stratton
Monthly Dividend Shares

The following information provides selected per share data and ratios for a share of the Fund outstanding throughout each year. The information for each of the five years in the period ended January 31, 1993 has been examined by Tait, Weller & Baker, certified public accountants, whose report thereon appears in the Fund's Statement of Additional Information dated June 1, 1993. This data should be read in conjunction with the other financial statements and notes thereto, also included in the Fund's Statement of Additional Information.

SELECTED PER SHARE DATA AND RATIOS
FOR A SHARE OUTSTANDING THROUGHOUT EACH YEAR

					Years Ended January 31					
	1993	1992	1991	1990	1989	1988[2][3]	1987[3]	1986[1]	1985[1]	1984[1]
Income and Expenses										
Investment income	$2.26	$2.29	$2.35	$2.40	$2.40	$2.39	$2.47	$2.16	$2.31	$2.21
Operating expenses	.32	.32	.30	.31	.30	.33	.38	.33	.35	.36
Net investment income	1.94	1.97	2.05	2.09	2.10	2.06	2.09	1.83	1.96	1.85
Dividends from net investment income	(1.94)	(1.95)	(2.20)	(2.05)	(2.08)	(2.06)	(2.28)	(2.17)	(2.05)	(1.93)
Capital Changes										
Distributions from net realized gains from security transactions	.00	.00	.00	.00	.00	(.27)	(.10)	.00	.00	.00
Distributions from paid-in capital[3]	.00	.00	.00	.00	.00	(.38)	(.40)	.00	.00	.00
Net realized and unrealized gain (loss) on investments	2.08	4.79	(1.33)	.03	(.70)	(5.33)	3.96	5.69	2.24	(.19)
Net increase (decrease) in net asset value	2.08	4.81	(1.48)	.07	(.68)	(5.98)	3.27	5.35	2.15	(.27)
Net Assets										
Beginning of year	27.83	23.02	24.50	24.43	25.11	31.09	27.82	22.47	20.32	20.59
End of year	$29.91	$27.83	$23.02	$24.50	$24.43	$25.11	$31.09	$27.82	$22.47	$20.32
Ratio of net operating expenses to average net assets	1.10%	1.23%	1.27%	1.25%	1.21%	1.21%	1.24%	1.49%	1.72%	1.74%
Ratio of net income to average net assets	6.74%	7.63%	8.79%	8.19%	8.54%	7.52%	6.90%	8.36%	9.77%	9.03%
Portfolio turnover	35.94%	43.55%	14.00%	39.10%	15.00%	24.44%	14.87%	13.62%	28.28%	30.00%
Number of shares outstanding at end of year	3,284,297	1,637,018	1,354,671	1,354,966	1,385,192	1,445,638	1,722,519	764,690	462,752	444,925

[1]Not covered by independent accountants' report.

[2]Per share income and expenses and net realized and unrealized gain (loss) on investments have been computed using the average number of shares outstanding during the period. These computations had no effect on net asset value per share.

[3]Distributions from paid-in capital result from the excess of taxable capital gains over gains available from book sources.

The Fund's portfolio turnover is calculated by dividing the lesser of the Fund's annual aggregate purchases or sales of its portfolio securities by the average monthly value of the Fund's portfolio securities during the year.

Source: Stratton Monthly Dividend Shares prospectus dated June 1, 1993

The fund also compares very well with the utilities group; it surpassed all but one fund in that group in both total return and yield in 1993 through April 30. The reason is that Stratton hunts for high yields among the smaller regional electric companies that are frequently overlooked. Recently, however, as investors have scrambled to find higher-yielding alternatives to low-paying certificates of deposit and money market funds, such issues have become newly popular and have enjoyed greater capital appreciation.

A problem the company may now face, with its growing asset base, is difficulty in being able to buy these smaller companies in sufficient quantities. The manager does not appear to be worried about this and continues to add new issues to the portfolio.

Stratton Monthly Dividend Shares has continued to do very well indeed, but it does have a weak spot. Its heavy exposure to utilities stocks makes the fund extremely sensitive to interest rates. If interest rates take a significant upturn, the fund could suffer considerable price depreciation.

Portfolio

Total stocks: 181 as of January 31, 1993

25 Largest Holdings

Rochester Gas & Electric	Washington Water Power
Texas Utilities	Meditrust
Northeast Utilities	Central Hudson Gas & Electric
Delmarva Power & Light	Lyondell Petrochemical
Public Service Enterprise	Health Care Real Estate Investment Trust
Long Island Lighting	TNP Enterprises
Puget Sound Power & Light	Dial Real Estate Investment Trust
Public Service of Colorado	Houston Industries
Ohio Edison	IBM
New York State Electric/Gas	Scana
Central Maine Power	Potomac Electric Power
American Health Property	Independence Bancorp
FPL Group	

Composition of Portfolio

As of December 31, 1992

Cash	4.7%	Preferreds	4.3%
Stocks	86.0	Convertibles	3.3
Bonds	1.7		

Sector Weightings

As of April 30, 1993

Natural Resources	4.1%
Industrial Products	2.5
Utilities	78.8
Finance	14.6

Other High-Performing Equity Income Funds

	Five-Year Growth of $10,000*
American Capital Equity Income Fund—Class A	$18,197
Capital Income Builder	19,204
Compass Capital Equity Income Fund	N/A
Cowen Income + Growth Fund	18,205
Evergreen Total Return Fund	**16,609**
Fidelity Equity Income Fund	**18,028**
Financial Industrial Income Fund	**22,531**
National Total Return Fund	18,686
One Group Income Equity Portfolio—Fiduciary Shares	**18,498**
Oppenheimer Equity Income Fund	16,474
Portico Income & Growth Fund	**N/A**
T. Rowe Price Equity Income Fund	**17,988**
Prudential Equity Income Fund—Class B	18,678
Royce Fund Equity Income Series	**N/A**
SAFECO Income Fund	**16,572**
Shearson Lehman Brothers Premium Total Return Fund—Class B	19,637
SteinRoe Total Return Fund	**17,901**
United Income Fund	20,009
USAA Mutual Income Stock Fund	**19,904**
Vanguard Equity Income Fund	**18,246**

*For the period ending April 30, 1993

Funds listed in **bold type** are available by direct purchase.

N/A indicates that the fund has not completed five full years of operation.

Summary

Equity income funds generally emphasize income and safety, not growth of capital. However, in recent years the group has enjoyed total returns as good or better than most other equity groups. The group's focus on income has made it a winner, as investors have scrambled for higher-yield investments that also have potential for price appreciation. Funds in this group that have stuck to their primary task of delivering income have performed well, while keeping their risk low.

Growth Funds

Usual Investment Objective of the Group

Growth funds invest in the common stock of well-established companies. Their primary aim is to produce an increase in the value of their investments—growth of capital—rather than a flow of dividends. Investors who buy a growth fund generally are more interested in seeing the fund's share price rise than in receiving income from dividends.

Survey of the Group

Funds in the growth fund category place primary emphasis on established companies that they believe to have favorable growth prospects. Common stocks usually constitute all or most of the investment portfolios, although many funds are free to invest in securities other than common stocks to achieve their objectives. Some funds will take substantial positions in securities convertible into common stocks, and may also purchase government securities, preferred stocks and other senior securities if the adviser believes they are likely to be the best-performing securities at that time. Funds may also hold short-term interest-bearing securities when the adviser wants to maintain a defensive position.

As a group, growth funds have rewarded their shareholders quite handsomely over many years. They delivered average total returns of 13.48 percent over the three-year period ending December 31, 1992, 13.28 percent over the same five-year period and 11.76 percent over ten years. It is interesting to note, however, that in each case this was less than the return of the S&P 500 stock index, which posted total returns of 13.57 percent, 14.77 percent and 14.4 percent, respectively. From 1983 to 1992, the group underperformed the S&P 500 in eight out of ten years.

The table below indicates the historical average total return of the growth fund group and of the S&P 500 Index for years ending December 31.

Growth Fund Group versus S&P 500 Index

	Group Total Return	S&P 500		Group Total Return	S&P 500
1983	21.32%	22.47%	1988	14.90%	16.60%
1984	−1.71	6.27	1989	26.65	31.68
1985	29.00	31.83	1990	−5.29	−3.12
1986	15.19	18.68	1991	36.41	30.48
1987	2.60	5.26	1992	8.52	7.62

Source: *Morningstar Mutual Funds*

Recommended Fund

Berger 100 Fund
210 University Boulevard, Suite 900
Denver, CO 80206
800-333-1001

Portfolio manager: William Berger (since 1974), Rod Linafelter (since 1990)
Investment adviser: Berger Associates
Sales fees: No-load
12b-1 fee: 0.75%
Management fee: 0.56%
Other expenses: 0.33%
Total operating expense: 1.64%
Minimum initial purchase: $250 (additional: $50)
Minimum IRA purchase: $250 (additional: $50)
Date of inception: August 1, 1966
Net assets of fund as of April 30, 1993: $863 million

Investment Objective

The primary investment objective of the Berger 100 Fund is capital appreciation. A secondary objective is to provide a moderate level of current income.

Investment Policy

Berger 100 Fund seeks to achieve its objectives by investing in common stocks of established companies that it believes to have favorable growth prospects. Common stocks usually constitute all or most of the fund's investment portfolio, but the fund may invest in securities other than common stocks, and will do so when deemed appropriate by the investment adviser to achieve its objective. The fund may also take substantial positions in securities convertible into common stocks, government securities, preferred stocks and other senior securities that are likely to be the best-performing securities at that time. The fund may also hold government securities and other short-term interest-bearing securities when market conditions warrant a defensive position.

Berger 100 Fund concentrates its investments in companies that produce a high after-tax return on shareholders' equity and that have a high reinvestment rate that may generate future growth.

Performance

The tables below indicate the annual total return of the Berger 100 Fund and the comparative results of the S&P 500 Index for years ending December 31, followed by total returns of the fund and the growth of $10,000 invested for different periods ending April 30, 1993.

Berger 100 Fund versus S&P 500 Index

	Fund Total Return	S&P 500		Fund Total Return	S&P 500
1983	16.99%	22.47%	1988	1.69%	16.60%
1984	−20.11	6.27	1989	48.31	31.68
1985	25.72	31.83	1990	−5.58	−3.12
1986	20.10	18.68	1991	88.81	30.48
1987	15.67	5.26	1992	8.53	7.62

Total Returns for Different Periods Ending April 30, 1993

	Fund Total Return	Growth of $10,000
3 Months	− 5.67%	$10,567
6 Months	6.34	10,634

1 Year	15.29	11,529
3-Year Average	25.21	19,629
5-Year Average	23.07	28,233
10-Year Average	13.51	35,509
15-Year Average	16.25	95,696

Source: *Morningstar Mutual Funds*

Financial History

Figure 17.3 illustrates selected per-share data and ratios for a share of Berger 100 Fund shares outstanding throughout each year ended September 30.

Comments

Berger 100 Fund has had a history of leading its group whenever growth stocks are in favor; it enjoyed huge gains in 1989 and 1991. When such stocks are out of favor, however, the fund can suffer disheartening losses. Investors jumped on the Berger 100 Fund bandwagon during the heady years of explosive gains. At the end of 1990, it had $15 million under management. By the end of 1991, its assets went to $192 million and then to $760 million by the end of 1992.

Since 1991 the fund has done a pretty good job of struggling through unfavorable markets. After a difficult first half of 1992, it recovered greatly and ended the year slightly ahead of its group's average. In 1993 Berger 100 managed to avoid losses in a chaotic market by picking many of the right stocks in otherwise unstable sectors. These included large holdings of technology, software and computer-services firms, all of which posted nice gains.

By the end of 1992, Berger 100 Fund had reduced its stake in health-care stocks to 6 percent of its assets, thereby avoiding the bloodbath in that sector. Since then the fund has begun buying cost-cutting health-care firms, particularly health maintenance organizations, believing they will benefit from President Clinton's health-care plan.

Good stock-picking has been as much of a factor in the fund's success over the years as has its growth-oriented strategy.

Portfolio

Total stocks: 83 as of March 31, 1993

25 Largest Holdings

Solectron	Pyxis
Conseco	Wellfleet Communications

FIGURE 17.3 Berger 100 Fund Per-Share Income and Capital Changes

BERGER 100 FUND
Per Share Income (Loss) and Capital Changes

For a Share Outstanding Throughout Fiscal Years Ended September 30,

	1992**	1991**	1990	1989	1988	1987	1986	1985	1984	1983
1. Investment income*	$ .14	$ .10	$ .04	$ .11	$ .02	$ .17	$ .11	$ .07	$ .21	$ .07
2. Expenses*	(.23)	(.20)	(.06)	(.16)	(.03)	(.20)	(.15)	(.10)	(.10)	(.10)
3. Net investment income (loss)*	(.09)	(.10)	(.02)	(.05)	(.01)	(.03)	(.04)	(.03)	.11	(.03)
4. Dividends from net investment income*	None	None	None	None	None	None	None	(.11)	None	(.04)
5. Net realized and unrealized gains (losses) on investments*	.86	5.15	(1.34)	2.92	(.48)	1.91	1.75	.33	(2.12)	2.50
6. Distributions from net realized gains on securities*	(.17)	(.59)	(.90)	(.08)	(1.58)	(.39)	None	None	None	None
7. Net increase (decrease) in net asset value*	.60	4.46	(2.26)	2.79	(2.07)	1.49	1.71	.19	(2.01)	2.43
8. Net asset value at beginning of period*	11.13	6.67	8.93	6.14	8.21	6.72	5.01	4.82	6.83	4.40
9. Net asset value at end of period*	$11.73	$11.13	$6.67	$8.93	$6.14	$8.21	$6.72	$5.01	$4.82	$6.83

Source: Berger 100 Fund prospectus dated July 5, 1993. Compliments of the Berger Funds

FIGURE 17.3 (continued)

10. Ratio of expenses to average net assets..........	1.89%	2.24%	2.13%	1.62%	1.72%	1.61%	1.71%	2.00%	1.90%	1.70%
11. Ratio of net investment income (loss) to average net assets	(.75)%	(1.06)%	(.71)%	(.54)%	(.57)%	(.27)%	(.47)%	(.59)%	1.95%	(.51)%
12. Portfolio turnover rate..........	51%	78%	145%	83%	166%	106%	122%	130%	272%	155%
13. Number of shares outstanding, at end of year (in thousands)*	32,740	6,905	1,941	1,569	1,725	1,425	1,572	1,785	1,986	2,112

*Per share amounts for periods 1983 through 1989 have been adjusted to reflect the 3 for 1 split which was effective December 15, 1989.

**Per share calculations for the period were based on average shares outstanding.

Cabletron Systems
Oracle Systems
Electronic Arts
American Power Conversion
Intel
Microsoft
Synoptics Communications
Countrywide Credit Industry
Cisco Systems
Motorola
Novell

Cott
Magna International
ECI Telecommunications
Home Depot
Broderbund Software
Autodesk
Applied Materials
PepsiCo
Peoplesoft
Medco Containment Services

Composition of Portfolio
As of March 31, 1993

Cash	20.0%	Preferreds	0.0%
Stocks	80.0	Convertibles	0.0
Bonds	0.0		

Sector Weightings
As of April 30, 1993

Natural Resources	0.9%
Industrial Products	30.5
Consumer Durables	19.4
Nondurables	8.6
Retail Trade	11.2
Services	11.8
Utilities	6.6
Finance	11.0

Other High-Performing Growth Funds

	Five-Year Growth of $10,000*
CGM Capital Development Fund (closed)	$30,554
Crabbe Huson Equity Fund	N/A
Delaware Value Fund	23,813
Equitable Growth Fund	23,813
Fidelity Advisor Equity Portfolio—Institutional Class	31,108
Fidelity Blue Chip Growth Fund	25,766
Fidelity Contrafund	31,145
Fidelity Disciplined Equity Fund	N/A

Fidelity Magellan Fund	**23,327**
Guardian Park Avenue Fund	20,832
Janus Twenty Fund (closed)	29,506
Lindner Fund	**17,797**
New York Venture Fund	24,227
Phoenix Capital Appreciation Fund	N/A
Portico Special Growth Fund	**N/A**
Vista Capital Growth Fund	31,482
Westcore MIDCO Growth Fund	26,023

*For the period ending April 30, 1993

Funds listed in **bold type** are available by direct purchase.

N/A indicates that the fund has not completed five full years of operation.

Summary

Mutual funds that place themselves in the growth group have an investment objective of long-term capital appreciation in well-established companies. Income is not an important consideration. These funds look for companies with growing earnings that will be reinvested with the expectation of future growth. The share prices of growth funds can be volatile, because they may often enjoy two or three years of spectacular returns that will be followed by a year or two of terrible results. However, investors who have hung on over both good and bad years have been amply rewarded over the long term.

Growth and Income Funds

Usual Investment Objective of the Group

Mutual funds included in this group seek capital appreciation and current income as nearly equal objectives, investing primarily in equity securities.

Survey of the Group

Growth and income funds invest mainly in the common stock of companies that have had increasing share value and also a solid record of paying dividends. Such funds attempt to combine long-term capital growth with a steady stream of income.

Over the last 12 to 18 months, as funds invested in smaller companies have been performing well, those funds investing in large capitalization blue chip stocks have done poorly. Top performers have been made up largely of value-oriented funds. These funds tend to overweight less-pricey companies in cyclical sectors, such as industrial cyclicals and consumer durables. Some of the best-performing funds have been those holding small to mid-capitalization companies.

The market's preference for smaller capitalization value funds over the last couple of years should not be taken as a signal to sell blue chip funds. Rather, it is a reminder that such funds are not always the "old faithfuls" they are often thought to be.

The average annual total return of the growth and income group has consistently come quite close to that of the S&P 500. In the 12 months ending May 31, 1993, the group's return of 11.67 percent was almost identical to the S&P's 11.60 percent. During longer periods, though, a negative gap appears, with a three-year return of 10.65 percent compared to 11.08 percent for the S&P 500. The five-year return of the group was 12.76 percent versus 15.17 for the S&P, ten years was 11.88 percent versus 14.81 percent, and the 15-year return was 13.72 percent versus 15.41 percent for the S&P 500.

The table below indicates the historical average total return of the growth and income group and the S&P 500 Index for years ending December 31.

Growth and Income Group versus S&P 500 Index

	Group Total Return	S&P 500		Group Total Return	S&P 500
1983	21.33%	22.47%	1988	14.83%	16.60%
1984	4.19	6.27	1989	23.47	31.68
1985	27.04	31.83	1990	−4.95	−3.12
1986	15.49	18.68	1991	28.96	30.48
1987	2.03	5.26	1992	8.17	7.62

Source: *Morningstar Mutual Funds*

Recommended Fund

Berger 101 Fund
210 University Boulevard, Suite 900
Denver, CO 80206
800-333-1001

Portfolio manager: William Berger (since 1974) and Rod Linafelter
(since 1990)
Investment adviser: Berger Associates
Sales fees: No-load
12b-1 fee: 0.75%
Management fee: 0.75%
Other expenses: 0.81%
Total operating expense: 2.31%
Minimum initial purchase: $250 (additional: $50)
Minimum IRA purchase: $250
Date of inception: August 1, 1966
Net assets of fund as of March 31, 1993: $61.5 million

Investment Objective
The primary investment objective of the Berger 101 Fund is capital appreciation. A secondary objective is to provide a moderate level of current income. The fund seeks to achieve its objectives primarily by investing in common stocks of established companies.

Investment Policy
In selecting its portfolio securities, the Berger 101 Fund places primary emphasis on securities that it believes offer favorable growth prospects and that, at the same time, will provide current income. The fund also invests in senior securities, such as government and municipal securities, corporate bonds, convertible securities or preferred stocks, as seems appropriate. Attention is given to the prospective reliability of income as well as to its indicated current level.

The fund may purchase put and call options on stock indexes for the purpose of hedging. To hedge the fund's portfolio against a decline in value, the fund may buy puts on stock indexes; to hedge against increases in prices of equities, pending investments in equities, the fund may buy calls on stock indexes. However, no more than 1 percent of the market value of the fund's net assets may be invested in put and call options.

The fund may invest in both domestic and foreign securities. It may purchase securities that are convertible into common stock when the manager believes they offer the potential for a higher total return than nonconvertible securities. The fund may also invest in zero-coupon bonds or "strips." These are bonds that do not make regular interest payments; rather, they are sold at a discount from face value. Principal and accreted discount (representing interest accrued but not paid) are paid at maturity.

Performance
The tables below indicate annual total returns for the fund for each year ending December 31 and comparative results for the S&P 500 Index, followed by total returns and the growth of $10,000 invested for different periods ending May 31, 1993.

Berger 101 Fund versus S&P 500 Index

	Fund Total Return	S&P 500		Fund Total Return	S&P 500
1983	34.99%	22.47%	1988	5.15%	16.60%
1984	−0.29	6.27	1989	20.32	31.68
1985	29.26	31.83	1990	−7.99	−3.12
1986	15.12	18.68	1991	60.97	30.48
1987	−2.88	5.26	1992	4.82	7.62

Total Returns for Different Periods Ending May 31, 1993

	Fund Total Return	Growth of $10,000
3 Months	11.36%	$10,284
6 Months	13.74	10,343
1 Year	17.06	11,706
3-Year Average	20.29	17,405
5-Year Average	17.09	22,009
10-Year Average	12.54	32,589
15-Year Average	13.28	64,908

Source: *Morningstar Mutual Funds*

Financial History
Figure 17.4 illustrates selected per-share data and ratios for a share of Berger 101 Fund shares outstanding throughout each year ended September 30.

Comments
Berger 101 Fund made a timely move that reaped important benefits in 1993. Usually investing in growth stocks and often in foreign

companies, the fund recently moved into domestic cyclical stocks. The managers search for companies that lead their industries and produce above-average earnings growth and profitability. Previously, these criteria led to an emphasis on growth companies, such as Pfizer and Gillette. In addition, the fund kept as much as 40 percent of its assets in foreign markets, especially in the fast-growing economies of Hong Kong and Mexico.

While this approach won huge gains in 1991, the fund ran into harder times in 1992. The U.S. market turned against growth stocks in favor of cyclicals, hurting both the Hong Kong and Mexican markets. About this time, Berger 101 cut its foreign stocks to 7 percent of assets and began to emphasize domestic cyclicals. These new holdings included such companies as Purolator and Echlin, both makers of auto parts, and Chrysler.

The fund's five-year record is outstanding. Returns rank near the top of the growth and income group, while risk has been average for the group. Its ten-year record has also been good, although there were some poor showings in the mid-1980s.

This is a well-managed fund suitable for investors who are looking for growth and income. Because of the annual 0.75 percent 12b-1 charge, however, operating expenses are higher than one might like.

Portfolio
Total stocks: 29 as of March 31, 1993
25 Largest Holdings

Kansas City Southern	Purolator Products
Trinity Industries	Hong Kong Telecommunications
Motorola	China Light & Power
Teléfonos De Mexico CL L	Echlin
Johnson Controls	Tyco Laboratories
Countrywide Credit Industry	New Zealand Telecom
Magna International CL A	Coca-Cola
Cooper Tire & Rubber	AT&T
Albertson's	Gillette
Resource Mortgage Capital	Tolmex CL B
CIFRA CL B	Hong Kong Electric
Telefonica De España	Briggs & Stratton
Ogden	

Composition of Portfolio
As of March 31, 1993

Cash	20.0%
Stocks	63.0

FIGURE 17.4 Berger 101 Fund Per-Share Income and Capital Changes

BERGER 101 FUND
Per Share Income (Loss) and Capital Changes

For a Share Outstanding Throughout
Fiscal Years Ended September 30,

	1992	1991	1990	1989	1988	1987	1986	1985	1984	1983
1. Investment income*	$.45	$.42	$.41	$.45	$.36	$.48	$.44	$.31	$.38	$.38
2. Expenses*	(.32)	(.24)	(.24)	(.13)	(.13)	(.15)	(.15)	(.14)	(.12)	(.13)
3. Net investment income (loss)*	.13	.18	.17	.32	.23	.33	.29	.17	.26	.25
4. Dividends from net investment income*	(.17)	(.11)	(.14)	(.44)	(.30)	(.30)	(.29)	(.22)	(.23)	(.24)
5. Net realized and unrealized gains (losses) on investments*	.54	3.25	(1.23)	.74	(1.40)	1.15	1.93	.56	(.34)	2.70
6. Distributions from net realized gains on securities*	(.74)	None	None	None	(.68)	(1.50)	(.15)	None	(.50)	None
7. Net increase (decrease) in net asset value*	(.24)	3.32	(1.20)	.62	(2.15)	(.32)	1.78	.51	(.81)	2.71
8. Net asset value at beginning of period*	9.20	5.88	7.08	6.46	8.61	8.93	7.15	6.64	7.45	4.74
9. Net asset value at end of period*	$8.96	$9.20	$5.88	$7.08	$6.46	$8.61	$8.93	$7.15	$6.64	$7.45

Source: Berger 101 Fund prospectus dated July 5, 1993. Compliments of the Berger
Funds

FIGURE 17.4 (continued)

10. Ratio of expenses to average net assets	2.56%	2.66%	2.48%	2.00%	1.79%	1.96%	2.00%	2.00%	2.00%
11. Ratio of net investment income (loss) to average net assets	1.05%	1.99%	1.74%	5.09%	4.04%	3.65%	2.42%	4.24%	3.75%
12. Portfolio turnover rate	42%	143%	139%	132%	241%	187%	166%	267%	168%
13. Number of shares outstanding at end of year (in thousands)*	3,675	443	709	260	334	324	304	224	210	176

*Per share amounts for periods 1983 through 1989 have been adjusted to reflect the 2 for 1 split which was effective December 15, 1989.

Bonds	2.0
Convertibles	14.0

Sector Weightings
As of March 31, 1993

Utilities	30.2%
Financials	10.1
Industrial Cyclicals	7.4
Consumer Durables	20.9
Consumer Staples	6.0
Services	7.4
Retail	4.0
Health	1.9
Technology	12.2

Other High-Performing Growth and Income Funds

	Five-Year Growth of $10,000*
AARP Growth & Income Fund	**$19,509**
AIM Charter Fund	22,684
AIM Value Fund	26,532
Clipper Fund	**19,991**
Fidelity Growth & Income Fund	**22,907**
MainStay Value Fund	22,254
Main Street Income & Growth Fund	30,408
Neuberger/Berman Guardian Fund	**21,313**
Scudder Growth & Income Fund	**19,262**
T. Rowe Price Growth & Income Fund	**19,457**
Vista Growth & Income Fund	32,857

*For the period ending June 30, 1993

Funds listed in **bold type** are available by direct purchase.

Summary

Conservative investors who look for growth of capital combined with a steady flow of dividend income have generally been rewarded when they have invested in one of the highly rated growth and income group funds. These funds normally invest in companies that have demonstrated an ability to produce solid dividends combined with adequate growth.

Small-Company Growth Funds

Usual Investment Objective of the Group

Funds included in the small-company growth fund category seek capital appreciation by investing primarily in stocks of small companies, as determined either by market capitalization or assets.

Survey of the Group

Small-company growth funds seek aggressive growth of capital by investing primarily in equity securities of relatively small companies with the potential for rapid growth. Small companies are usually those in the emerging or developing states of their life cycle. Shares of these companies often trade in over-the-counter markets and may be relatively thinly traded. Such shares may be subject to more abrupt and erratic market movement than those of large corporations or the market in general. Small companies are usually not included in the top 500 in sales, market capitalization, revenues or other standard measures.

Growth has recently regained some of its success in the small-company group. Technology stocks with high price/earnings multiples have performed well, as have telecommunications equipment firms. As the economy continues to grow slowly, economically sensitive stocks turn in strong performances. These include select retailers, heavy machinery makers and companies in the areas of consumer durables, auto parts, energy and financials.

Because of a slowly growing economy in 1993, the small-company fund group moved erratically.

The table below indicates the historical average total return of the small-company group and the S&P 500 Index for years ending December 31.

Small-Company Growth Fund Group versus S&P 500 Index

	Group Total Return	S&P 500		Group Total Return	S&P 500
1983	26.18%	22.47%	1988	19.58%	16.60%
1984	−7.04	6.27	1989	24.01	31.68
1985	30.96	31.83	1990	−9.57	−3.12
1986	10.21	18.68	1991	51.58	30.48
1987	−2.09	5.26	1992	13.32	7.62

Source: *Morningstar Mutual Funds*

Recommended Fund

Twentieth Century Ultra Investors
P.O. Box 419200
Kansas City, MO 64141-6200
800-345-2021

Portfolio manager: Management Team
Investment adviser: Investors Research
Sales fees: No-load
Management fee: 1.00% flat fee
Annual brokerage cost: 0.21%
Minimum initial purchase: $1,000 (additional: $25)
Minimum IRA purchase: None (additional: $25)
Date of inception: November 2, 1981
Net assets as of July 31, 1993: $6,541.5 million

Investment Objective
Twentieth Century Ultra Investors Fund seeks capital growth by investing in securities, primarily common stocks, that have better than average potential for appreciation. Current income is not a consideration.

Investment Policy
The fund selects securities of companies whose earnings and revenue trends meet management's standards of selection, which will generally be medium-size and smaller companies.

So long as a sufficient number of such securities are available, Twentieth Century intends to stay fully invested in these securities regardless of the movement of stock prices generally. In most circumstances, the fund's actual level of cash and cash equivalents will fluctuate between 0 percent and 10 percent of assets, with 90–100 percent of its assets committed to equity investments. The fund may purchase securities only of companies that have a record of at least three years of continuous operation, and their securities must have, in the opinion of management, a fair degree of marketability.

Performance
The following tables indicate annual total returns of the fund for each year ending December 31 and comparative results for the S&P 500 Index, followed by total returns and the growth of $10,000 invested for different periods ending July 31, 1993.

Twentieth Century Ultra Investors Fund versus S&P 500 Index

	Fund Total Return	S&P 500		Fund Total Return	S&P 500
1983	26.89%	22.47%	1988	13.32%	16.60%
1984	−19.45	6.27	1989	36.94	31.68
1985	26.37	31.83	1990	9.36	−3.12
1986	10.26	18.68	1991	86.45	30.48
1987	6.69	5.26	1992	1.27	7.62

Total Returns for Different Periods Ending as of July 31, 1993

	Fund Total Return	Growth of $10,000
3 Months	15.09%	$11,509
6 Months	9.86	10,986
1 Year	30.63	13,063
3-Year Average	29.17	21,550
5-Year Average	25.89	31,617
10-Year Average	14.41	38,416

Source: *Morningstar Mutual Funds*

Financial History

Figure 17.5 illustrates selected per-share data and ratios for a share of Twentieth Century Ultra Investors outstanding throughout each year ending October 31.

Comments

The popularity of Twentieth Century Ultra Investors has increased dramatically, as evidenced by the expansion of its net assets under management from $247 million in 1987 to $2.9 billion in 1991 and $6.5 billion by mid-1993. The fund had remarkable returns of 36.9 percent in 1989 and a huge 86.5 percent in 1991.

The fund's excellent returns are the result of its aggressive growth strategy, whereby management seeks firms with rapidly accelerating earnings. In addition, it buys only stocks that it deems already have begun their upward trend (based on increased trading volume). The result is a portfolio that is full of high fliers in the priciest, most aggressive sectors, especially in technology (39 percent of assets) and health care (9 percent).

The flip side of this policy is a high-risk portfolio, causing the fund to plummet when the market doesn't go its way. The fund's volatility has been increased by its emphasis on small capitalization stocks, especially in its earlier years. Since 1990, however, the fund has moved

FIGURE 17.5 Twentieth Century Ultra Selected Per-Share Data and Ratios

SELECTED PER SHARE DATA AND RATIOS

The Selected Per-Share Data and Ratios for each of the periods presented have been examined by Baird, Kurtz & Dobson, independent certified public accountants, whose report thereon appears in the corporation's annual report which accompanies the statement of additional information.

Ultra Investors Year Ended Oct. 31,	INCOME AND EXPENSE				CAPITAL CHANGES								
	Investment Income	Expenses	Net Investment Income (Loss)	Dividends from Net Investment Income	Net Realized and Unrealized Gains or (Losses) on Investments	Distributions from Net Realized Gains on Investments	Net Increase (Decrease) in Net Asset Value	Net Asset Value at Beginning of Period	Net Asset Value at End of Period	Ratio of Operating Expenses to Average Net Assets	Ratio of Net Investment Income (Loss) to Average Net Assets	Portfolio Turnover Rate	Shares Outstanding at End of Period (in Thousands)
1983	$.03	$.05	$(.02)	—	$2.580	—	$2.56	$5.42	$7.98	1.02%	(.4%)	58%	63,406
1984	.04	.06	(.02)	—	(1.132)	$(.258)	(1.41)	7.98	6.57	1.01%	(.3%)	93%	67,826
1985	.09	.08	.01	—	.550	—	.56	6.57	7.13	1.01%	.1%	100%	54,060
1986	.27	.27	.00	$(.010)	1.940	—	1.93	7.13	9.06	1.01%	—	99%	34,743
1987	.06	.13	(.07)	(.007)	(.220)	—	(.30)	9.06	8.76	1.00%	(.5%)	137%	26,940
1988	.05	.07	(.02)	—	1.380	(3.258)	(1.90)	8.76	6.86	1.00%	(.3%)	140%	37,680
1989	.28	.09	.19	—	2.580	—	2.77	6.86	9.63	1.00%	2.2%	132%	36,041
1990	.05	.08	(.03)	(.196)	(.730)	(.947)	(1.90)	9.63	7.73	1.00%	(.3%)	141%	42,713
1991	.04	.07	(.03)	—	7.860	(.028)	7.80	7.73	15.53	1.00%	(.5%)	42%	138,289
1992	.08	.13	(.05)	—	(.020)	—	(.07)	15.53	15.46	1.00%	(.4%)	59%	276,547

*Annualized

Source: Twentieth Century Investors, Inc. prospectus dated March 1, 1993

more toward mid-capitalization size companies in the interest of greater liquidity.

Holding the stocks of larger companies has not yet had the effect of reducing its volatility very much; it lost more than 17 percent in the first half of 1992, when the market turned against high prices. Then 22 percent was gained back in 1992's second half. While volatility may moderate in the future, if assets continue to grow, investors should consider the fund as a powerful capital-appreciation vehicle, demanding a long-term commitment and steady nerves.

Over recent years the fund has had an outstanding performance record, beating the S&P 500 Index in all periods during the five years ending July 31, 1993. In the 12 months ending on that date, the fund's total return of 30.63 percent was significantly better than the S&P's 8.71 percent. Over three years, the fund's average return was 29.17 percent versus 11.41 percent for the S&P, and over five years the fund's return was 25.89 percent versus 14.20 for the S&P. However, the comparison changes over the long term; the ten-year average annual return achieved by Twentieth Century Ultra of 14.41 percent was nearly identical to the S&P 500's average annual return of 14.7 percent.

Portfolio
Total stocks: 83 as of April 30, 1993

25 Largest Holdings

Cisco Systems	Microelectronique Horlogerie
Oracle Systems	Tele-Communications CL A
Intel	Electronic Arts
Synoptics Communications	3COM
Newbridge Networks	Promus
International Game Technology	Parametric Technology
Sega Enterprises	Cabletron Systems
DSC Communications	United Healthcare
Applied Materials	Circuit City Stores
Wellfleet Communications	Office Depot
Sybase	Immunex
Compaq Computer	Triton Energy
Medco Containment Services	

Composition of Portfolio
As of April 30, 1993

Cash	5.6%
Stocks	94.4

Sector Weightings
As of April 30, 1993

Utilities	17.0%
Energy	2.9
Financials	1.4
Industry Cyclicals	5.4
Consumer Durables	6.9
Services	7.7
Retail	10.8
Health	8.6
Technology	39.4

Other High-Performing Small-Company Funds

	Five-Year Growth of $10,000*
Acorn Fund	$23,149
FAM Value Fund	**22,447**
Fidelity Low-Priced Stock Fund	**N/A**
Founders Discovery Fund	**N/A**
John Hancock Special Equities Fund—Class A	30,375
MFS Lifetime Emerging Growth Fund	26,651
PBHG Growth Fund	**26,951**
Skyline Special Equities Portfolio	25,768
Twentieth Century Giftrust Investors	29,372

*For the period ending July 31, 1993

Funds listed in **bold type** are available by direct purchase.
N/A indicates the fund was not in operation for five full years.

Summary

Small-company growth funds will tend to be more volatile than funds investing in much larger blue chip stocks, often reacting to changes in market direction with sharp movements, both up and down. Because of a slowly growing economy in recent years, the group has tended to move in fits and starts, with generally lackluster returns.

Chapter 18

International Stock Funds: Investing for Growth in the Global Market

Europe Stock Funds

Usual Investment Objective of the Group

Most mutual funds included in the Europe stock group seek long-term capital growth as their investment objective. Current income is normally not a consideration in the selection of securities. Funds in this group invest primarily in equity securities of issuers located in Europe, normally maintaining at least 65 percent of their assets in that market.

Survey of the Group

In the first six months of 1993, Europe stock funds finally pulled ahead of the U.S. market, which they had trailed for five consecutive years. The average fund in this group had a total return of 8.36 percent for the six months ending June 30. This was significantly better than the S&P 500 Index, which was up only 4.86 percent during the same period. The European markets finally came to life as investors bid up equity prices in hopes of economic recovery, and interest rates began to decline from their steep levels. The peripheral markets—those that pulled out of the Exchange Rate Mechanism in 1992 and/or devalued their currencies—enjoyed the biggest gains because of their newfound freedom to cut interest rates.

One of the funds that took advantage of these trends was Paine-Webber Europe Growth Fund, which placed 12 percent of its assets in Italy and boosted its holdings in Scandinavia. This helped make the fund one of the top performers in the group for the first six months of 1993. Similarly, G.T. Europe Growth Fund scored a nice gain by investing in resurging Spanish and Italian stocks.

Many investment managers are optimistic about the European markets, but their future is far from assured. In addition, European stock funds have historically been about 30 percent more volatile than the average equity fund, making them appropriate only for investors who can tolerate losses. Generally reliable offerings include INVESCO Europe Fund and Merrill Lynch Euro-Fund. And a top performer over the last few years has been Vanguard International Equity Index Fund—European Portfolio, which is my recommended fund.

Despite the 1993 rally in the Tokyo stock market, the three developed regions—the United States, Japan and Europe—are still waiting for a strong resurgence in their economies. Many emerging markets are surging ahead but experiencing the usual choppiness along the way.

The table below indicates the historical average annual total returns of the Europe stock group and the S&P 500 Index for years ending December 31.

Europe Stock Group versus S&P 500 Index

	Group Total Return	S&P 500		Group Total Return	S&P 500
1986	17.21%	18.68%	1990	−5.78%	−3.12%
1987	10.11	5.26	1991	7.11	30.48
1988	8.26	16.60	1992	−6.66	7.62
1989	22.41	31.68			

Source: *Morningstar Mutual Funds,* Morningstar, Inc., 225 W. Wacker Dr., Chicago, IL 60606; 312-696-6532

Investments in foreign stock markets can be as volatile, if not more volatile, than investments in U.S. markets. To illustrate the volatility of European stock market returns for the U.S. dollar–based investor, the table below sets forth the extremes, as well as average annual returns, for the period from 1970 to 1992, as measured by the Morgan Stanley Capital International (MSCI) Europe Index as calculated for a U.S.-dollar investor. The MSCI-Europe Index, which includes common stocks that U.S. investors cannot purchase, is shown here in lieu of the MSCI-Europe (Free) Index, which was initiated only in January 1988. The "Free" Index includes only shares that U.S. investors are "free to purchase." The index excludes restricted shares in Finland, Norway, Sweden and Switzerland.

Average Annual MSCI-Europe Stock Market Returns (1970–1992)

	1 Year	5 Years	10 Years
Best	78.6%	32.3%	19.3%
Worst	−22.6	−1.2	5.5
Average	13.4	13.2	13.5

Source: Vanguard International Equity Index Fund dated April 26, 1993

●───

Recommended Fund

Vanguard International Equity Index Fund European Portfolio
Vanguard Financial Center
P.O. Box 2600
Valley Forge, PA 19482
800-662-7447

Portfolio manager: George U. Sauter
Investment adviser: Vanguard's Core Management Group
Sales fees: No-load
Annual account maintenance fee: $10
12b-1 fees: None
Investment management fee: 0.06%
Other expenses: 0.26%
Total operating expense: 0.32%
Minimum initial purchase: $3,000 (additional: $100)
Minimum IRA purchase: $500 (additional: $100)
Date of inception: June 18, 1990
Net assets of fund as of April 30, 1993: $371.3 million

Investment Objective
Vanguard International Equity Index Fund European Portfolio seeks to replicate the aggregate price and yield performance of the Morgan Stanley Capital International Europe (Free) Index, a diversified, capi-

talization-weighted index comprising companies located in 13 European countries.

Investment Policy

The fund is not managed according to traditional methods of active investment management, which involve the buying and selling of securities based upon economic, financial and market analysis and investment judgment. Instead, the Europe portfolio utilizes a passive or indexing investment approach, attempting to approximate the investment performance of the MSCI-Europe (Free) through statistical procedures. The fund is managed without regard to tax ramifications.

The European portfolio invests in a statistically selected sample of approximately 575 stocks included in MSCI-Europe (Free) located in 13 European countries. Three countries—the United Kingdom, Germany and France—dominate MSCI-Europe (Free), with 40 percent, 14 percent and 14 percent of the market capitalization of the index, respectively. The ten other countries are individually much less significant to the index and, consequently, the portfolio.

The portfolio's policy is to remain fully invested in common stocks. Under normal circumstances, at least 80 percent of the assets will be invested in stocks that are represented in the index. It may invest in certain short-term fixed-income securities, such as cash reserves, although cash or cash equivalents are expected to represent less than 1 percent of the portfolio's assets. The portfolio may also invest in stock futures contracts, options and warrants in order to invest uncommitted cash balances, maintain liquidity to meet shareholder redemptions, or minimize trading costs.

The portfolio will not invest in cash reserves or other instruments as part of a temporary defensive strategy, such as lowering its investment in common stocks, to protect against potential stock market declines. Rather, the portfolio intends to remain fully invested, to the extent practicable, in a pool of securities that will approximate the investment characteristics of its index.

Performance

The tables below indicate annual total returns of the fund for each full year of operation ending December 31 and comparative results for the S&P 500 Index and the MSCI-Europe (Free) Index, followed by total returns and the growth of $10,000 invested in the fund for different periods ending June 30, 1993.

**Vanguard International Equity Index Fund
European Portfolio versus S&P 500 Index
and MSCI-Europe (Free) Index**

	Fund Total Return	S&P 500	MSCI Europe
1991	12.40%	30.48%	13.11%
1992	−3.32	7.62	−4.71

**Total Returns for Different Periods Ending
June 30, 1993**

	Fund Total Return	Growth of $10,000
3 Months	2.33%	$10,233
6 Months	8.47	10,847
1 Year	−2.32	9,768
3-Year Average	1.90	10,582

Source: *Morningstar Mutual Funds*

Financial History
Figure 18.1 provides information on selected per-share data and ratios for a share outstanding for each year ended December 31.

Comments
Vanguard International Equity Index Fund European Portfolio makes sense for the investor who wants to participate in Europe. A passively managed vehicle that attempts to replicate the performance of the MSCI Europe (Free) Index, the fund is firmly rooted in the efficient-market hypothesis: i.e., all the information known about a company is automatically reflected in its stock price.

There is no reason to dispute the assertion that large European stocks trade efficiently, making it difficult, if not impossible, for an active investment manager to consistently surpass a passively managed index. Currency risk makes the job even more challenging. If local currencies weaken relative to the dollar, U.S.-based investors suffer lower returns. The cost of hedging against this risk is quite high, though, and it cuts into performance when the dollar declines. As a result, no Europe stock fund has topped the index over the last five years.

The fund is not only good in theory; it is good in practice. Rather than investing in all 600 stocks in the index, it uses statistical sampling to build a portfolio that closely resembles the index in terms of country allocations, market capitalizations, industry weightings and portfolio

FIGURE 18.1 Vanguard International Equity Index Fund European
Portfolio Selected Per-Share Data and Ratios

	European Portfolio		
	Year ended December 31, 1992	1991	May 1† to December 31, 1990
Net Asset Value, Beginning of Period.............	$ 9.92	$ 9.06	$10.00
Investment Activities			
Income...	.28	.29	.18
Expenses......................................	(.03)	(.03)	(.02)
Net Investment Income	.25	.26	.16
Net Realized and Unrealized Gain (Loss) on Investments	(.58)	.86	(.94)
Total from Investment Activities	(.33)	1.12	(.78)
Distributions			
Net Investment Income	(.26)	(.26)	(.16)
Realized Net Gain	—	—	—
Total Distributions	(.26)	(.26)	(.16)
Net Asset Value, End of Period	$ 9.33	$ 9.92	$ 9.06
Ratio of Expenses to Average Net Assets	.32%	.33%	.40%*
Ratio of Net Investment Income to Average Net Assets	3.05%	3.06%	3.68%*
Portfolio Turnover Rate	1%	15%**	3%
Number of Shares Outstanding, End of Period (thousands)	27,489	16,204	10,577

Annualized
**Portfolio turnover rates for 1991 excluding in-kind redemptions were 3%.
Portfolio.
† Commencement of operations

Source: Vanguard International Equity Index Fund dated April 26, 1993

statistics. This approach has worked well; the fund's returns have
tracked the index fairly closely. Another factor working in the fund's
favor is its total operating expenses of 0.32 percent, by far the lowest
in the Europe stock group.

Overall, Vanguard International Equity Index Fund European Portfolio is one of the best choices available for investors who seek
exposure to European stocks.

Portfolio
Total stocks: 401 as of March 31, 1993
25 Largest Holdings

Royal Dutch Petroleum
British Telecommunications
Allianz Holding
Glaxo Holdings
British Petroleum
Siemens
B-A-T Industries
Deutsche Bank
British Gas
Unilever (NV)
Roche Holding
Daimler-Benz
Nestle

Nationale Elf Aquitaine
BTR
Electrabel
Assicurazioni Generali
Alcatel Alsthom
Hanson
HSBC Holdings (UK)
Union Bank of Switzerland
Guinness
Marks & Spencer
Unilever (UK)
BSN Groupe

Composition of Portfolio
As of March 31, 1993

Stocks	100%

Sector Weightings
As of March 31, 1993

Utilities	15.4%
Energy	8.4
Financials	22.5
Industrial Cyclicals	14.7
Consumer Durables	6.4
Consumer Staples	12.5
Services	6.9
Retail	3.7
Health	7.1
Technology	2.4

Other Europe Stock Funds

	Five-Year Growth of $10,000*
Alliance New Europe Fund—Class A	N/A
DFA Continental Small-Company Portfolio	**$13,735**
DFA United Kingdom Small-Company Portfolio	**10,385**

Fidelity Europe Fund	**14,759**
G.T. Europe Growth Fund—Class A	13,231
INVESCO European Fund	**14,321**
Merrill Lynch EuroFund—Class B	14,752
PaineWebber Europe Growth Fund—Class A	N/A
T. Rowe Price European Stock Fund	**N/A**

*For the period ending June 30, 1993

Funds listed in **bold type** are available by direct purchase.
N/A indicates that the fund did not have five full years of operation.

Summary

While many investment managers are optimistic about the European markets, their future is far from assured. Europe stock funds have historically been about 30 percent more volatile than the average equity fund, making them appropriate only for investors who can tolerate some losses. For long-term investors who want to participate in the entire European market, Vanguard International Equity Index European Portfolio is one of the best choices available.

Foreign Stock Funds

Usual Investment Objective of the Group

Most mutual funds included in the foreign stock group seek long-term capital growth as their primary investment objective. Additionally, some seek current income and growth of income. Funds in this group normally maintain at least 65 percent of their assets invested in securities of companies that have their principal business activities outside of the United States. Such securities are likely to be in any combination of a broad range of equity and debt securities.

Survey of the Group

With many brokers and investment advisers encouraging investors to consider overseas investment opportunities, foreign stock funds are taking off, in terms of both popularity and returns. The assets of this group have soared over the last decade, from less than $1 billion in

1983 to over $22 billion by mid-1993. For example, in just three months the assets of Fidelity International Growth and Income Fund grew from $85 million in April to more than $215 million at the end of June 1993.

Investors were well rewarded in the first six months of 1993, with the foreign stock group posting an average gain of 15 percent. This compared with a 5 percent return on the S&P 500 Index but followed four years during which the group's average return was significantly below that of the S&P. Over most historical periods the group has had difficulty in competing with the S&P 500. Over the five years ending June 30, 1993, the foreign stock group had an average total return of 7.21 percent, compared with 14.21 percent for the S&P 500. Likewise, over ten years ending June 30, 1993, the group earned 12.66 percent versus 14.4 percent for the S&P. The 15-year average return for the group was 12.18 percent versus 15.55 percent for the S&P 500.

Emerging-markets funds hold the potential for explosive growth but also can be extremely volatile. Fidelity Overseas Fund had returns of more than 78 percent in 1985 and more than 69 percent in 1986, but posted losses of over 6 percent in 1990 and over 11 percent in 1992. Then they soared by nearly 20 percent in the first six months of 1993 alone. So the jury is still out as to what the future may hold for investors in the foreign arena. While some funds in this group could conceivably perform very well, long-term results have tended to favor the U.S. market.

Best-performing funds over time have generally been those that stick to more traditional, liquid markets. For long-term strength, it's hard to beat Templeton Foreign Fund or Harbor International Fund (my recommended fund), both of which hold the bulk of their assets in established European markets.

The following table indicates the historical average annual total return of the foreign stock group and the S&P 500 Index for years ending December 31.

Foreign Stock Group versus S&P 500 Index

	Group Total Return	S&P 500		Group Total Return	S&P 500
1983	27.73%	22.47%	1988	17.42%	16.60%
1984	−4.51	6.27	1989	21.98	31.68
1985	44.44	31.83	1990	−12.07	−3.12
1986	44.58	18.68	1991	12.51	30.48
1987	6.95	5.26	1992	−4.54	7.62

Source: *Morningstar Mutual Funds*

Recommended Fund

Harbor International Fund
One SeaGate
Toledo, OH 43666
800-422-1050

Portfolio manager: Hakan Castegren
Investment adviser: Harbor Capital Advisors
Sales fees: No-load
Management fee: 0.00%
Investment advisory fee: 0.85%
Other expenses: 0.43%
Total operating expense: 1.28%
Minimum initial purchase: $2,000 (additional: $500)
Minimum IRA purchase: $500 (additional: $100)
Date of inception: December 29, 1987
Net assets of fund as of June 30, 1993: $1.44 billion

Investment Objective
The investment objective of Harbor International Fund is to seek long-term growth of capital through investment in a portfolio consisting of non-U.S. equity securities. Current income is a secondary consideration.

Investment Policy
Harbor International Fund pursues its investment objective by investing its assets in common stocks and comparable equity securities of issuers that do business primarily outside the United States. The fund will be invested in a minimum of three countries exclusive of the United States, and currently intends to invest primarily in equity securities of issuers located in Europe, the Pacific Basin and the more highly developed emerging industrialized countries, which it believes present favorable investment opportunities.

Under exceptional conditions abroad or when it is believed that economic or market conditions warrant, the fund may temporarily invest part or all of its portfolio in equity securities of U.S. issuers, notes and bonds that are rated BBB or higher by Standard & Poor's Corporation or Baa or higher by Moody's Investors Service, and cash or cash equivalents of U.S. or foreign issuers.

In addition, for temporary defensive or hedging purposes, the fund may purchase options on foreign currencies; enter into forward foreign currency exchange contracts and contracts for future delivery of foreign currencies; and purchase options on such futures contracts.

Performance

The tables below indicate annual total returns of the fund for each full year of operation ending December 31 and comparative results for the S&P 500 Index, followed by total returns and the growth of $10,000 invested in the fund for different periods ending June 30, 1993.

Harbor International Fund versus S&P 500 Index

	Fund Total Return	S&P 500		Fund Total Return	S&P 500
1988	37.71%	16.60%	1991	21.46%	30.48%
1989	36.86	31.68	1992	−0.21	7.62
1990	−9.76	−3.12			

Total Returns for Different Periods Ending June 30, 1993

	Fund Total Return	Growth of $10,000
3 Months	6.37%	$10,637
6 Months	16.83	11,683
1 Year	8.51	10,851
3-Year Average	6.08	11,939
5-Year Average	15.65	20,692

Source: *Morningstar Mutual Funds*

Financial History

Figure 18.2 illustrates per-share data for a share outstanding throughout each period and selected ratio information for Harbor International Fund for each year ended October 31.

Comments

In its short history, Harbor International Fund has had a very respectable performance. In its first two full years of operation, it did significantly better than the S&P 500 Index, with back-to-back returns of more than 37 percent in 1988 and more than 36 percent in 1989. The fund beat the S&P by more than 21 percentage points in 1988 and by more than five points in 1989. Compared with the Morgan Stanley Capital International (MSCI) Europe, Australia and Far East Index

FIGURE 18.2 Harbor International Fund Selected Per-Share Data and Ratios

Year (Period) Ended	Investment Income	Operating Expenses	Interest Expense	Net Investment Income
Harbor International Fund				
October 31, 1992	$.40	$.16	—	$.24
October 31, 1991	.28	.12	—	.16
October 31, 1990	.55	.18*	—	.37
October 31, 1989	.32	.14*	—	.18
October 31, 1988**	.21	.14*	—	.07

	Net Asset Value		Ratio of Operating Expenses to Average Net Assets (%)
	Beginning of Period	End of Period	
Harbor International Fund			
October 31, 1992	$17.69	$16.77	1.28%
October 31, 1991	15.74	17.69	1.35
October 31, 1990	15.99	15.74	1.40*
October 31, 1989	13.00	15.99	1.15*
October 31, 1988**	10.00	13.00	1.78†*

Source : Harbor Fund prospectus dated June 25, 1993

(EAFE), an index of international equity securities, Harbor International Fund did very well over the five years that ended June 30, 1993. Its average annual return of 15.65 percent easily outpaced the index, which had an average return of 3.63 percent.

Much of the fund's success has come from avoiding overpriced trouble spots. Low exposure to Japan left the fund relatively unmarked as that equity market declined from 1990 through 1992. Although the Japanese market strengthened in 1993, Mr. Castegren remains cautious of its high prices and kept the fund's exposure to only 8 percent of assets.

For the future, management sees attractive long-term potential in Eastern Europe and indirectly invests in that region through Switzerland, which has been a successful area for the fund and which continues to top the fund's country exposure.

It is interesting to look at the historical results of the major indexes to which investors compare their returns. Indexes can often provide a valuable means of measuring the effectiveness of professional investment managers. The following table provides the historic average total

FIGURE 18.2 *(continued)*

Dividends From		Net Realized and Unrealized Gains (Losses) on Investments Futures, Options and Forward Currency Contracts	Net Increase (Decrease) in Net Asset Value
Net Investment Income	Net Realized Capital Gains		
$(.21)	$ —	$ (.95)	$ (.92)
(.34)	(.34)	2.47	1.95
(.17)	(.72)	.27	(.25)
(.10)	(.76)	3.67	2.99
—	—	2.93	3.00

Ratio of Interest Expense to Average Net Assets (%)	Ratio of Net Investment Income to Average Net Assets (%)	Portfolio Turnover (%)	Number of Shares Outstanding at End of Period (000's)
—	1.98%	24.67%	41,782
—	1.76	18.63	11,627
—	2.82*	28.28	4,049
—	1.56*	21.05	1,815
—	0.87†*	26.66	796

returns for five investment categories for the 30 years ending December 31, 1992.

Average Annual Returns for Five Investment Categories

	30 Years (1963–1992) Annual Rates
Morgan Stanley Capital International Europe, Australia and Far East Index	11.18%
Standard & Poor's 500 Index	10.87
Domestic Bonds (intermediate and long blended historic data)	7.51
90-Day U.S. Treasury Bills	6.66
Consumer Price Index	5.27

Source: Harbor Fund Semiannual Report dated April 30, 1993

The record of Harbor International Fund says it all. It has shown itself to be one of the best ways for investors to enhance their exposure to international markets.

Portfolio

Total stocks: 88 as of May 28, 1993

25 Largest Holdings

Hutchison Whampoa

Roche Holding

Keppel

CS Holding

Sony

Total B

Lasmo

Sandoz

Nestle

Astra Class A Free

SMH

Hong Kong Electric

Swire Pacific Class A

British Petroleum

Bridgestone

National Westminster

Saga Petroleum Class A

Nintendo

Malayan Banking

Jurong Shipyard

Credit Lyonnais

Hong Kong Telecommunications

RTZ

Telekom Malaysia

FUJI Photo Film

Composition of Portfolio

As of March 31, 1993

Cash	3.3%
Stocks	96.7

Sector Weightings

As of March 31, 1993

Utilities	15.7%
Energy	10.4
Financials	23.2
Industrial Cyclicals	16.3
Consumer Durables	13.0
Services	1.9
Health	10.4
Technology	2.3

Other High-Performing Foreign Stock Funds

	Five-Year Growth of $10,000*
Babson-Stewart Ivory International Fund	**$15,719**
EuroPacific Growth Fund	17,980
GAM International Fund	19,125
Ivy International Fund	17,294

Lexington Worldwide Emerging Markets Fund	**15,151**
T. Rowe Price International Stock Fund	**15,519**
Scudder International Fund	**15,389**
Smith Barney World Funds International Equity	
Portfolio—Class A	18,603
Templeton Foreign Fund	18,368

*For the period ending June 30, 1993

Funds listed in **bold type** are available by direct purchase.

Summary

Diversifying internationally has become a wise trend recently. The top-rated funds tend to be those that stick to more traditional, liquid markets. While emerging-markets funds hold the potential for explosive growth, they can also be extremely volatile.

Pacific Stock Funds

Usual Investment Objective of the Group

Mutual funds included in the Pacific stock fund group seek capital appreciation. Current income is normally not an important consideration. Funds in this group invest primarily in companies that have their principal business activities in the Pacific Basin. Such countries include Japan, Australia, Hong Kong, Singapore, Malaysia, New Zealand and the Philippines. For defensive purposes, funds may invest in fixed-income securities denominated in the currencies of Pacific Basin countries and in U.S. dollars.

Survey of the Group

The annual performance of funds in this group has to a large extent been determined by their level of exposure to Japan. Unlike the precipitous decline experienced in 1990 and, to a lesser extent, in 1992, funds heavily weighted with Japanese securities bounced back with a vengeance in the first half of 1993; DFA Japanese Small-Company Portfolio was up more than 50 percent through June. The average total return for the group in the first six months of 1993 was over 25 percent, benefiting from the Tokyo exchange's tremendous rally. Other Japan-focused funds such as Nomura Pacific Basin (my recommended fund) and The Japan Fund also produced big returns during this period.

A subset of funds in this group spurn Japanese stocks, preferring to seeks investments in Hong Kong, Singapore, Malaysia and other emerging markets. Funds that mostly avoid Japan include Merrill Lynch Dragon Fund—Class B, Morgan Stanley Institutional Fund Asian Equity Portfolio, Newport Tiger Fund and T. Rowe Price New Asia Fund. Funds that avoided Japan outperformed the Japan-focused funds during that country's long and brutal recession. While these funds did not participate in the 1993 rally in the Tokyo market, they still show promise, as returns from exchanges throughout the region have continued to easily outpace the S&P 500 index.

Funds invested in the Pacific Basin have sharply increased in number. From three funds as recently as 1984, the number grew to ten in 1988, 15 in 1991 and at least 26 in late 1993. New investment monies have continued to pour into the region.

Investors considering the purchase of funds in this arena should consider where they want their money placed. For example, many of the broad-based Pacific funds have stakes in Japan totaling more than 70 percent of assets. Other funds avoid the gigantic Japan market altogether. Investors who want more control over how their funds are divided may opt for one Japan and one non-Japan fund. And they should consider how much of their investment, if any, should be exposed to the smaller, less-developed markets.

The following table indicates the historical average total return of the Pacific stock group and the S&P 500 for years ending December 31.

Pacific Stock Group versus S&P 500 Index

	Group Total Return	S&P 500		Group Total Return	S&P 500
1983	35.14%	22.47%	1988	22.72%	16.60%
1984	−0.55	6.27	1989	27.70	31.68
1985	28.93	31.83	1990	−20.00	−3.12
1986	71.98	18.68	1991	11.84	30.48
1987	32.57	5.26	1992	−6.20	7.62

Source: *Morningstar Mutual Funds*

Recommended Fund

Nomura Pacific Basin Fund
180 Maiden Lane
New York, NY 10038
800-833-0018

Portfolio manager: Takeo Nakamura
Investment adviser: Nomura Capital Management
Sales fees: No-load
Management fee: 0.75%
Other expenses: 0.76%
Total operating expense: 1.51%
Minimum initial purchase: $1,000 (additional: $0)
Minimum IRA purchase: $1,000 (additional: $0)
Date of inception: July 8, 1985
Net assets of fund as of April 30, 1993: $51.4 million

Investment Objective

Nomura Pacific Basin Fund's investment objective is long-term capital appreciation primarily through investments in equity securities of corporations domiciled in Japan and other Far Eastern and Western Pacific (Pacific Basin) countries, including Japan, Australia, Hong Kong, Korea, Malaysia, New Zealand, Singapore, Taiwan, Thailand and the Philippines. Current income from dividends and interest is not an important consideration in selecting securities.

Investment Policy

The fund anticipates that under normal conditions at least 70 percent of its assets will consist of Pacific Basin corporate securities, primarily common stock and, to a lesser extent, securities convertible into common stock and rights to subscribe for common stock. It is expected that the fund's investment in securities of Japanese corporations will constitute a substantial part of its assets under normal circumstances due to the size and liquidity of the Japanese market, availability of investment alternatives and growth potential of technology-oriented companies in Japan.

The fund will attempt to maximize opportunity and reduce risk by investing in a diversified portfolio of companies in different stages of development. Portfolio companies will range from large, well-established companies to medium-size companies and smaller, less seasoned companies in an earlier stage of development.

For defensive purposes, the fund may invest in nonconvertible fixed-income securities denominated in currencies of Pacific Basin countries and in U.S. dollars. The fund may also hold cash in U.S. or Pacific Basin currencies, or short-term securities denominated in such currencies to provide for redemptions. It is not expected that such reserve for redemptions will exceed 10 percent of the fund's assets.

Performance

The tables below indicate annual total returns of Nomura Pacific Basin Fund during its full years of operation ending December 31 and comparative results of Standard & Poor's 500 Index, followed by total return and growth of $10,000 for different periods ending June 30, 1993.

Nomura Pacific Basin Fund Versus S&P 500 Index

	Fund Total Return	S&P 500		Fund Total Return	S&P 500
1986	74.27%	18.68%	1990	−15.51%	−3.12%
1987	34.90	5.26	1991	11.93	30.48
1988	15.18	16.60	1992	−12.74	7.62
1989	22.91	31.68			

Total Returns for Different Periods Ending June 30, 1993

	Fund Total Return	Growth of $10,000
3 Months	12.63%	$11,263
6 Months	27.69	12,769
1 Year	25.61	12,561
3-Year Average	3.63	11,130
5-Year Average	6.89	13,951

Source: *Morningstar Mutual Funds*

Financial History

Figure 18.3 illustrates per-share data for a share outstanding throughout each period and selected ratio information for each year ended March 31.

Comments

Based in New York, Nomura Pacific Basin Fund is committed to managing a portfolio in which Japanese holdings are predominant. The fund's substantial exposure to Japan does not exceed the amount this huge market occupies in the Morgan Stanley Capital International Index (MSCI), although its stake in the Tokyo exchange has dipped recently below 70 percent of the fund's equity assets.

The fund's total return for the 12 months ended June 30, 1993, was 25.6 percent, whereas for the five-year period ending on the same date, the average annual return was but 6.9 percent. This reflects substantial losses in 1990 and 1992 that resulted mainly from the fund's heavy commitment to Japanese stocks, which were badly hit in those years. Thus, investors should be aware that as Japan goes, to a large extent, so goes the fund.

Japanese stocks made a strong recovery in early 1993; therefore, it is no surprise that Nomura Pacific Basin Fund did well in the first six months of the year. Because its exposure to Japan is so predominant, its 25.6 percent surge was significantly better than funds that avoid Japan. On the other hand, Japan-only funds, such as DFA Japanese Small-Company Portfolio, with more than 50 percent total return, were the obvious leaders in the Pacific stock group.

Actually, Nomura Pacific Basin Fund closely resembles the MSCI Pacific Index. Still, over extended time periods, the fund has not been able to add significant value relative to that index. Since inception, the fund's average annualized return of 20.4 percent barely beats the index's 20 percent annualized gain for the same time period. While the fund doesn't have any sales fee, its annual expense ratio of 1.5 percent helps make a persuasive case for the Vanguard Pacific Index offering over this fund.

The fund has exhibited one important advantage over index funds. Using stock selection, modified allocations and cash reserves, the fund withstood the sharp recession problems in 1990 much better than the MSCI Pacific Index, outperforming it by almost 19 percentage points.

Portfolio

Total stocks: 181 as of March 31, 1993

25 Largest Holdings

Tohoku Electric Power	Seino Transportation
Mabuchi Motor	News
National Australia Bank	Yamato Setubi Construction
Toray Industries	Mitsui Marine & Fire Insurance
Secom	Hong Kong & Shanghai Banking
Hitachi	Kokuyo
Sony	Tokyo Steel Manufacturing
Seven-Eleven Japan	Yamanouchi Pharmaceutical
Mitsui	Ito-Yokado

FIGURE 18.3 Nomura Pacific Basin Fund Per-Share Data and Selected Ratios

Selected data for a share of common stock outstanding throughout each period:

	Year ended March 31,							7/8/85* to 3/31/86
	1993	1992	1991	1990	1989	1988	1987	
Net asset value, beginning of period	$12.49	$15.19	$15.36	$19.15	$20.59	$24.20	$15.68	$10.00
Income from investment operations:								
Net investment income (loss)	0.00††	0.00††	0.04	0.08	0.03	0.06††	0.03††	0.06††
Net realized and unrealized gain (loss) on investments and foreign currencies	1.87††	(1.84)††	2.53§	0.20	(0.21)	6.87††	8.85††	5.62††
Total from investment operations	1.87††	(1.84)††	2.57§	0.28	(0.18)	6.93††	8.88††	5.68††
Distributions to shareholders from:								
Net investment income	(0.02)	(0.01)	(0.04)	(0.10)	(0.05)	(0.08)	0.00	0.00
Net realized capital gains	(0.01)	(0.85)	(2.70)§	(3.97)	(1.21)	(10.46)	(0.36)	0.00
Total distributions	(0.03)	(0.86)	(2.74)§	(4.07)	(1.26)	(10.54)	(0.36)	0.00
Net asset value, end of period	$14.33	$12.49	$15.19	$15.36	$19.15	$20.59	$24.20	$15.68

Source: Nomura Pacific Basin Fund, Inc. prospectus dated July 29, 1993

FIGURE 18.3   (continued)

Total investment return	15.0%	(12.9%)	17.4%	(1.7%)	(0.9%)	35.3%	57.6%	56.8%
Ratio to average net assets/supplemental data:								
Net assets, end of period (in 000)	46,095	43,203	54,274	53,933	73,169	94,786	81,850	32,426
Average net assets (in 000)	43,456	52,253	54,329	69,459	83,420	91,562	53,958	13,803
Operating Expenses	1.51%	1.46%	1.42%	1.25%	1.25%	1.22%	1.45%	1.50%†**
Net investment income	0.01%	0.00%	0.28%	0.40%§	0.07%	0.28%	0.14%	0.88%**
Portfolio turnover	55%	41%	76%	46%	37%	61%	46%	3%

*Commencement of operations.
**Annualized.
§Amounts restated.
†Net of expense reimbursement which amounted to $0.06** per share and 0.62% of average net assets.
††Based on average shares outstanding.

Suzuki Motor	Adyama Trading
Tanjong	Rohm
Mitsubishi Heavy Industries	Mitsubishi Bank
TDK	

Composition of Portfolio
As of July 9, 1993

Cash	15.0%
Stocks	85.0

Sector Weightings
As of April 30, 1993

Utilities	7.6%
Financials	17.3
Industrial Cyclicals	22.9
Consumer Durables	13.8
Consumer Staples	1.5
Services	14.0
Retail	7.1
Health	4.7
Technology	11.1

Other Pacific Stock Funds

	Five-Year Growth of $10,000*
DFA Japanese Small-Company Portfolio	**$11,386**
Fidelity Pacific Basin Fund	**11,356**
G.T. Japan Growth Fund—Class A	10,996
G.T. Pacific Growth Fund—Class A	16,849
The Japan Fund	**11,734**
Merrill Lynch Dragon Fund—Class B **	N/A
Merrill Lynch Pacific Fund—Class A	16,380
Morgan Stanley Institutional Fund Asian Equity Portfolio ($500,000 minimum initial investment)	**N/A**
Newport Tiger Fund	N/A
T. Rowe Price New Asia Fund	**N/A**
Vanguard International Equity Index Fund Pacific Portfolio	**N/A**

*For the period ending June 30, 1993
**This fund is closed to new purchases.

Funds listed in **bold type** are available by direct purchase.

N/A indicates that the fund has not completed five full years of operation.

Summary

The relative year-to-date performance of the individual funds in the Pacific stock group is often determined by their level of exposure to Japan. Many of the broad-based Pacific funds have stakes in Japan totaling more than 70 percent of assets. Other funds avoid that gigantic market altogether. Investors in the Pacific Basin should consider how much of their investment, if any, should be exposed to the smaller, less-developed markets.

World Stock Funds

Usual Investment Objective of the Group

Mutual funds included in the world stock group seek long-term capital growth as their primary investment objective. Some funds also seek current income and growth of income. Funds in this group invest primarily in equity securities of issuers located throughout the world, maintaining a percentage of their assets (usually 25–50 percent) in the United States. Such securities are likely to be a flexible portfolio of equity and debt securities.

Survey of the Group

World stock funds saw a number of market reversals in 1993. In 1992, the Japanese market was the world's biggest loser, dropping 26 percent in dollar terms. After a few years of such beatings, many funds, such as IDS International Fund, decided to cut back longstanding Japan holdings. Unhappily, those funds missed out in 1993, as the Japanese government's fiscal stimulus caused both the Nikkei market and the yen to soar. During the first six months of 1993, Japan was the world's best performer, gaining more than 40 percent in dollar terms. The United States, on the other hand, which had been one of the safer places to be in 1992, turned out to be one of the worst performers in 1993; it gained less than 5 percent through June.

Europe did better in early 1993 than in 1992, when the European Rate Mechanism collapsed. The stronger performances were centered in peripheral markets like Italy, which posted a 19 percent gain as a result of its rate drop and its anti-corruption campaign. Scandinavia was also a strong region, due to falling interest rates and an expected boost to corporate profits from its devalued currencies. Meanwhile, the major markets of Germany, France and the United Kingdom each gained less than 5 percent in the first six months of 1993 as their economies continued to drag.

Many Pacific Rim markets, such as Hong Kong and Malaysia, performed strongly in the first half of 1993. The only big net loser during that period was Mexico, dropping 10 percent because of uncertainty surrounding the passage of the North American Free Trade Agreement.

With the exception of the first half of 1993, the world stock group has underperformed the Standard & Poor's 500 Index over most extended time frames. The average annual total return of the group was 7.85 percent during the five years ended June 30, 1993, versus 14.21 percent for the S&P 500. For the ten-year period ending on the same date, the group return averaged 10.96 percent versus 14.40 for the S&P. The gap continues to narrow over the fifteen-year period, when the group averaged 14.43 percent versus 15.54 percent for the S&P.

Despite the 1993 rally in the Tokyo stock market, the three developed regions—the United States, Japan and Europe—are still waiting for a strong resurgence in their economies. Many emerging markets are surging ahead but experiencing the usual choppiness along the way.

The following table indicates the historical average total return of the world stock group and the S&P 500 Index for years ending December 31.

World Stock Funds Group versus S&P 500 Index

	Group Total Return	S&P 500		Group Total Return	S&P 500
1983	26.82%	22.47%	1988	14.23%	16.60%
1984	−5.81	6.27	1989	21.57	31.68
1985	40.00	31.83	1990	−10.70	−3.12
1986	31.17	18.68	1991	19.15	30.48
1987	5.16	5.26	1992	−0.66	7.62

Source: *Morningstar Mutual Funds*

●
——

Recommended Fund

Scudder Global Fund
175 Federal Street
Boston, MA 02110
800-225-2470

Portfolio manager: J. Garret and William Holzer
Investment adviser: Scudder Investor Services
Sales fees: No-load
12b-1 fees: None
Investment management fee: 1.00%
Other expenses: 0.48%
Total operating expense: 1.48%
Minimum initial purchase: $1,000 (additional: $100)
Minimum IRA purchase: $500 (additional: $50)
Date of inception: July 23, 1986
Net assets of fund as of June 30, 1993: $575.6 million

Investment Objective

Scudder Global Fund seeks long-term growth of capital through a diversified portfolio of marketable securities, primarily equity securities, including common stocks, preferred stocks and debt securities convertible into common stocks. The fund invests on a worldwide basis in equity securities of companies that are incorporated in the United States or in foreign countries. It also may invest in the debt securities of U.S. and foreign issuers. Income is an incidental consideration.

Investment Policy

The fund invests in companies expected to benefit from global economic trends, promising technologies or products, and specific-country opportunities resulting from changing geopolitical, currency or economic relationships. Investments will normally be spread broadly around the world and are expected to be invested in securities of at least three countries, one of which may be the United States. The fund may be invested 100 percent in non-U.S. issues, and for temporary defensive purposes it may be invested 100 percent in U.S. issues. However, under normal circumstances it is expected that both foreign and U.S. companies of varying size, as measured by assets, sales or capitalization, will be represented in the fund's portfolio.

Scudder Global Fund generally invests in equity securities but may also invest in debt securities convertible into common stock, convertible and nonconvertible preferred stock, and fixed-income securities of governments, government agencies, supranational agencies and companies when the investment manager believes the potential for appreciation will equal or exceed that available from equities.

In addition, the fund may invest in cash equivalents, such as bankers' acceptances, certificates of deposit, commercial paper, short-term government and corporate obligations, and repurchase agreements, for temporary defensive purposes and for liquidity.

Performance
The tables below indicate annual total returns for the fund for each full year of operation ending December 31 and comparative results for the S&P 500 Index, followed by total returns and the growth of $10,000 invested for different periods ending June 30, 1993.

Scudder Global Fund versus S&P 500 Index

	Fund Total Return	S&P 500		Fund Total Return	S&P 500
1987	3.03%	5.26%	1990	−6.40%	−3.12%
1988	19.19	16.60	1991	17.07	30.48
1989	37.41	31.68	1992	4.49	7.62

Total Returns for Different Periods Ending June 30, 1993

	Fund Total Return	Growth of $10,000
3 Months	4.95%	$10,495
6 Months	11.96	11,196
1 Year	13.40	11,340
3-Year Average	7.04	12,265
5-Year Average	12.77	18,236

Source: *Morningstar Mutual Funds*

Financial History
Figure 18.4 illustrates per share data for a share outstanding throughout each period and selected ratio information for each year ended June 30.

Comments
Scudder Global Fund stands the test of time, having managed to establish a better, more consistent performance than most of its peers

in the world stock fund group. This fund has delivered the best record in its group over the five years ending June 30, 1993, with a 12.77 percent average annual return.

The fund's strategy has always been to identify broad growth themes. It currently favors issues with below-market price/earnings multiples in such areas as information delivery, infrastructure-related companies and banks. The fund's performance in early 1993 was enhanced by holdings in foreign markets; its Asian stake did particularly well. For example, the fund's Japanese holdings soared as the Nikkei market rebounded, and its holdings in Hong Kong benefited from the good performance in that market.

Scudder Global Fund is well diversified. On June 30, 1993, its portfolio included weightings of 38.3 percent in North America, 33.6 percent in Europe, 13.0 percent in Japan, 12.9 percent in the Pacific Basin and 2.2 percent in South America.

The fund's management believes that there is substantial opportunity for long-term capital growth from a professionally managed portfolio of securities selected from U.S. and foreign markets. It has designed its fund for investors seeking worldwide equity opportunities in developed, newly industrialized and developing countries.

The strategy of investment manager William Holzer to blend value-oriented issues with growth themes has served shareholders well. The fund has a good combination of below-average risk, solid returns and low expenses. It provides an excellent diversification tool for an investor's portfolio.

The record of Scudder Global Fund says it all. It has shown itself to be one of the best ways for investors to enhance their exposure to world markets.

Portfolio

Total stocks: 112 as of December 31, 1992

25 Largest Holdings

Comerica	Lasmo
Union Bank of Switzerland	United Healthcare
Tokyo Marine & Fire Insurance	Nestle
Exel	JP Morgan
MBIA	Texas Instruments
Chemical Banking	Jardine Matheson Holdings
MCI Communications	Eurotunnel
Destec Energy	RWE
Astra Class A Free	Reuters Holdings Class B

FIGURE 18.4 Scudder Global Fund Per-Share Data and Selected Ratios

Selected data (for a share outstanding throughout each period) and ratios are as follows (audited):

	For the Years Ended June 30,					For the Period July 23, 1986 (commencement of operations) to June 30, 1987
	1992	1991	1990	1989	1988	
Income and expenses						
Income	$ .50	$ .74	$ .41	$ .51	$ .47	$ .19
Operating expenses, net	(.28)	(.31)	(.20)	(.30)	(.27)	(.13)
Foreign taxes withheld	(.03)	(.03)	(.02)	(.02)	(.02)	(.01)
Net investment income	.19	.40	.19	.19	.18	.05
Dividends from net investment income	(.31)	(.37)	(.20)	(.14)	(.06)	—
Capital changes						
Net realized and unrealized gain (loss) on investments and foreign currency related transactions	2.28	(1.50)	3.28	3.20	(.82)	3.37
Distributions from net realized gains on investments and foreign currency related transactions	(.66)	(.83)	(.55)	(.08)	(.25)	—

Source: Scudder Global Fund prospectus dated November 1, 1993.

FIGURE 18.4 (continued)

Net increase (decrease) in net asset value	1.50	(2.30)	2.72	3.17	(.95)	3.42
Net asset value:						
Beginning of period	18.06	20.36	17.64	14.47	15.42	12.00
End of period	$19.56	$18.06	$20.36	$17.64	$14.47	$15.42
Ratio of operating expenses, net, to average net assets (%)	1.59	1.70	1.81	1.98	1.71 (b)	1.84* (a)
Ratio of net investment income to average net assets (%)	1.09	2.21	1.77	1.22	1.23	.63*
Portfolio turnover rate (%)	44.6	85.0 (c)	38.3	30.7	53.8	32.2*
Number of shares outstanding at end of period (000 omitted)	18,957	14,826	12,623	5,140	5,576	6,608

* Annualized

(a) The Adviser did not impose all of its management fee during the period July 23, 1986 (commencement of operations) to December 31, 1986 amounting to $.01 per share.

(b) The Adviser absorbed a portion of the Fund's expenses exclusive of management fees, amounting to $.03 per share.

(c) The portfolio turnover rate on equity securities and debt securities was 62.7% and 174.4%, respectively, based on average monthly equity holdings and average monthly debt holdings.

Sandoz
American President
Commonwealth Edison
LaFarge

Banco Latinoamer de Export E
First Union
Bank of Montreal

Composition of Portfolio
As of March 31, 1993

Cash	10.0%
Stocks	87.0
Convertibles	2.0

Sector Weightings
As of March 31, 1993

Utilities	16.8%
Energy	3.9
Financials	33.9
Industrial Cyclicals	13.6
Consumer Staples	2.7
Services	11.3
Retail	2.8
Health	8.1
Technology	7.0

*Other High-Performing World Stock Funds**

	Five-Year Growth of $10,000**
Dreyfus Strategic World Investing	$16,257
G.T. Worldwide Growth Fund—Class A	17,345
MFS Lifetime Worldwide Equity Fund	14,964
New Perspective Fund	17,263
Oppenheimer Global Fund	17,041
Putnam Global Growth Fund—Class A	15,717
Templeton Growth Fund	18,148
Templeton Smaller Companies Growth Fund	16,713
Templeton World Fund	16,206

*For the period ending June 30, 1993
**Funds listed above are not available by direct purchase.

Summary

Funds in the world stock fund group invest globally, including in U.S. markets. This diversification permits investors to participate in global economic trends, technologies, products and specific-country opportunities on a worldwide basis. It should be noted, though, that over most time periods during the last 15 years the average returns of the group significantly trailed that of the Standard & Poor's 500 Index of major U.S. companies.

Chapter 19

Investing in Specialty Stock Funds

Financial Services Funds

Usual Investment Objective of the Group

Funds in this group seek capital appreciation by investing primarily in equity securities of financial service companies, including banks, brokerage firms and insurance companies. Current income is a secondary consideration for some funds.

Survey of the Group

Funds in the financial services group invest in the securities of financial services companies, such as commercial and industrial banks, savings and loan associations, consumer and industrial finance companies, leasing companies, securities-brokerage companies and insurance companies. The share prices of financial funds are sensitive to interest rate changes, much like those of certain other fund groups, such as fixed-income and utility offerings. Share values will tend to move inversely to the direction of interest rates.

There are approximately 90 funds in the financial group. Over extended periods of time, the group has slightly exceeded the S&P 500 in total return, with an average return of 15.7 percent over ten years and 15.99 percent over 15 years (as of June 30, 1993), versus 14.4 percent and 15.54 percent, respectively, for the S&P. The group significantly outperformed the S&P over shorter periods of time, with returns of 31.56 percent for one year, 26.89 percent for three years and 20.07 percent for five years. The heaviest gains came in 1991 and 1992 as a result of falling interest rates and rising profit margins.

While the financial group's performance has soared recently, investors should keep in mind that all good things eventually come to an end.

The following table indicates the historical average total return of the financial services group and the S&P 500 Index for years ending December 31.

Financial Services Group versus S&P 500 Index

	Group Total Return	*S&P 500*		*Group Total Return*	*S&P 500*
1983	26.42%	22.47%	1988	18.92%	16.60%
1984	15.17	6.27	1989	24.84	31.68
1985	39.79	31.83	1990	−15.65	−3.12
1986	15.14	18.68	1991	59.34	30.48
1987	−11.49	5.26	1992	34.82	7.62

Source: *Morningstar Mutual Funds,* Morningstar, Inc. 225 W. Wacker Dr., Chicago, IL 60606; 312-696-6532

Recommended Fund

INVESCO Strategic Financial Services Portfolio
P.O. Box 173706
Denver, CO 80217-3706
800-525-8085

Portfolio manager: Douglas N. Pratt
Investment adviser: INVESCO Funds Group
Sales fees: No-load, 0.02% administrative fee
Management fee: 0.75% maximum/0.55% minimum
Total operating expense: 1.07%
Minimum initial purchase: $1,000 (additional: $50)
Minimum IRA purchase: $250
Date of inception: June 2, 1986
Net assets of fund as of June 30, 1993: $387 million

Investment Objective
The investment objective of INVESCO Strategic Financial Services Portfolio is to seek capital appreciation by investing primarily in securities of financial services companies.

Investment Policy
The fund normally invests at least 80 percent of its assets in the equity securities of financial services companies. Such companies include commercial and industrial banks, savings and loan associations, consumer and industrial finance companies, leasing companies, securities-brokerage companies and insurance companies.

Performance
The tables below indicate annual total returns of the fund for each full year of operation ending December 31 and comparative results for the S&P 500 Index, followed by total returns and the growth of $10,000 invested for different periods ending June 30, 1993.

INVESCO Strategic Services Portfolio versus S&P 500 Index

	Fund Total Return	S&P 500		Fund Total Return	S&P 500
1987	−11.01%	5.26%	1990	−7.16%	−3.12%
1988	17.15	16.60	1991	74.00	30.48
1989	36.90	31.68	1992	26.78	7.62

Total Returns for Different Periods Ending June 30, 1993

	Fund Total Return	Growth of $10,000
3 Months	−2.53%	$ 9,747
6 Months	11.60	11,160
1 Year	30.39	13,039
3-Year Average	31.44	22,709
5-Year Average	24.99	30,507

Source: *Morningstar Mutual Funds*

Financial History
Figure 19.1 illustrates per-share data for a share outstanding throughout each period and selected ratio information for each year ended October 31.

Comments
After several years of outstanding results and substantially outperforming the S&P 500 in 1991 and 1992, the investment manager

FIGURE 19.1 INVESCO Strategic Financial Services Portfolio Per-Share Data and Selected Ratios

	Financial Services Year Ended October 31						Period Ended October 31
	1992	1991	1990	1989	1988	1987	1986⁻
PER SHARE DATA							
Net Asset Value — Beginning of Period	$14.665	$ 7.185	$ 9.045	$ 7.552	$ 6.372	$ 7.738	$ 8.000
OPERATIONS							
Investment Income	0.360	0.176	0.218	0.296	0.261	0.159	0.059
Expenses	(0.163)	(0.069)	(0.233)	(0.208)	(0.139)	(0.089)	(0.033)
Net Investment Income (Loss)	0.197	0.107	(0.015)	0.088	0.122	0.070	0.026
Net Realized and Unrealized Gain (Loss) on Investments	1.520	7.555	(1.817)	2.304	1.188	(1.253)	(0.263)
Total from Operations	1.717	7.662	(1.832)	2.392	1.310	(1.183)	(0.237)
DISTRIBUTIONS							
Net Investment Income	(0.199)	(0.080)	(0.007)	(0.091)	(0.130)	(0.060)	(0.025)
Net Realized Gain on Investments	(0.906)	(0.102)	(0.021)	(0.808)	0.000	(0.123)	0.000
Total Distributions	(1.105)	(0.182)	(0.028)	(0.899)	(0.130)	(0.183)	(0.025)
Net Change in Net Asset Value	0.612	7.480	(1.860)	1.493	1.180	(1.366)	(0.262)
Net Asset Value — End of Period	$15.277	$14.665	$ 7.185	$ 9.045	$ 7.552	$ 6.372	$ 7.738
RATIOS							
Ratio of Expenses to Average Net Assets	1.07%	1.13%	2.50%	2.50%	1.95%	1.50%	1.50%*
Ratio of Net Investment Income (Loss) to Average Net Assets	1.28%	1.76%	-0.16%	1.05%	1.71%	1.18%	0.48%
Portfolio Turnover Rate	208%	249%	528%	217%	175%	284%	76%
Shares Outstanding at End of Period (000 Omitted)	12,418	6,488	183	244	307	188	70

⁻ From June 2, 1986, commencement of operations, to October 31, 1986.

* Annualized

Source: INVESCO Strategic Financial Services prospectus dated July 1, 1993

believes that the tremendous appreciation of U.S. financial stocks over recent years has peaked and that future earnings will not be sufficient to sustain the sector's price level. To counter that, he cut back holdings in U.S. banks and increased foreign holdings, expecting to continue that trend. He thinks that if European rates decline, the resulting rise in bank profits may offset any possible currency losses.

Some high-quality thrifts, insurance and brokerage stocks have been added to the portfolio. Securities industry stocks have helped to boost returns, as brokerage firms such as Merrill Lynch have enjoyed higher commissions from increased trading.

To a large extent, the fund's future performance will depend on how the shift into foreign securities pans out.

This is a well-managed fund suitable for investors who are looking for growth and believe that interest rates will not begin a dramatic upward trend.

Portfolio

Total stocks: 57 as of March 31, 1993

25 Largest Holdings

Citicorp	Merrill Lynch
Primerica	Advanta CL B
Greentree Financial	First USA
Household International	Wells Fargo
Allmerica Property/Casualty	JP Morgan
Norwest	FHLMC
Michigan National	First Commerce
Fleet Financial Group	Chase Manhattan
Countrywide Credit Industry	CCP Insurance
Torchmark	Bankers Life Holding
Bank of New York	Comerica
NationsBank	First of America Bank
ICH	

Composition of Portfolio

As of March 31, 1993

Cash	26.3%
Stocks	73.7
Convertibles	14.0

Sector Weightings

As of March 31, 1993

Financials	99.6%
Technology	0.4

Other Financial Services Funds

	*Five-Year Growth of $10,000**
Century Shares Fund	**$23,180**
Fidelity Select Financial Services Fund	**23,037**
Fidelity Select Home Finance Fund	**26,888**
Fidelity Select Regional Banks Fund	**28,544**
John Hancock Freedom Regional Bank Fund—Class B	26,511
PaineWebber Regional Financial Growth Fund—Class A	26,524
SIFE Trust Fund	19,651

*For period ending June 30, 1993

Funds listed in **bold type** are available by direct purchase.

Summary

Investors seeking capital appreciation, who prefer to invest in a specific sector and who believe that interest rates will stay relatively level or continue their downward trend, may find the financial services group to be rewarding. As in the case of any specialty fund, prudent strategy dictates allocating only a small portion of one's capital to this area.

Health-Care Funds

Usual Investment Objective of the Group

Mutual funds included in the health-care group seek capital appreciation by investing primarily in equity securities of health-care companies, including drug manufacturers, hospitals and biotechnology companies.

Survey of the Group

Health-care funds invest in stocks of companies in the medical industry. Individual funds may emphasize a limited portion of the broad health-care and biotechnology field, which ranges from large pharmaceutical companies to service companies that supply laundry to hospitals and nursing homes, to start-up medical research firms.

Investors' patience has been sorely tested with health-care funds. Because of the uncertainty surrounding pressure to regulate medical costs, as well as a shift in the market's focus from growth to cyclical stocks, the average health-care fund lost 6.54 percent in 1992, lagging the overall market by 14 percentage points. And 1993 wasn't any easier. Some health-care stocks, particularly in the biotechnology sector, outperformed the S&P 500, but most did worse.

Shareholders responded to the negative conditions by bailing out in large numbers. According to *Morningstar Mutual Funds,* total assets of the 13 health-care funds they follow declined to about $3.8 billion— nearly 40 percent lower than their 1991 peak.

It is easy to understand why some investors have fled this volatile group. Although health-care funds have enjoyed attractive returns in the past, especially from 1989 through 1991, their future is disturbingly uncertain. Government policy and particularly the Clinton administration's health-care plan leave investors wary.

Despite the current difficulties, most portfolio managers remain optimistic for the long term. The aging of the American population should boost demand for health-care products and services. Technological advances should keep the industry competitive. Nevertheless, cautious investors should use specialty health-care funds only as a small, long-term portion of their diversified fund portfolio.

The table below indicates the historical average total return of the health-care group and the S&P 500 Index for years ending December 31.

Health-Care Group versus S&P 500 Index

	Group Total Return	S&P 500		Group Total Return	S&P 500
1983	6.11%	22.47%	1988	10.46%	16.60%
1984	−3.56	6.27	1989	36.99	31.68
1985	39.92	31.83	1990	14.61	−3.12
1986	17.08	18.68	1991	69.02	30.48
1987	0.26	5.26	1992	−6.54	7.62

Source: *Morningstar Mutual Funds*

Recommended Fund

Vanguard Specialized Health-Care Portfolio
Vanguard Financial Center
P.O. Box 2600
Valley Forge, PA 19482
800-662-7447

Portfolio manager: Edward P. Owens
Investment adviser: Wellington Management
Sales fees: No-load
Redemption fee: 1.00%
Management fee: 0.16%
Total operating expenses: 0.22%
Minimum initial purchase: $3,000 (additional: $100)
Minimum IRA purchase: $500
Date of inception: May 23, 1984
Net assets as of June 30, 1993: $523.7 million

Investment Objective
Vanguard Specialized Health-Care Portfolio seeks to provide long-term capital appreciation. Although the portfolio may generate dividend income to a limited extent, current income will be secondary to the primary objective of capital appreciation.

Investment Policy
The fund normally invests at least 80 percent of its assets in equity securities of companies engaged in the development, production or distribution of products and services related to the treatment or prevention of diseases and other medical infirmities. These companies include pharmaceutical firms, medical supply firms, and companies that operate hospitals and other health-care facilities. The fund will also consider companies engaged in medical, diagnostic, biochemical and biotechnological research and development.

Performance
The tables below indicate annual total returns for the fund for each full year of operation ending December 31 and comparative results for the S&P 500 Index, followed by total returns and the growth of $10,000 invested for different periods ending June 30, 1993.

Vanguard Specialized Health-Care Portfolio versus S&P 500 Index

	Fund Total Return	S&P 500		Fund Total Return	S&P 500
1985	46.75%	31.83%	1989	32.95%	31.68%
1986	21.42	18.68	1990	16.79	-3.12
1987	-0.50	5.26	1991	46.32	30.48
1988	28.41	16.60	1992	-1.57	7.62

Total Returns for Different Periods Ending June 30, 1993

	Fund Total Return	Growth of $10,000
3 Months	5.97%	$10,597
6 Months	-2.35	9,765
1 Year	5.76	10,576
3-Year Average	13.77	14,725
5-Year Average	17.75	22,634

Source: *Morningstar Mutual Funds*

Financial History

Figure 19.2 illustrates per-share data for a share outstanding throughout each period and selected ratio information for each year ended January 31.

Comments

Despite the shadow that political uncertainty has cast over the entire health-care sector, the Vanguard Specialized Health-Care Portfolio has held up remarkably well. It outperformed nearly every other health-care fund in the first half of 1993 despite remaining fully invested. Some of its peers took huge losses despite sitting on very large cash positions.

Manager Edward Owens follows a conservative, value-oriented approach. Like most of the Wellington managers, he refuses to pay up for the promise of accelerated earnings. Instead, he buys stocks that are cheap relative to earnings, cash flow, or research and development costs.

This emphasis on value means that the portfolios's price multiples are relatively low. As a result, the fund's holdings haven't had as much room to fall as pricier issues. Industry allocations have also helped. The portfolio has had fairly light weightings in volatile biotechnology and medical-devices stocks, which have recently lost more than pharmaceuticals.

FIGURE 19.2 Vanguard Specialized Health-Care Portfolio Per-Share Data and Selected Ratios

					HEALTH CARE PORTFOLIO				May 23, 1984,
					Year ended January 31,				to Jan. 31, 1985
	1993	1992	1991	1990	1989	1988	1987	1986	
Net Asset Value, Beginning of Period	$35.54	$27.32	$22.16	$19.46	$17.53	$19.53	$15.61	$11.85	$10.00
Investment Activities									
Income	.77	.61	.60	.56	.48	.46	.35	.20	.11
Expenses	(.07)	(.08)	(.08)	(.08)	(.12)	(.11)	(.10)	(.07)	(.02)
Net Investment Income	.70	.53	.52	.48	.36	.35	.25	.13	.09
Net Realized and Unrealized Gain (Loss) on Investments	(1.68)	8.75	6.03	3.43	3.20	(.39)	4.60	3.81	1.76
Total From Investment Activities	(.98)	9.28	6.55	3.91	3.56	(.04)	4.85	3.94	1.85
Distributions									
Net Investment Income	(.70)	(.53)	(.55)	(.49)	(.34)	(.57)	(.13)	(.07)	—
Realized Net Gain	(1.20)	(.53)	(.84)	(.72)	(1.29)	(1.39)	(.80)	(.11)	—
Total Distributions	(1.90)	(1.06)	(1.39)	(1.21)	(1.63)	(1.96)	(.93)	(.18)	—
Net Asset Value, End of Period	$32.66	$35.54	$27.32	$22.16	$19.46	$17.53	$19.53	$15.61	$11.85
Ratio of Expenses to Average Net Assets	.22%	.30%	.36%	.39%	.62%	.51%	.61%	.83%	.59%*
Ratio of Net Investment Income to Average Net Assets	2.06%	1.98%	2.54%	2.34%	1.85%	1.65%	1.47%	1.52%	2.41%*
Portfolio Turnover Rate	13%	7%	17%	28%	19%	41%	27%	59%	23%*
Number of Shares Outstanding, End of Period (Thousands)	17,204	15,566	6,937	3,432	2,977	3,092	2,516	1,442	231

Annualized.

Source: Vanguard Specialized Health Care Portfolio prospectus dated May 31, 1993

The fund has also tended to do well in past bear markets. It put in strong showings when health-care stocks fell from favor in 1988 and 1992. Even though the fund doesn't top the charts when health-care stocks are in vogue, it has still received competitive returns over the last five years.

This is a well-managed, low-cost fund suitable for investors who are looking for a long-term investment in the health-care industry.

Portfolio

Total stocks: 75 as of March 31, 1993

25 Largest Holdings

Beckman Instruments	Biogen
Pfizer	Syntex
CIBA-Geigy	FHP International
Schering	Advanced Technology Labs
Bristol-Myers Squibb	Imperial Chemical Industries
Johnson & Johnson	Galen Health Care
Warner-Lambert	Becton Dickinson
Abbott Laboratories	Allergan
AL Laboratories CL A	Humana
Eli Lilly	Merck
Imcera Group	Sandoz
McKesson	American Cyanamid
DeKalb Genetics, CL B	

Composition of Portfolio
As of March 31, 1993

Cash	2.0%
Stocks	98.0

Sector Weightings
As of March 31, 1993

Industrial Cyclicals	6.4%
Consumer Staples	2.7
Services	0.9
Health	81.4
Technology	8.7

Other Health-Care Funds

	*Five Year Growth of $10,000**
Fidelity Select Biotechnology Portfolio	$31,849
Fidelity Select Health-Care Portfolio	24,190
Fidelity Select Medical Delivery Portfolio	24,830
G.T. Global Health Care Fund—Class A	N/A
INVESCO Strategic Portfolios Health Sciences	28,974
Merrill Lynch Health-Care Fund—Class A	14,500
Oppenheimer Global Bio-Tech Fund	20,133
Putnam Health Sciences Trust—Class A	20,532

*For the period ending June 30, 1993

Funds listed in **bold type** are available by direct purchase.
N/A indicates that a fund did not have five full years of operation.

Summary

While some investors have been losing patience with health-care funds, these funds provide an excellent way for the "patient" investor to participate in the growing health-care industry. The aging of the American population should boost demand for health-care products and services, and technological advances should keep the industry competitive. However, the prudent investor will use specialty health-care funds only as small, long-term components of a diversified fund portfolio.

Natural Resources Funds

Usual Investment Objective of the Group

Most mutual funds included in the natural resources group seek capital appreciation as their primary investment objective. These funds normally invest at least 65 percent of their assets in common stock of companies that explore, develop, produce and/or distribute natural resources. Such companies may also develop energy-efficiency technologies and other processing systems. Natural resource industries include precious metals, minerals, water, timber, oil, natural gas, coal, uranium and other such industries.

Survey of the Group

While the natural resources group had an average total return of more than 19 percent in the first six months of 1993, significantly outperforming the S&P 500, over longer periods its results have been less rewarding. According to *Morningstar Mutual Funds,* the group underperformed the S&P by over five percentage points in the three years that ended June 30, 1993, and by over six percentage points in the five-year period and five points in the ten-year period ending on that date.

Funds in this group with a portfolio holding that emphasized energy stocks did very well in early 1993, responding to rising natural gas prices. Gas prices rose from a low of about $1.50 per million British thermal units (BTUs) to a record $2.80 by the end of April. The funds that benefited most from gas-price increases were those favoring energy-services and exploration-and-production (E&P) firms. When fuel prices move up, E&P becomes profitable and energy services do very well. Fidelity Select Energy Services Portfolio, which focuses primarily on E&P and energy services, posted a huge 35 percent gain through June of 1993. Of course, when natural gas prices fall, E&P stops and energy services starve. In 1991 Fidelity shares lost over 23 percent of their value, while the S&P 500 *gained* over 30 percent.

Natural gas prices have fallen from their $2.80 high, but if the prices remain stable, drilling should accelerate. Still, risk-averse investors should stay away from funds that are highly leveraged to fuel prices; they are very volatile. Funds that diversify among nonenergy resources, such as Dean Witter Natural Resource Development Securities, offer a safer means of accessing natural resources exposure.

The following table indicates the historical average annual total return of the natural resources group and the S&P 500 Index for years ending December 31.

Natural Resources Group versus S&P 500 Index

	Group Total Return	S&P 500		Group Total Return	S&P 500
1983	20.48%	22.47%	1988	10.63%	16.60%
1984	−8.98	6.27	1989	28.38	31.68
1985	16.21	31.83	1990	−8.40	−3.12

| 1986 | 12.07 | 18.68 | 1991 | 7.07 | 30.48 |
| 1987 | 8.25 | 5.26 | 1992 | 2.54 | 7.62 |

Source: *Morningstar Mutual Funds*

Recommended Fund

Vanguard Specialized Energy Portfolio
Vanguard Financial Center
P.O. Box 2600
Valley Forge, PA 19482
800-662-7447

Portfolio manager: Ernst H. von Metzsch
Investment adviser: Wellington Management
Sales fees: No-load (there is a 1% redemption fee)
Management fee: 0.00%
Investment advisory fee: 0.16%
Other expenses: 0.05%
Total operating expense: 0.21%
Minimum initial purchase: $3,000 (additional: $100)
Minimum IRA purchase: $500 (additional: $100)
Date of inception: May 23, 1984
Net assets of fund as of June 30, 1993: $251.7 million

Investment Objective
Vanguard Specialized Energy Portfolio seeks to provide long-term capital appreciation. Although the portfolio may generate income to a limited extent, current income will be secondary to the primary objective of achieving capital appreciation.

Investment Policy
Under normal circumstances, the portfolio will invest at least 80 percent of its net assets in the common stocks and securities convertible into common stocks of companies engaged in energy-related activities: the production, transmission, marketing, control or measurement of energy or energy fuels; the making of component products for such activities; energy research or experimentation; and activities related to energy conservation and pollution control. Such activities may involve newer sources of energy, such as geothermal, nuclear and solar power, as well as more traditional sources of energy, such as oil, natural gas

and coal. The portfolio will not purchase the securities of electric utility companies, although it may invest in natural gas distributors and natural gas pipeline concerns.

Besides investing primarily in equity securities, the portfolio may hold certain short-term fixed-income securities as cash reserves, and it may also invest in stock futures contracts and options to a limited extent.

Performance

The tables below indicate annual total returns for the fund for each full year of operation ending December 31 and comparative results for the S&P 500 Index, followed by total returns and the growth of $10,000 invested for different periods ending June 30, 1993.

Vanguard Specialized Energy Portfolio versus S&P 500 Index

	Fund Total Return	S&P 500		Fund Total Return	S&P 500
1985	14.63%	31.83%	1989	43.45%	31.68%
1986	12.70	18.68	1990	−1.37	−3.12
1987	6.13	5.26	1991	0.28	30.48
1988	21.37	16.60	1992	6.18	7.62

Total Returns for Different Periods Ending June 30, 1993

	Fund Total Return	Growth of $10,000
3 Months	7.82%	$10,782
6 Months	30.78	13,078
1 Year	37.07	13,707
3-Year Average	10.27	13,408
5-Year Average	15.28	20,361

Source: *Morningstar Mutual Funds*

Financial History

Figure 19.3 illustrates per-share data for a share outstanding throughout each period and selected ratio information for each year ended January 31.

Comments

While volatile, Vanguard Specialized Energy Portfolio has turned in a very satisfactory performance during its short history. Over the five years ended June 30, 1993, the fund outperformed the S&P 500 Index,

FIGURE 19.3 Vanguard Specialized Energy Portfolio Per-Share Data and Selected Ratios

	ENERGY PORTFOLIO Year ended January 31,								May 23, 1984, to Jan. 31, 1985
	1993	1992	1991	1990	1989	1988	1987	1986	
Net Asset Value, Beginning of Period	$12.73	$13.39	$14.94	$12.29	$10.22	$12.42	$9.93	$9.81	$10.00
Investment Activities									
Income	.37	.46	.50	.43	.41	.67	.21	.54	.18
Expenses	(.03)	(.04)	(.05)	(.05)	(.05)	(.06)	(.03)	(.09)	(.02)
Net Investment Income	.34	.42	.45	.38	.36	.61	.18	.45	.16
Net Realized and Unrealized Gain (Loss) on Investments	1.29	(.24)	(.66)	3.20	2.08	(.64)	2.80	(.11)	(.35)
Total From Investment Activities	1.63	.18	(.21)	3.58	2.44	(.03)	2.98	.34	(.19)
Distributions									
Net Investment Income	(.36)	(.42)	(.46)	(.36)	(.37)	(.76)	(.44)	(.14)	—
Realized Net Gain	(.18)	(.42)	(.88)	(.57)	—	(1.41)	(.05)	(.08)	—
Total Distributions	(.54)	(.84)	(1.34)	(.93)	(.37)	(2.17)	(.49)	(.22)	—
Net Asset Value, End of Period	$13.82	$12.73	$13.39	$14.94	$12.29	$10.22	$12.42	$9.93	$ 9.81
Ratio of Expenses to Average Net Assets	.21%	.30%	.35%	.38%	.40%	.38%	.65%	.92%	.55%*
Ratio of Net Investment Income to Average Net Assets	2.47%	2.78%	3.24%	3.05%	3.07%	3.70%	3.43%	4.40%	3.75%*
Portfolio Turnover Rate	.37%	42%	40%	44%	46%	84%	34%	156%	34%*
Number of Shares Outstanding, End of Period (Thousands)	11,844	9,729	8,474	5,363	3,536	3,484	2,300	207	97

*Annualized.

Source: Vanguard Specialized Portfolios prospectus dated May 31, 1993

delivering an average annual return of 15.28 percent versus 14.21 percent for the S&P, and beating the index in four out of eight years.

The fund's strong record is a result of Mr. von Metzsch's care in diversifying the portfolio and in seeking good value in his stock purchases. The portfolio is overweighted in sectors where prices have already dropped and where the manager thinks a turnaround is possible in one or two years. This contrarian strategy sometimes fails in the short run but tends to do well over the long term. In 1991 the fund bought cheap energy service companies and in early 1992 some low-priced natural gas firms. In late 1992 and early 1993, the heavy gas commitment paid off when natural gas prices jumped, helping the fund to return over 37 percent in the 12 months ended June 30, 1993.

The fund recently reduced its exposure to natural gas and increased its leverage from oil prices, which have dropped, betting that oil prices will rise substantially in the next year or so. However, some analysts predict that oil may continue to fall.

Vanguard Specialized Energy Portfolio is not for the faint of heart. While it turned in an over 43 percent return in 1989, this was followed by a negative performance in 1990, an essentially flat performance in 1991 and then 6 percent in 1992. Patience was again rewarded by a nearly 31 percent return in the first half of 1993. However, investors seeking broad energy exposure with a contrarian strategy should take a careful look at this fund.

Portfolio

Total stocks: 61 as of March 31, 1993

25 Largest Holdings

Phillips Petroleum	Maxus Energy
Kerr-McGee	Chevron
Unocal	Mobil
British Petroleum	Amoco
Pennzoil	Exxon
USX-Marathon Group	Santa Fe Energy Resources
Amerada Hess	Oryx Energy
Texaco	Union Texas Petroleum
Baker Hughes	Diamond Shamrock
Norsk Hydro	Ashland Oil
Seagull Energy	Enron Oil & Gas
Total Petroleum	Dresser Industries
Repsol	

Composition of Portfolio
As of July 15, 1993

Cash	5.0%
Stocks	95.0

Sector Weightings
As of July 15, 1993

Utilities	2.6%
Energy	91.5
Industrial Cyclicals	2.8
Services	3.1

Other Natural Resources Funds

	Five Year Growth of $10,000*
American Gas Index Fund	**N/A**
Dean Witter Natural Resource Development Securities	$15,593
Fidelity Select Energy Portfolio	**16,416**
Fidelity Select Energy Service Portfolio	**16,114**
Fidelity Select Paper and Forest Products Portfolio	**13,712**
INVESCO Strategic Portfolios Energy Fund	**13,433**
Merrill Lynch Natural Resources Trust—Class B	11,985
New Alternatives Fund	15,945
PaineWebber Global Energy Fund Class B	16,055
T. Rowe Price New Era Fund	**14,066**
Putnam Energy Resources Trust	18,552

*For the period ending June 30, 1993

Funds listed in **bold type** are available by direct purchase.

N/A indicates that the fund has not completed five full years of operation.

Summary

Through 1992, the average fund in the natural resources group was outperformed by the S&P 500 in nine out of ten years. Risk-averse investors should stay away from the funds in this group that are highly leveraged to fuel prices; they are very volatile. Nevertheless, for broad energy exposure with a contrarian bent, investors will like the Vanguard Specialized Energy Portfolio.

Precious Metals Funds

Usual Investment Objective of the Group

Precious metals funds seek capital appreciation by investing primarily in equity securities of companies engaged in the mining, distribution or processing of precious metals.

Survey of the Group

Precious metals funds normally invest at least two-thirds of their portfolios in bullion or securities associated with gold, silver and other precious metals. Some funds will restrict their investments to preclude any securities related to the Republic of South Africa, while other funds will favor South African investments.

Funds in this group were severely hurt during most of the period from 1984 through 1992, showing negative total returns of more than minus 17 percent in 1988, minus 23 percent in 1990, minus 4 percent in 1991 and minus 15 percent in 1992. However, as the price of gold climbed to the $400-per-ounce range in 1993, the funds in this group had a gain averaging 63 percent through the end of June. This placed them at the head of the entire mutual fund pack.

Those funds with the biggest gains have maintained large positions in South African securities. The mining operations in that country tend to be highly leveraged to the price of gold. Thus, when the price of gold bullion moves up, these securities can make huge gains. Of course, the reverse is true when gold prices fall. An example of the riskiness of concentrating in South African issues is Lexington Strategic Investments, which invests strictly in South African gold-mining operations. It gained 199 percent in the first six months of 1993, after losing 61 percent in 1992.

The precious metals group offers a wide array of choices, but investors should remember that even the safest alternative can lose a lot of money when the price of gold tumbles. For the prudent investor, gold funds should be used only in small doses and only for hedging purposes.

The following table indicates the historical average annual total return of the precious metals group and the S&P 500 Index for years ending December 31.

Precious Metals Group versus S&P 500 Index

	Group Total Return	S&P 500		Group Total Return	S&P 500
1983	1.90%	22.47%	1988	−17.73%	16.60%
1984	−26.82	6.27	1989	25.64	31.68
1985	−9.35	31.83	1990	−23.94	−3.12
1986	34.06	18.68	1991	−4.33	30.48
1987	−17.73	5.26	1992	−15.18	7.62

Source: *Morningstar Mutual Funds*

●——————————————————————————————————————

Recommended Fund

Vanguard Specialized Gold and Precious Metals Portfolio
Vanguard Financial Center
P.O. Box 2600
Valley Forge, PA 19482
800-662-7447

Portfolio manager: David J. Hutchins
Investment adviser: M&G Investment Management
Sales fees: No-load (1% redemption fee)
Investment advisory fee: 0.28%
Other expenses: 0.08%
Total operating expenses: 0.36%
Annual brokerage cost: 0.12%
Minimum initial purchase: $3,000 (additional: $100)
Minimum IRA purchase: $500
Date of inception: May 23, 1984
Net assets as of June 30, 1993: $454 million

Investment Objective
Vanguard Specialized Gold and Precious Metals Portfolio seeks to provide long-term capital appreciation. Current income is not a consideration in the selection of securities.

Investment Policy
The fund invests in equity securities traded in the United States and, to a limited extent, in foreign securities markets. Normally, at least 80 percent of the fund's assets are invested in equity securities of companies involved in the exploration for, mining, processing or distribution

of gold, silver, platinum, diamonds or other precious and rare metals and minerals. The fund may also invest up to 20 percent of its assets directly in gold, silver or other precious metal bullion and coins.

Performance
The tables below indicate annual total returns for the fund for each full year of operation ending December 31 and comparative results for the S&P 500 Index, followed by total returns and the growth of $10,000 invested for different periods ending June 30, 1993.

Vanguard Specialized Gold and Precious Metals Portfolio versus S&P 500 Index

	Fund Total Return	S&P 500		Fund Total Return	S&P 500
1985	−5.03%	31.83%	1989	30.43%	31.68%
1986	49.88	18.68	1990	−19.86	−3.12
1987	38.73	5.26	1991	4.37	30.48
1988	−14.19	16.60	1992	−19.41	7.62

Total Returns for Different Periods Ending June 30, 1993

	Fund Total Return	Growth of $10,000
3 Months	31.28%	$13,128
6 Months	65.19	16,519
1 Year	35.63	13,563
3-Year Average	10.09	13,342
5-Year Average	6.26	13,549

Source: *Morningstar Mutual Funds*

Financial History
Figure 19.4 illustrates per-share data for a share outstanding throughout each period and selected ratio information for each year ended January 31.

Comments
The industry risks of the Vanguard Specialized Gold and Precious Metals Portfolio include the sharp price volatility of gold and other precious metals and of mining company shares. Investments related to gold or other precious metals are affected by a host of worldwide economic, financial and political factors. Prices of gold and other precious metals may fluctuate sharply over short periods due to several factors: changes in inflation or expectations regarding inflation in

FIGURE 19.4 Vanguard Specialized Gold and Precious Metals Portfolio Per-Share Data and Selected Ratios

	GOLD & PRECIOUS METALS PORTFOLIO Year ended January 31,								May 23, 1984, to Jan. 31, 1985
	1993	1992	1991	1990	1989	1988	1987	1986	
Net Asset Value, Beginning of Period	$9.41	$8.29	$12.49	$ 9.65	$9.35	$10.50	$ 7.60	$6.60	$10.00
Investment Activities									
Income	.22	.27	.33	.31	.32	.41	.24	.24	.11
Expenses	(.03)	(.03)	(.04)	(.04)	(.05)	(.06)	(.04)	(.04)	(.02)
Net Investment Income	.19	.24	.29	.27	.27	.35	.20	.20	.09
Net Realized and Unrealized Gain (Loss) on Investments	(2.13)	1.13	(4.17)	2.91	.29	.12	2.91	.86	(3.49)
Total From Investment Activities	(1.94)	1.37	(3.88)	3.18	.56	.47	3.11	1.06	(3.40)
Distributions									
Net Investment Income	(.18)	(.25)	(.32)	(.34)	(.26)	(.48)	(.21)	(.06)	—
Realized Net Gain	—	—	—	—	—	(1.14)	—	—	—
Total Distributions	(.18)	(.25)	(.32)	(.34)	(.26)	(1.62)	(.21)	(.06)	—
Net Asset Value, End of Period	$7.29	$9.41	$ 8.29	$12.49	$9.65	$ 9.35	$10.50	$7.60	$ 6.60
Ratio of Expenses to Average Net Assets	.36%	.35%	.42%	.45%	.48%	.47%	.59%	.73%	.87%*
Ratio of Net Investment Income to Average Net Assets	2.50%	2.54%	2.78%	3.01%	2.67%	2.71%	3.36%	3.86%	3.25%*
Portfolio Turnover Rate	2%	3%	10%	17%	18%	44%	32%	40%	11%*
Number of Shares Outstanding, End of Period (Thousands)	24,055	18,888	17,383	17,824	13,097	13,695	6,653	4,007	1,050

*Annualized.

Source: Vanguard Specialized Gold and Precious Metals Portfolio prospectus dated May 31, 1993

various countries; currency fluctuations; metal sales by governments, central banks or international agencies; investment speculation; changes in industrial and commercial demand; and government prohibitions or restrictions on the private ownership of certain precious metals or minerals.

At present, there are only four major producers of gold bullion. In order by production volume, they are the Republic of South Africa, Russia, Canada, and the United States. Political and economic conditions in these gold-producing countries may have a direct effect on the mining and distribution of gold and, therefore, its price.

The Vanguard Specialized Gold and Precious Metals Portfolio has consistently been one of the best performers among its peers. Over the five-year period ending June 30, 1993, the fund achieved an average annual total return of 6.26 percent, versus an average for the precious metals group of 2.03 percent. Over the three-year period ending on the same date, the fund returned an average of 10.09 percent versus the group's average return of 5.70 percent. The fund's six-month return of 65.19 percent was just slightly better than the group's average return of 62.83 percent.

While the volatility of precious metals funds is apparent, Vanguard's fund is one of the most conservative of the group. The fund's management has proven its ability to ride out gold's misfortunes while still taking advantage of rallies. Nevertheless, precious metals is another of those investment avenues that is not appropriate for the faint of heart.

Portfolio
Total stocks: 54 as of March 31, 1993
25 Largest Holdings

Royal Oak Mines	Randfontein Estates Gold
Franco-Nevada Mining	Freeport-McMoran Copper/Gold
American Barrick Resources	Cambior
Placer Dome	LAC Minerals
Western Mining	Homestake Mining
Minorco	Newmont Mining
RTZ	Highland Gold
Pegasus Gold	Plutonic Resources
Euro-Nevada Mining	Kloof Gold Mining
Poseidon Gold	CRA
De Beers Centenary South Africa	Normandy Poseidon
Free State Consolidated	Driefontein Consolidated
Gold Mines	Newcrest Mining

Composition of Portfolio

As of June 30, 1993

Cash	16.0%
Stocks	84.0

Other Precious Metals Funds

	Five-Year Growth of $10,000*
Benham Gold Equities Index Fund	N/A
Bull & Bear Gold Investors Fund	$12,140
Fidelity Select American Gold Portfolio	13,007
Fidelity Select Precious Metals and Minerals Portfolio	12,990
INVESCO Strategic Portfolios Gold	10,980
Keystone Precious Metals Holdings	12,910
Lexington Goldfund	10,996
Shearson Lehman Brothers Precious Metals and Mining Fund—Class A	10,206
USAA Investment Trust Gold Fund	10,639
Van Eck Gold/Resources Fund	11,257

*For the period ending June 30, 1993

Funds listed in **bold type** are available by direct purchase.
N/A indicates the fund was not in operation for five full years.

Summary

Precious metals funds tend to be among the most volatile of mutual funds. While the group offers a wide array of choices, investors should keep in mind that even the safest alternative can lose money quickly when the price of gold tumbles. Prudent investors should use these funds in small doses and only for hedging purposes.

Technology Funds

Usual Investment Objective of the Group

Mutual funds in the technology group seek capital appreciation by investing primarily in equity securities of companies engaged in the development, distribution or servicing of technology-related equipment or processes.

Survey of the Group

Technology securities funds emphasize companies that develop new processes, technologies or products in a variety of fields, from agriculture to manufacturing to communications. These companies will often be small growth companies or companies investing heavily in research and development where untried technologies hold great promise, but whose commercial success is not yet established.

In recent years, funds in the technology group have invested extensively in the networking and semiconductor industries while tending to avoid health care. Expanded uses for personal computers have driven demand, and thus earnings, for networking and semiconductor stocks. The strength of these industries has made technology a very attractive place to be. Funds that emphasize those types of firms have turned in top performances during the last several years.

Funds that have avoided the health-care sector have also benefited from that decision. Whereas health-care stocks helped performances in the late 1980s, they have not been so kind lately. Since 1992, investors have been worried about the earnings-dampening effects of potential health-care reform, which has led them to pull money from the sector, thus knocking down stock prices. Funds holding significant health-care positions in the last couple of years have generally lagged their peers.

This is not to say that funds holding health-care securities should be avoided. Actually, their diversification helped them until 1992. And those funds that focus exclusively on the high-growth, high-tech companies have to contend with the risks associated with high stock prices. The ambitious expectations associated with high-priced stocks mean that if those expectations are not met, the issues can plummet.

The technology group as a whole is far riskier for the investor than the overall equity fund universe. Investors seeking a lower-risk introduction to the field might look at Franklin DynaTech Fund and

Vanguard Specialized Technology Fund. These funds follow more cautious, diversified investment strategies, which help counter the sector's inherent volatility.

The table below indicates the historical average total return of the technology group and the S&P 500 Index for years ending December 31.

Technology Group versus S&P 500 Index

	Group Total Return	S&P 500		Group Total Return	S&P 500
1983	26.28%	22.47%	1988	5.16%	16.60%
1984	−9.44	6.27	1989	22.48	31.68
1985	18.53	31.83	1990	−4.58	−3.12
1986	6.61	18.68	1991	44.76	30.48
1987	−0.04	5.26	1992	12.27	7.62

Source: *Morningstar Mutual Funds*

Recommended Fund

INVESCO Strategic Technology Fund
P.O. Box 173706
Denver, CO 80217-3706
800-525-8085

Portfolio manager: Daniel B. Leonard
Investment adviser: INVESCO Funds Group
Sales fees: No-load (0.02% administrative fee)
Management fee: 0.75%
Other expenses: 0.37%
Total operating expenses: 1.12%
Annual brokerage cost: 0.91%
Minimum initial purchase: $1,000 (additional: $50)
Minimum IRA purchase: $250 (additional: none)
Date of inception: January 19, 1984
Net assets as of June 30, 1993: $235 million

Investment Objective
INVESCO Strategic Technology Fund seeks capital appreciation by investing primarily in securities of companies principally engaged in

the development, distribution or servicing of technology-related equipment or processes.

Investment Policy
The fund normally invests at least 80 percent of its assets in the equity securities of companies engaged in technology-related fields. These related areas may include computers, communications, video, electronics, oceanography, office and factory automation, and robotics. The fund will not invest more than 25 percent of its assets in any one technology-related industry.

Performance
The tables below indicate annual total returns for the fund for each full year of operation ending December 31 and comparative results for the S&P 500 Index, followed by total returns and the growth of $10,000 invested for different periods ending June 30, 1993.

INVESCO Strategic Technology versus S&P 500 Index

	Fund Total Return	S&P 500		Fund Total Return	S&P 500
1985	27.71%	31.83%	1989	21.44%	31.68%
1986	21.82	18.68	1990	8.59	−3.12
1987	−5.30	5.26	1991	76.88	30.48
1988	14.21	16.60	1992	18.81	7.62

Total Returns for Different Periods Ending June 30, 1993

	Fund Total Return	Growth of $10,000
3 Months	10.62%	$11,062
6 Months	3.26	10,326
1 Year	34.09	13,409
3-Year Average	22.77	18,277
5-Year Average	21.51	26,485

Source: *Morningstar Mutual Funds*

Financial History
Figure 19.5 illustrates per-share data for a share outstanding throughout each period and selected ratio information for each year ended October 31.

Comments
Unlike many funds, whose managers state that they try to hit singles or doubles to build up a strong long-term record, manager Daniel

Leonard clearly goes for home runs, and he often succeeds. This fund's manager since its inception in 1984, Leonard follows an aggressive strategy combining small-capitalization stocks, the technology sector and high-price multiples into a successful whole.

The result of this approach is that the fund has been in the top half of its group every year since its inception until the first half of 1993, when several of the fund's smaller holdings caved in. Much of the gains in such winners as Newbridge Networks and Adobe Systems were wiped out. But the long-term performance has been excellent, with the fund still in the top 5 percent of the group over a five-year period.

Management moderates the risk that usually accompanies small, pricey stocks by holding larger positions in better-known, more liquid stocks, such as Cisco Systems. The smaller, less popular stocks are relegated to smaller positions in the portfolio.

Also, the fund generally holds a large 20–30 percent position in stocks that are only indirectly linked to the technology sector. These would include firms such as York International (which makes CFC-free air-conditioners), which benefit from technological advances but are not necessarily going to fall out of bed when the high-tech stocks do. Such diversification holds down risk. The fund's historical risk is only slightly higher than its average technology peer, despite its aggressive style.

The cautious investor should remember that technology funds as a group are much riskier than most other equity funds. But for investors willing to take on such risk, this fund has provided very high returns.

Portfolio
Total stocks: 60 as of March 31, 1993

25 Largest Holdings

ALC Communications	Pitney Bowes
First Pacific Networks	Chipcom
Newbridge Networks	Sony
Spectrum Information Tech	Oracle Systems
Thermo Electron	Ionics
ICN Pharmaceuticals	Ericsson CL B
Solectron	LDDS Communications CL A
Telefonos de Chile	Informix
Sensormatic Electronics	Novell
Digi International	Read-Rite
General Instrument	Vishay Intertechnology
Cisco Systems	Geotek Industries
Adobe Systems	

FIGURE 19.5 INVESCO Strategic Tehnology Fund Per-Share Data and Selected Ratios

	Technology ◆ Year Ended October 31								Period Ended October 31
	1992	1991	1990	1989	1988	1987	1986	1985	1984⁻
PER SHARE DATA									
Net Asset Value — Beginning of Period	$ 18.103	$ 11.608	$ 12.657	$ 10.106	$ 8.492	$ 9.293	$ 7.587	$7.110	$ 8.000
OPERATIONS									
Investment Income	0.132	0.116	0.175	0.447	0.265	0.125	0.049	0.066	0.066
Expenses	(0.221)	(0.210)	(0.183)	(0.733)	(0.555)	(0.232)	(0.093)	(0.065)	(0.045)
Net Investment Income (Loss)	(0.089)	(0.094)	(0.008)	(0.286)	(0.290)	(0.107)	(0.044)	0.001	0.021
Net Realized and Unrealized Gain (Loss) on Investments	2.184	10.975	(1.041)	2.837	1.904	(0.687)	2.817	0.476	(0.891)
Total from Operations	2.095	10.881	(1.049)	2.551	1.614	(0.794)	2.773	0.477	(0.870)
DISTRIBUTIONS									
Net Investment Income	0.000	0.000	0.000	0.000	0.000	0.000	0.000	0.000	(0.020)
Net Realized Gain on Investments	0.000	(4.386)	0.000	0.000	0.000	(0.007)	(1.067)	0.000	0.000
Total Distributions	0.000	(4.386)	0.000	0.000	0.000	(0.007)	(1.067)	0.000	(0.020)
Net Change in Net Asset Value	2.095	6.495	(1.049)	2.551	1.614	(0.801)	1.706	0.477	(0.890)
Net Asset Value — End of Period	$ 20.198	$ 18.103	$ 11.608	$ 12.657	$ 10.106	$ 8.492	$ 9.293	$7.587	$ 7.110

Source: INVESCO Strategic Technology Fund prospectus dated July 1, 1993

FIGURE 19.5 *(continued)*

RATIOS									
Ratio of Expenses to Average Net Assets	1.12%	1.19%	1.25%	1.59%	1.72%	1.47%	1.50%	1.50%	1.50%*
Ratio of Net Investment Income (Loss) to Average Net Assets	−0.45%	−0.53%	−0.06%	−0.62%	−0.90%	−0.68%	−0.71%	0.03%	0.55%
Portfolio Turnover Rate	169%	307%	345%	259%	356%#	556%	368%	175%	91%
Shares Outstanding at End of Period (000 Omitted)	8,173	3,487	1,739	674	955	1,094	505	335	138

◆ The per share information for 1992, 1991 and 1990 was computed based on weighted average shares.

~ From January 19, 1984, commencement of operations, to December 31, 1984.

* Annualized

For the year ended October 31, 1988, the value of securities acquired in connection with the acquisition of the net assets of World of Technology, Inc. was excluded when computing the Portfolio turnover rate.

Composition of Portfolio
As of March 31, 1993

Cash	2.9%
Stocks	96.7
Convertibles	0.4

Sector Weightings
As of March 31, 1993

Utilities	29.4%
Industrial Cyclicals	7.3
Consumer Durables	6.0
Services	1.2
Health	6.0

Other High-Performing Technology Funds

	Five-Year Growth of $10,000*
Alliance Technology Fund	$17,349
Fidelity Select Developing Communications Portfolio	**N/A**
Fidelity Select Electronics Portfolio	**19,553**
Fidelity Select Software and Computer Services Portfolio	**26,112**
Fidelity Select Technology Portfolio	**22,906**
Seligman Communication and Information Fund—Class A	23,381
T. Rowe Price Science and Technology Fund	**27,721**
United Science & Energy Fund	18,624
Vanguard Specialized Technology Portfolio	**16,804**

*For the period ending June 30, 1993

Funds listed in **bold type** are available by direct purchase.
N/A indicates the fund was not in operation for five full years.

Summary

Technology funds may often invest in small growth companies or companies that invest heavily in research and development where untried technologies hold great promise, but whose commercial success is not yet established. As a result, such funds are far riskier than the overall equity universe. The flip side of this is that some funds have turned in spectacular performances.

●———————————————————————————————————

Utilities Funds

Usual Investment Objective of the Group

Mutual funds included in the utilities category primarily seek current income. Capital appreciation is a secondary objective.

Survey of the Group

Historically, utility stocks have been known to be less volatile than other types of common stocks. The higher dividends that utility companies pay can provide an important income cushion to help moderate stock market fluctuations. Thus, utility share prices may not fall as fast or as far as the prices of common stocks in general. Conversely, utility share prices may not rise as quickly in periods of stock market growth.

Funds in this category invest primarily in public utility companies. The group's asset base has soared to over $25 billion as more and more investors have been lured by the group's superior payouts. Its approximate 4 percent yield is quite attractive in today's low-interest environment. In addition, the group has enjoyed capital appreciation well above that of the broad market averages.

During the year ended June 30, 1993, the group had an average total return of 21.35 percent—almost eight percentage points higher than the S&P 500. While the utility group has been strong, some observers worry about the relationship between interest rates and the funds' performance. Their attraction because of high yields depends to a large extent on the availability of other mostly fixed-income investments. If interest rates climb, enthusiasm for utility funds is likely to decline.

The prices of the stocks underlying utility funds have become atypically high, leaving room for speculation on just how long the funds can continue to appreciate in value. Thus, it's not clear if the group's total returns will be able to rely as heavily on price appreciation in the future. Investors must decide how important it is for their utilities fund to achieve relatively superior growth of income or of capital.

The following table indicates the historical average total return of the utilities group and the S&P 500 Index for years ending December 31.

Utilities Group versus S&P 500 Index

	Group Total Return	S&P 500		Group Total Return	S&P 500
1983	11.80%	22.47%	1988	15.29%	16.60%
1984	18.94	6.27	1989	30.71	31.68
1985	27.17	31.83	1990	–3.01	–3.12
1986	21.26	18.68	1991	20.58	30.48
1987	–4.83	5.26	1992	9.46	7.62

Source: *Morningstar Mutual Funds*

Recommended Fund

Fidelity Utilities Income Fund
82 Devonshire Street
Boston, MA 02109
800-544-8888

Portfolio manager: John Muresianu
Investment adviser: Fidelity Management & Research
Sales fees: No-load
Management fee: 0.53%
Total fund operating expenses: 0.87%
Minimum initial purchase: $2,500 (additional: $250)
Minimum IRA purchase: $500
Date of inception: November 27, 1987
Net assets as of June 30, 1993: $1,378.6 million

Investment Objective

Fidelity Utilities Income Fund seeks a high level of current income by investing primarily in equity securities of public utility companies. When consistent with this goal, the fund may also consider the potential for growth of income and capital appreciation.

Investment Policy

The fund normally invests at least 65 percent of its assets in public utility companies. These companies include providers of electricity, natural gas, water, sanitary services, telephone or telegraph service, or other communications services.

The fund will spread investment risk by limiting its holdings in any one company. With respect to 75 percent of its total assets, the fund may not own more than 10 percent of the outstanding voting securities of a single issuer and may not own 5 percent or more of the outstanding voting securities of more than one public utility company. The fund also may not invest more than 25 percent of its total assets in any one industry (other than public utility companies). These limitations do not apply to U.S. government securities.

The fund may invest only in debt securities and convertible bonds that are rated A or better by Moody's Investors Service or Standard & Poor's Corporation, or are judged by the portfolio manager to be of equivalent quality if unrated.

The fund may borrow up to one-third of its total assets for temporary or emergency purposes. It may borrow from banks or from other funds advised by the investment manager, or through reverse repurchase agreements. As a means of earning income, the fund may lend securities to broker-dealers and institutions. Loans, in the aggregate, may not exceed one-third of the fund's total assets.

Performance

The tables below indicate annual total returns for the fund for each full year of operation ending December 31 and comparative results for the S&P 500 Index, followed by total returns and the growth of $10,000 invested for different periods ending June 30, 1993.

Fidelity Utilities Income Fund versus S&P 500 Index

	Fund Total Return	S&P 500		Fund Total Return	S&P 500
1988	14.77%	16.60%	1991	21.18%	30.48%
1989	25.92	31.68	1992	10.90	7.62
1990	1.85	−3.12			

Total Returns for Different Periods Ending June 30, 1993

	Fund Total Return	Growth of $10,000
3 Months	4.00%	$10,400
6 Months	13.69	11,369
1 Year	24.44	12,444
3-Year Average	17.45	16,201
5-Year Average	15.33	20,404

Source: *Morningstar Mutual Funds*

FIGURE 19.6 Fidelity Utilities Income Fund Per-Share Data and
Selected Ratios

Per-Share Data						
Fiscal years ended January 31	1988†	1989	1990	1991	1992	1993
Investment income	$ .08	$ .74	$ .84	$ .78	$ .75	$ .73
Expenses	.02††	.14	.12	.11	.12	.12
Net investment income	.06	.60	.72	.67	.63	.61
Distributions from net investment income	(.04)	(.52)	(.76)	(.69)	(.63)	(.60)
Net realized & unrealized gain (loss) on investments	.92	.11	1.21	.10	1.38	1.37
Distributions from net realized gain on investments	—	(.03)	(.31)	(.30)	(.18)	(.38)
Net increase (decrease) in net asset value	.94	.16	.86	(.22)	1.20	1.00
Net asset value (NAV) beginning of year	10.00	10.94	11.10	11.96	11.74	12.94
Net asset value at end of year	$10.94	$11.10	$11.96	$11.74	$12.94	$13.94
Ratios						
Ratio of expenses to average net assets	2.00%*††	1.47%	1.02%	.94%	.95%	.87%
Ratio of net investment income to average net assets	5.36%*	6.14%	6.19%	5.93%	5.11%	4.57%
Ratio of management fee to average net assets	.59%*	.56%	.56%	.54%	.54%	.53%
Portfolio turnover rate	0%	10%	61%	43%	39%	73%
Shares outstanding at end of year (in thousands)	2,812	11,650	13,093	18,749	50,016	71,888

*Annualized
†From November 27, 1987 (commencement of operations) to January 31, 1988
†† During the period November 27, 1987 (commencement of operations) to January 31, 1988, expenses
were limited to a percentage of average net assets in accordance with a state expense limitation regulation.
Expenses borne by the investment adviser during the period amounted to $.006 per share.

Source: Fidelity Utilities Income Fund prospectus dated March 31, 1993

Financial History
Figure 19.6 illustrates per-share data for a share outstanding
throughout each period and selected ratio information for each year
ended January 31.

Comments
The primary objective of this fund is the pursuit of income, but its
recent performance indicates an emphasis on capital appreciation also.

The fund's 12-month yield is about average for a utility fund. Still, in terms of total return, the fund outgained all but a few of the other funds in the utility group. This results from the fund's greater investments in growing cellular operations (through its telephone holdings) and to the natural gas sector, both of which have been outgaining even the rapidly appreciating electric utilities.

While current income is the primary objective of this fund, the manager apparently believes that adding stocks with greater growth potential doesn't necessarily place limits on income.

The Fidelity Utilities Income Fund is appropriate for conservative stock market investors looking for income with some potential for capital growth.

Portfolio

Total stocks: 103 as of March 31, 1993

25 Largest Holdings

Bell Atlantic	GTE
Ameritech	Pacific Telesis Group
NYNEX	BellSouth
Southwestern Bell	Entergy
US West	Nipsco Industries
Gulf States Utilities	Illinois Power
Houston Industries	Central & Southwest
DQE	Western Resources
Pacific Gas & Electric	General Public Utilities
DPL	Niagara Mohawk Power
Westcoat Energy	Enron
Sonat	MCN
Northeast Utilities	

Composition of Portfolio

As of December 31, 1992

Cash	9.0%
Stocks	91.0

Sector Weightings

As of December 31, 1992

Utilities	93.5%
Energy	5.0
Financials	1.1
Industrial Cyclicals	0.4

Other High-Performing Utilities Funds

	Five-Year Growth of $10,000*
Colonial Utilities Fund—Class A	$19,553
Dean Witter Utilities Fund	18,612
Eaton Vance Total Return Trust	20,423
Fidelity Select Utilities Portfolio	**22,277**
Fortress Utility Fund	**20,268**
Franklin Utilities Series	19,405
Global Utility Fund—Class A	N/A
INVESCO Strategic Portfolio Utilities	**20,241**
Liberty Utility Fund	20,142
Shearson Lehman Brothers Utilities Fund—Class B	18,673

*For the period ending June 30, 1993

Funds listed in **bold type** are available by direct purchase.
N/A indicates the fund was not in operation for five full years.

Summary

Utility funds are designed for the conservative investor who is interested primarily in income with a secondary objective of capital appreciation. Historically, utility companies have gradually increased their dividends over the years. Investors in utility funds should expect an increasing income stream that typically has grown at about 6 percent yearly. The value of utility fund shares will be affected inversely by the direction of interest rates in the economy. Falling interest rates will tend to cause shares to rise, while rising rates will have the opposite effect.

Chapter 20

Investing in
Hybrid Funds

Asset Allocation Funds

Usual Investment Objective of the Group

Funds included in the asset allocation group generally distribute their assets among domestic and foreign stocks, bonds and short-term instruments. Managers of these funds shift the investment mix as market conditions change, seeking high total return with reduced risk over the long term.

Survey of the Group

The asset allocation group tends to be safer than funds in general, but because investment styles vary considerably, investors should definitely look closely before committing assets to any particular fund.

There are about 61 funds in the asset allocation group. Because they rotate assets among stock, fixed-income securities and cash, the funds in this group tend to be less risky than the average equity fund or the S&P 500 Index. The funds' returns, while rarely spectacular, usually put them consistently near the average for all equity and fixed-income funds.

Certain funds share the general characteristics of the group. Vanguard Allocation Fund is a straightforward fund that uses a relative-valuation model to weight long U.S. Treasury bonds against the S&P 500. This has resulted in higher returns than the group without an increase in risk.

Other asset allocation funds are more far-reaching. SoGen International, Blanchard Global Growth, Fremont Global, Merrill Lynch Global Allocation and Fidelity Asset Manager all diversify into foreign stocks and bonds. Even within these funds, styles differ significantly. While Blanchard maintains a large holding in emerging markets but holds mostly large capitalization companies, SoGen has remained in major markets but focused on small, often obscure firms.

Some of the funds that remain entirely in the domestic universe also can be quite unusual. While the group on average holds about 50 percent of its assets in stocks, Flex-funds Growth Fund occasionally holds up to 90 percent in equities and has a risk profile much like the S&P 500. Perhaps the riskiest of all funds in the asset allocation group is United Gold & Government Fund. It holds nearly 70 percent of its assets in volatile gold-mining stocks.

The most successful funds in the group on a long-term basis have been funds like Fidelity Asset Manager (my recommended fund) and Stagecoach Asset Allocation Fund. They usually maintain a conservative balance of stocks and bonds. However, for those investors who want to move in a particular direction, the asset allocation group offers many variations to choose from.

The following table indicates historical average annual total returns of the asset allocation group and the S&P 500 Index for years ending December 31.

Asset Allocation Group versus S&P 500 Index

	Group Total Return	S&P 500		Group Total Return	S&P 500
1983	21.39%	22.47%	1988	8.22%	16.60%
1984	−0.32	6.27	1989	16.30	31.68
1985	23.50	31.83	1990	−0.46	−3.12
1986	16.73	18.68	1991	22.17	30.48
1987	10.74	5.26	1992	6.25	7.62

Source: *Morningstar Mutual Funds,* Morningstar, Inc., 225 W. Wacker Dr., Chicago, IL 60606; 312-696-6532

Recommended Fund

Fidelity Asset Manager
82 Devonshire Street
Boston, MA 02109
800-544-8888

Portfolio manager: Robert A. Beckwitt
Investment adviser: Fidelity Management & Research
Sales fees: No-load
Management fee: 0.74%
12b-1 fee: None
Other expenses: .43%
Total operating expense: 1.17%
Annual brokerage cost: 0.12%
Minimum initial purchase: $2,500 (additional: $250)
Minimum IRA purchase: $500 (additional: $250)
Date of inception: December 28, 1988
Net assets of fund as of July 31, 1993: $5.7 billion

Investment Objective
Fidelity Asset Manager seeks high total return with reduced risk over the long term by allocating its assets among stocks, bonds and short-term instruments.

Investment Policy
The fund diversifies across stocks, bonds and short-term instruments, both domestic and foreign. It normally stays within the following limits: 10–60 percent in stocks, 20–60 percent in bonds and 0–70 percent in short-term fixed-income instruments. A mix considered neutral would consist of 40 percent stocks, 40 percent bonds and 20 percent money market instruments. The bond portion consists of securities of varying quality; maturities are greater than three years. A single reallocation may not involve more than 10 percent of assets.

Performance
The tables below indicate annual total returns of Fidelity Asset Manager for each full year of operation ending December 31 and comparative results for the S&P 500 Index, followed by total returns and the growth of $10,000 invested for different periods ending July 31, 1993.

Fidelity Asset Manager versus S&P 500 Index

	Fund Total Return	S&P 500		Fund Total Return	S&P 500
1989	15.62%	31.68%	1991	23.64%	30.48%
1990	5.38	–3.12	1992	12.75	7.62

Total Returns for Different Periods Ending July 31, 1993

	Fund Total Return	Growth of $10,000
3 Months	4.98%	$10,498
6 Months	10.02	11,002
1 Year	16.81	11,681
3-Year Average	16.96	16,002

Source: *Morningstar Mutual Funds*

Financial History

Figure 20.1 illustrates per-share data for a share outstanding throughout each period and selected ratio information for each year ended September 30.

Comments

The fund generally tends to be quite cautious, unlike the first group of asset allocation funds, which made rapid-fire shifts among asset classes in hope of capturing market trends. Fidelity Asset Manager, on the other hand, keeps its portfolio composition fairly constant. Rather than trying to predict which types of securities will earn the best returns, the investment manager makes gradual adjustments based on relative valuations. In 1993, for example, Beckwitt cut back on bonds, because the tax-adjusted differential between the yield on long-term bonds and inflation was at its lowest point in 25 years.

The fund's asset mix tends to be relatively conservative. It usually operates around a neutral mix of 30 percent in stocks, 40 percent in bonds and 30 percent in money market instruments. This essentially makes Fidelity Asset Manager a fixed-income fund with an equity kicker. Even when the manager is most bullish, the fund will not invest more than 60 percent of its assets in stocks. This investment policy requirement has kept the fund one of the least risky of the asset allocation group.

Still, the fund takes advantage of opportunities when they become available. More than one-third of the portfolio's equity component is invested in foreign securities. And its 30 percent bond position includes

FIGURE 20.1 Fidelity Asset Manager Fund Per-Share Data and
Selected Ratios

Per-Share Data				
Fiscal periods ended September 30	1989†	1990	1991	1992
Investment income	$.34	$.70	$.66	$.56
Expenses	.07	.12	.11	.10
Net investment income	.27	.58	.55	.46
Distributions from net investment income	–	(.38)	(.65)	(.45)
Net realized & unrealized gain (loss) on investments	1.12	(.71)	2.48	.97
Distributions from net realized gain on investments	–	(.24)	–	(.50)
Net increase (decrease) in net asset value	1.39	(.75)	2.38	.48
Net asset value (NAV) beginning of period	10.00	11.39	10.64	13.02
Net asset value at end of period	$11.39	$10.64	$13.02	$13.50
Ratios				
Ratio of net investment income to average net assets	5.88%*	5.89%	5.74%	5.58%
Ratio of expenses to average net assets	1.58%*	1.17%	1.17%	1.17%
Ratio of management fee to average net assets	.75%*	.75%	.75%	.74%
Portfolio turnover rate	167%*	105%	134%	134%
Shares outstanding at end of period (in thousands)	21,524	32,516	57,089	204,626

*Annualized
† From December 28, 1988 (commencement of operations) to September 30, 1989

Source: Fidelity Asset Manager prospectus dated January 31, 1993

domestic "junk" bonds, European bonds, emerging market debt, and a small stake in structured notes tied to European short-term interest rates.

By utilizing Fidelity's strengths—research and securities selection—rather than trying to outguess the market, the fund has become the most successful of the asset allocation offerings. Fidelity Asset Manager could well be considered the flagship of the entire group.

Portfolio

Total stocks: 767 as of March 31, 1993

Total fixed-income securities: 146 as of March 31, 1993

25 Largest Holdings

Security	Maturity
Government of Mexico Brady FRN	12/31/19
U.S. Treasury Bond 8%	11/15/21
Banco International Mexico 0%	12/08/94
Argentina Republic Bote FRN	05/31/96
U.S. Treasury Bond 8.125%	08/15/19
U.S. Treasury Bond 8.125%	08/15/21
German Government 8%	07/22/02
Kroger 11.8%	12/15/04
U.S. Treasury Note 8.875%	11/15/97
Government of Mexico FRN	06/30/94
Wilton Investments 0%	06/03/94
Argentina Republic Brady 0%	12/31/22
FNMA	
GNMA 9%	10/15/19
Chrysler	
UNISYS 9.75%	09/15/96
Philip Morris	
News America Holdings 8.5%	02/15/05
Embassy Suites 8.75%	03/15/00
Government of France BTAN 8.5%	03/12/97
Morocco Trust FRN	01/03/09
CEMEX 9.41%	05/21/96
Citicorp	
Intel	
UAL	

Composition of Portfolio

As of March 31, 1993

Cash	15.6%
Stocks	49.4
Bonds	35.0

Sector Weightings

As of March 31, 1993

Utilities	4.5%
Energy	5.3
Financials	18.4

Industrial Cyclicals	21.3
Consumer Durables	12.3
Consumer Staples	4.1
Services	9.7
Retail	6.3
Health	5.7
Technology	12.6

Other High-Performing Asset Allocation Funds

	Five-Year Growth of $10,000*
Connecticut Mutual Total Return Account	$19,596
Flex-funds Muirfield Fund	N/A
Merrill Lynch Global Allocation Fund—Class B	N/A
Overland Express Asset Allocation Fund—Class A	17,045
Phoenix Total Return Fund	19,115
Prudential FlexiFund Conservatively Managed Portfolio—Class B	17,124
Quest for Value Opportunity Fund	N/A
Smith Barney Shearson Strategic Investors Fund—Class B	18,654
Stagecoach Asset Allocation Fund	18,039
Strong Investment Fund	**15,988**
Vanguard Asset Allocation Fund	N/A

*For the period ending July 31, 1993

Funds listed in **bold type** are available by direct purchase.

N/A indicates that the fund has not had five full years of performance history.

Summary

The asset allocation group offers a place for conservative investors to place funds that will generally be managed with a lower degree of risk than average equity funds and the S&P 500 Index. But since investment styles differ widely, care should be taken; certain funds can be highly speculative. The most successful funds on a long-term basis have been those that maintain a conservative balance of stocks and bonds.

Balanced Funds

Usual Investment Objective of the Group

Mutual funds included in the balanced fund group seek total return by investing in a relatively fixed combination of both stocks and bonds. Normally, these funds will hold a minimum of 25 percent in stocks and 25 percent in bonds at any time.

Survey of the Group

Balanced funds generally have a three-part investment objective: to conserve the investor's initial principal, to pay current income and to promote long-term growth of both principal and income. Such funds have a portfolio mix of bonds, preferred stocks and common stocks.

Balanced funds frequently perform in the middle of the pack. These funds do not usually try to shoot for the top of the fund charts. Rather, their goal is to provide investors with a cautious, diversified exposure to both the stock and bond markets. The result is a fairly consistent middle-of-the-road performance, which is counted as success. This objective has historically provided as much return as the typical specialized fund, but with less risk.

In recent years, funds with more conservative stock portfolios have had superior performances. These funds have been price-conscious, with heavy weightings in typical value stocks, such as financials and industrial cyclicals. Funds with large bond positions have also outperformed, as interest rates continued their downward trend, pushing bond prices up.

Many balanced funds, such as Fidelity Balanced and CGM Mutual, have served their shareholders well over the longer term.

The following table indicates the historical average total return of the balanced fund group and the S&P 500 Index for years ending December 31.

Balanced Fund Group versus S&P 500 Index

	Group Total Return	S&P 500		Group Total Return	S&P 500
1983	17.29%	22.47%	1988	12.18%	16.60%
1984	7.75	6.27	1989	19.29	31.68
1985	27.94	31.83	1990	−0.76	−3.12

| 1986 | 17.40 | 18.68 | 1991 | 26.23 | 30.48 |
| 1987 | 1.85 | 5.26 | 1992 | 7.10 | 7.62 |

Source: *Morningstar Mutual Funds*

●──

Recommended Fund

Evergreen Foundation Fund
2500 Westchester Avenue
Purchase, NY 10577
800-235-0064

Portfolio manager: Stephen A. Lieber
Investment adviser: Evergreen Asset Management
Sales fees: No-load
12b-1 fee: None
Management fee: 0.875%
Other expenses: 0.555%
Total operating expenses: 1.43%
Annual brokerage cost: 0.43%
Minimum initial purchase: $500 (additional: none)
Minimum IRA purchase: None (additional: none)
Date of inception: January 2, 1990
Net assets as of July 31, 1993: $133 million

Investment Objective
The objectives of Evergreen Foundation Fund, in order of priority, are reasonable income, conservation of capital and capital appreciation. The fund invests principally in income-producing common and preferred stocks, securities convertible into or exchangeable for common stocks, and fixed-income securities.

Investment Policy
The fund invests in a combination of dividend-paying common stocks, preferred stocks, convertible securities, high-quality corporate and U.S. debt obligations, and short-term debt instruments. Normally, at least 25 percent of the fund's assets are in fixed-income securities; the balance is invested in income-producing equity securities. In order to generate additional income and to offset expenses, the fund may lend portfolio securities.

To maintain portfolio diversification and attempt to reduce investment risk, the fund has adopted a number of specific investment restrictions. Specifically, the fund may not invest 25 percent or more of its total assets in the securities of any one industry, nor may it invest more than 5 percent of its total assets in the securities of any one issuer, or purchase more than 10 percent of any class of securities of any one issuer. These restrictions do not apply to obligations issued or guaranteed by the U.S. government or its agencies or instrumentalities. The fund may not invest in securities that are not readily marketable or in securities of companies that have not been in continuous operation for at least three years.

Performance
The tables below indicate the annual total returns for the fund for each full year of operation ending December 31 and comparative results for the S&P 500 Index, followed by total returns and the growth of $10,000 invested for different periods ending July 31, 1993.

Evergreen Foundation Fund versus S&P 500 Index

	Fund Total Return	S&P 500		Fund Total Return	S&P 500
1990	6.60%	−3.12%	1992	19.99%	7.62%
1991	36.36	30.48	1993	15.71	10.06

Total Returns for Different Periods Ending July 31, 1993

	Fund Total Return	Growth of $10,000
3 Months	4.76%	$10,476
6 Months	7.39	10,739
1 Year	17.68	11,768
3-Year Average	20.73	17,597

Source: *Morningstar Mutual Funds*

Financial History
Figure 20.2 illustrates per-share data for a share outstanding throughout each period and selected ratio information for each year ended December 31.

Comments
Evergreen Foundation Fund is part of the series of Evergreen Foundation Trust, a diversified, open-end investment company. The fund's objectives, in order of priority, are reasonable income, conservation of

capital and capital appreciation. The fund invests principally in in-come-producing common and preferred stocks, securities convertible into or exchangeable for common stocks, and fixed-income securities.

Since its inception on January 2, 1990, through June 30, 1993, the Evergreen Foundation Fund has had an average annual compounded rate of return of 19.9 percent, outperforming all 55 other balanced funds tracked by Lipper Analytical Services for that period.

The fund has built a solid record with an interest rate focus. Many investment decisions are based on the manager's outlook for future interest rates, which caused him to overweight financial stocks and U.S. Treasury long-term bonds. Both choices were successful, as interest rates continued to decline during most of the fund's lifetime.

The fund's strategy isn't based entirely on interest rate moves. Seeing opportunity in recent weakness in the health-care sector, the manager has been acquiring health-care issues, which by July 1993 made up over 17 percent of the fund's equity assets. The fund has also been successful in seeking out turnaround situations. Stocks such as Sears Roebuck and Eastman Kodak have risen as restructuring efforts for those firms have paid off.

Management states that the fund's investments are designed to form the foundation of an investor's portfolio, investing in "a mix of stocks and bonds so that it offers a diversified and balanced portfolio for results-oriented asset allocation within one investment vehicle." The fund is structured to provide wide diversification by investment in an equity portfolio with higher-than-average yields and an appreciation-driven selection policy; convertible bonds offering income as well as capital gains potential; and an investment-grade bond sector managed with an emphasis on investment timing.

Evergreen Foundation Fund appears to have good potential for the future, although share prices could be hurt if interest rates should rise quickly.

Portfolio

Total stocks: 87 as of March 31, 1993

Total fixed-income securities: 17 as of March 31, 1993

25 Largest Holdings

Security	Maturity
U.S. Treasury Bond 7.25%	05/15/16
U.S. Treasury Bond 8.375%	08/15/08
U.S. Treasury Bond 8%	11/15/21

FIGURE 20.2 Evergreen Foundation Fund Per-Share Data and
Selected Ratios

Per Share Data	Year Ended December 31, 1993	1992	1991	For the Period January 2, 1990* to December 31, 1990
Net asset value, beginning of year	$11.98	$10.75	$8.95	$10.00
Income (loss) from investment operations:				
Net investment income	.31	.27	.33	1.23†
Net realized and unrealized gain (loss) on investments	1.55	1.83	2.77	(.59)
Total from investment operations	1.86	2.10	3.10	.64
Less distributions to shareholders from:				
Net investment income	(.31)	(.24)	(.33)	(1.17)
Realized gains	(.41)	(.63)	(.97)	(.52)
Total distributions	(.72)	(.87)	(1.30)	(1.69)
Net asset value, end of year	$13.12	$11.98	$10.75	$8.95
Total Return††	15.7%	20.0%	36.4%	6.6%
Ratios & Supplemental Data				
Net assets, end of year (000's omitted)	$240,391	$64,455	$10,661	$2,239
Ratios to average net assets:				
Expenses	1.20%	1.40%(1)	1.20%(2)	– (3)
Net investment income	2.81%	2.93%(1)	2.86%(2)	15.07%(3)†
Portfolio turnover rate	60%	127%	178%	131%

Source: Evergreen Foundation Fund prospectus dated May 3, 1993

FIGURE 20.2 *(continued)*

(1) Net of voluntary expense limitation by the Adviser equal to .03% of average daily net assets.

(2) Net of voluntary expense limitation and absorption of expenses by the Adviser equal to 1.38% of average daily net assets.

(3) Annualized and net of the absorption of all Fund expenses by the Adviser equal to 3.64% of average daily net assets.

† Includes receipt of a special dividend representing $.62 per share net investment income and 7.59% of average net assets.

†† Total return is calculated for the periods indicated and is not annualized.

* Commencement of operations.

U.S. Treasury Bond 13.75%	08/15/04
Intel	
JC Penney	
U.S. Treasury Bond 8.5%	02/15/20
AMP	
U.S. Treasury Bond 7.125%	02/15/23
Medtronic	
MGIC Investment	
U.S. Treasury Bond 15.75%	11/15/01
Household International	
Johnson & Johnson	
Caremark	
U.S. Treasury Bond 10.625%	08/15/15
Sears Roebuck	
American Home Products	
U.S. Treasury Bond 10%	05/15/10
Pacific Telesis Group	
Corestates Financial	
JP Morgan	
International Flavors & Fragrances	
Bristol-Myers Squibb	
FNMA 8.1%	08/12/19

Composition of Portfolio
As of July 31, 1993

Cash	7.4%
Stocks	60.1
Bonds	28.9
Convertibles	3.6

Sector Weightings
As of July 31, 1993

Utilities	5.0%
Financials	28.0
Industrial Cyclicals	13.6
Consumer Durables	5.8
Consumer Staples	1.4
Services	8.5
Retail	7.6
Health	17.4
Technology	12.7

Other High-Performing Balanced Funds

	Five-Year Growth of $10,000*
CGM Mutual Fund	**$21,541**
Dodge & Cox Balanced Fund	**18,961**
Fidelity Advisor Income & Growth Portfolio	**20,819**
Fidelity Balanced Fund	**19,482**
IDS Mutual Fund	17,692
Kemper Investment Portfolios Total Return Portfolio	19,282
Kemper Retirement Fund Series I	N/A
MainStay Total Return Fund	18,577
National Income & Growth Fund—Class A	19,532
Vanguard STAR Fund	**17,494**

*For the period ending July 31, 1993

Funds listed in **bold type** are available by direct purchase.
N/A indicates the fund was not in operation five full years.

Summary

Balanced funds generally are managed to be less volatile than many other hybrid funds. Their three-part investment objective is to conserve the investor's initial principal, to pay current income and to promote long-term growth. They will normally have a portfolio mix of bonds, preferred stocks and common stocks.

Income Funds

Usual Investment Objective of the Group

Mutual funds in the income group invest in both equity and debt securities primarily for the purpose of realizing current income. These funds generally will not invest more than 50 percent of their assets in equities.

Survey of the Group

Income is the primary objective for funds in this broadly defined group. To achieve this goal, funds use a wide variety of investment styles, asset mixes and levels of risk-tolerance. Income can come from a variety of sources, with widely differing risks. The volatility of individual funds will vary depending on the source of their income. For example, Oppenheimer Strategic Income Fund, with a yield of 11.6 percent, has almost 90 percent of its assets in bonds. Value Line Income Fund has about 75 percent of its funds in stocks and delivers an income that is under 4 percent.

The different charters of funds in this group result in quite different asset mixes that may not overlap at all. Investors looking for income may want to think twice before simply choosing the highest payer. They should consider whether a given fund will not only add income to their portfolio, but will also add diversity—not duplication.

In early 1993, funds with lower-quality bonds have done well, benefiting from the continuing decline in interest rates, which has attracted new money into that sector. Funds such as Franklin Income Fund, with a 29 percent position in high-yield corporate bonds, enjoyed substantial total returns, while funds that avoid the low-quality sector lagged (such as Mutual of Omaha Income Fund). But funds with higher-quality issues are designed for investors who don't want to face relatively higher volatility.

Within the income funds group are funds to suit almost every investor, but it means that investors must look closely for the fund with the asset mix, return and risk level to meet their particular needs.

The following table indicates the historical average total return of the Income Group and the S&P 500 Index for years ending December 31.

Income Group versus S&P 500 Index

	Group Total Return	S&P 500		Group Total Return	S&P 500
1983	15.73%	22.47%	1988	11.33%	16.60%
1984	10.63	6.27	1989	14.63	31.68
1985	20.98	31.83	1990	−0.16	−3.12
1986	13.28	18.68	1991	22.57	30.48
1987	−0.45	5.26	1992	9.60	7.62

Source: *Morningstar Mutual Funds*

Recommended Fund

USAA Mutual Fund Income Fund
USAA Building
San Antonio, TX 78288
800-382-8722

Portfolio manager: John W. Saunders, Jr.
Investment adviser: USAA Investment Management
Sales fees: No-load
Management fee: 0.24%
12b-1 fee: None
Other expenses: 0.18%
Total fund operating expenses: 0.42%
Annual brokerage cost: 0.01%
Minimum initial purchase: $1,000 (additional: $50)
Minimum IRA purchase: $1,000 (additional: $50)
Date of inception: March 4, 1974
Net assets as of July 31, 1993: $1,642 million

Investment Objective
USAA Mutual Fund Income Fund seeks current income without undue risk to principal. Investments are primarily in income-producing securities.

Investment Policy
The fund invests primarily in investment-grade debt securities. These securities may include U.S. government obligations mortgage-backed securities, corporate debt, U.S. bank obligations and asset-backed securities. In addition, the fund may purchase convertible securities, common stocks and preferred stocks. For temporary purposes, the fund may invest up to 100 percent of its assets in high-quality, short-term debt instruments.

The debt securities must be investment grade at the time of purchase. Investment-grade securities are those issued or guaranteed by the U.S. government, its agencies and instrumentalities, those rated at least Baa by Moody's Investors Service, BBB by Standard and Poor's Corporation, BBB by Fitch Investors Service or BBB by Duff & Phelps, or those judged to be of equivalent quality by the portfolio manager if not rated.

Performance

The tables below indicate annual total returns of USAA Mutual Fund Income Fund for each year ending December 31 and comparative results for the S&P 500 Index, followed by total returns and the growth of $10,000 invested for different periods ending July 31, 1993.

USAA Mutual Fund Income Fund versus S&P 500 Index

	Fund Total Return	S&P 500		Fund Total Return	S&P 500
1983	10.68%	22.47%	1988	9.98%	16.60%
1984	14.24	6.27	1989	16.30	31.68
1985	19.18	31.83	1990	7.69	–3.12
1986	12.74	18.68	1991	19.38	30.48
1987	3.43	5.26	1992	8.37	7.62

Total Returns for Different Periods Ending July 31, 1993

	Fund Total Return	Growth of $10,000
3 Months	3.33%	$10,333
6 Months	6.62	10,662
1 Year	11.96	11,196
3-Year Average	13.68	14,691
5-Year Average	12.84	18,293
10-Year Average	12.64	32,879
15-Year Average	11.41	50,565

Source: *Morningstar Mutual Funds*

Financial History

Figure 20.3 illustrates per-share data for a share outstanding throughout each period and selected ratio information for each year ended September 30.

Comments

With a record of consistent gains year after year, USAA Mutual Fund Income Fund is a good place for the investor seeking low risk and above-average returns. This history has been put together by manager John Saunders by utilizing a very conservative combination of Treasury bonds, mortgage pass-throughs and a small position in utility stocks. The fund emphasizes bonds far more than its average peer does. Whereas the typical income fund maintains only about 50 percent of its assets in bonds, this fund stays with about 80 percent bonds in its portfolio.

FIGURE 20.3 USAA Mutual Fund Income Fund Per-Share Data and Selected Ratios

Income Fund

					Fiscal Year Ended					
	1992	1991	1990	1989	1988	1987	1986	1985	1984	1983
Investment income	$ 1.00	$ 1.03	$ 1.09	$ 1.11	$ 1.13	$ 1.14	$ 1.23	$ 1.31	$ 1.23	$ 1.26
Expenses	(.05)	(.05)	(.06)	(.06)	(.07)	(.07)	(.08)	(.08)	(.08)	(.12)
Net investment income	.95	.98	1.03	1.05	1.06	1.07	1.15	1.23	1.15	1.14
Distributions from net investment income	(.93)	(.99)	(1.03)	(1.05)	(1.06)	(1.24)	(1.12)	(1.21)	(1.06)	(1.05)
Net realized and unrealized gain (loss)	.64	1.09	(.44)	.30	.57	(.96)	.61	.76	(.22)	.50
Distributions of realized capital gains	(.01)	–	(.03)	–	(.26)	(.06)	(.02)	–	(.12)	–
Net change in net asset value	.65	1.08	(.47)	.30	.31	(1.19)	.62	.78	(.25)	.59
Net asset value:										
Beginning of period	12.11	11.03	11.50	11.20	10.89	12.08	11.46	10.68	10.93	10.34
End of period	$12.76	$12.11	$11.03	$11.50	$11.20	$10.89	$12.08	$11.46	$10.68	$10.93
Ratio of expenses to average net assets (%)	.42	.47	.53	.57	.61	.61	.65	.68	.75	1.09
Ratio of net investment income to average net assets (%)	7.78	8.61	9.19	9.36	9.57	9.13	9.69	10.96	10.97	10.58
Portfolio turnover (%)	21.78	15.45	12.07	13.79	10.66	35.90	37.58	78.57(b)	116.20	165.59
Shares outstanding at end of period (000's)	106,531	68,306	39,406	28,877	25,408	22,961	17,680	12,113	8,620	3,569

Source: USAA Mutual Fund Income Fund prospectus dated June 1, 1993

The fund's main attraction has always been its low risk. While bonds are not risk-free, they tend to be much more stable than stocks, and this offering is much quieter than its peers that hold larger equity positions. The other side of the coin is that this fund gives up some of the appreciation potential of stocks—but it avoids their downside risk. For example, in the market crash of October 1987, this fund enjoyed more than a 2 percent positive return, while the average income fund was down by 7.8 percent.

Mutual Income's bond position is made up of both Treasury bonds and a variety of mortgage pass-throughs. Mortgages are heavily weighted, making up more than three-quarters of the fund's bonds. This emphasis retarded returns somewhat in early 1993, as mortgage holders rushed to refinance at low interest rates, causing prepayments to rise, thereby tempering gains from dropping interest rates. While this was happening, the Treasury bonds and interest rate–sensitive utilities stocks surged in the falling-rate environment. The bullish bond market of the 1980s and early 1990s allowed Mutual Income to deliver more than a decade of positive annual returns.

All of these factors make this fund look very attractive on the basis of risk and return. Investors have clearly recognized the fund's strengths. Its assets have grown from $12.9 million in 1981 to $138.8 million in 1985, $356 million in 1989 and $1.452 billion in 1992. The economies of scale resulting from that asset base make possible the fund's very low expense ratio of .42 percent.

Portfolio

Total stocks: 14 as of March 31, 1993

Total fixed-income securities: 45 as of March 31, 1993

25 Largest Holdings

Security	Maturity
FNMA 7.5%	02/01/23
U.S. Treasury Bond 7.875%	02/15/21
FNMA 8%	12/01/22
FHLMC 8%	01/01/21
FHLMC 8.5%	09/01/20
FNMA 8.5%	05/01/22
FHLMC 10%	09/01/20
GNMA 8.5%	02/15/17
FHLMC 9.5%	01/01/21
GNMA 7.5%	12/15/22
Public Service Enterprise	

Allegheny Power System
Northeast Utilities
Long Island Lighting
FNMA 7%   04/01/23
American Electric Power
Cincinnati Gas & Electric
Houston Industries
FHLMC 9%   10/01/20
FPL Group
New York State Electric/Gas
FHLMC 7.5%   10/01/09
CIPSCO
ITT 9.75%   02/15/21
Southwestern Public Service

Composition of Portfolio
As of August 10, 1993

Stocks	18%
Bonds	82

Sector Weightings
As of August 10, 1993

Utilities	100.0%

Other High-Performing Income Funds

	Five Year Growth of $10,000*
Advantage Income Fund	$17,597
Berwyn Income Fund	**19,089**
Colonial Strategic Income Fund—Class A	16,275
First Prairie Diversified Asset Fund	18,272
Founders Equity Income Fund	**17,709**
Franklin Income Series	19,515
Income Fund of America	18,582
Lindner Dividend Fund	19,085
Mutual of Omaha Income Fund	17,720
National Multi-Sector Fixed-Income Fund—Class A	N/A
Oppenheimer Strategic Income Fund—Class A	N/A
T. Rowe Price Spectrum Income Fund	**N/A**
Putnam Diversified Income Trust—Class A	N/A
Seligman Income Fund—Class A	18,003

Smith Barney Shearson Diversified Strategic Income Fund—Class B	N/A
Value Line Income Fund	**18,171**
Vanguard Preferred Stock Fund	**18,852**
Vanguard/Wellesley Income Fund	**19,220**

*For the five-year period ending July 31, 1993

Funds listed in **bold type** are available by direct purchase.
N/A indicates less than five full years of operation.

Summary

Income funds generally attempt to deliver a high level of current income. But investment styles, asset mixes and levels of risk tolerance vary widely. So while the range of funds in the income category means that there is something in it for almost every investor, it is also true that investors must check closely to select the fund with the right asset mix, returns and risk level to meet their needs.

Chapter 21

Investing in Specialty Bond Funds

Convertible Bond Funds

Investment Policy of the Group

Funds included in the convertible bond group generally invest in bonds, notes, debentures and, to some extent, preferred stock that can be exchanged for a set number of shares of common stock in the issuing company at a prestated price or exchange ratio. As such, they have characteristics similar to both fixed-income and equity securities.

Survey of the Group

The popularity of convertible bond funds has been growing. The funds were generally ignored in the late 1980s in favor of pure stock and bond funds, but their recent positive performance has led many investors to take a second look.

As interest rates declined, the securities market poured forth a spate of new convertibles in 1993, providing investors hungry for yields with a steady flow of instruments to choose from. Such heavy demand, plus a strong equity market, allowed convertible bond funds to stand out.

For the three-year period ending July 31, 1993, the group returned an attractive 14.38 percent, compared with 11.29 percent for diversified equity funds and 10.73 percent for bond funds.

The appeal of convertible bonds arises from their dual identity. They combine elements of both stock and bond performance, providing income without sacrificing appreciation potential. This gives managers of convertible bond funds a good deal of flexibility in assembling their portfolios—a fact that fund investors should carefully consider before making a selection.

The manager of Pacific Horizon Capital Income, for example, has achieved total return success by focusing on the issues of rapid growth companies. SBSF Convertible Securities and Gabelli Convertible Securities, on the other hand, focus their efforts on finding fairly valued issues with high coupons—a strategy that places them among the group's yield leaders.

However, funds that emphasize small companies and "junk" securities have continued to hold the group's top total return positions. MainStay Convertible climbed to the top echelon in 1993 in terms of three-year performance by holding half of its assets in small capitalization companies and an additional 40 percent in non-investment-grade issues. Fidelity Convertible Securities, our recommended fund, has been consistently at or near the top. It holds nearly all of its portfolio in lower-grade securities.

Investors should be aware, though, that while convertible securities offer the best features of bonds and stocks, they are also subject to the difficulties of both. These securities are often at the mercy of interest-rate fluctuations, credit risk or the failing strength of their underlying equities.

The following table indicates the historical average annual total return of the convertible bond group and the Lehman Brothers Corporate Bond Index for years ending December 31.

Convertible Bond Group versus
Lehman Brothers Corporate Bond Index

	Group Total Returns	LBCB Index		Group Total Returns	LBCB Index
1983	19.99%	9.27%	1988	12.74%	9.22%
1984	2.12	16.62	1989	15.45	13.98
1985	23.71	24.06	1990	−5.73	7.15
1986	15.19	16.54	1991	29.78	18.50
1987	−4.66	2.56	1992	13.46	8.70

Source: *Morningstar Mutual Funds,* Morningstar, Inc., 225 W. Wacker Dr., Chicago, IL 60606; 312-696-6532

Recommended Fund

Fidelity Convertible Securities Fund
82 Devonshire Street
Boston, MA 02109
800-544-8888

Portfolio manager: Andrew Offit
Investment adviser: Fidelity Management & Research
Sales fees: No-load
Management fee: 0.54%
12b-1 fee: None
Other expenses: 0.42%
Total operating expense: 0.96%
Annual brokerage cost: 0.24%
Minimum initial purchase: $2,500 (additional: $250)
Minimum IRA purchase: $500 (additional: $250)
Date of inception: January 5, 1987
Net assets of fund as of July 31, 1993: $869 million

Investment Objective

Fidelity Convertible Securities Fund seeks a high level of total return through a combination of current income and capital appreciation by investing primarily in convertible securities.

Investment Policy

The fund normally invests at least 65 percent of its assets in convertible securities. The balance of assets may be invested in corporate or U.S. debt securities, common stocks, preferred stocks, and money market instruments. The fund may invest in lower-quality, high-yielding securities, although the fund currently expects that its fixed-income securities are primarily rated B or better. The fund may write covered call options or buy put options.

Performance

The tables below indicate total annual returns of Fidelity Convertible Securities Fund for each full year of operation ending December 31 and comparative results for the Lehman Brothers Corporate Bond Index, followed by total returns and the growth of $10,000 invested for different periods ending July 31, 1993.

Fidelity Convertible Securities Fund versus Lehman Brothers Corporate Bond Index

	Fund Total Returns	LBCB Index		Fund Total Returns	LBCB Index
1988	15.89%	16.60%	1991	38.74%	30.48%
1989	26.28	31.68	1992	22.02	7.62
1990	−2.89	−3.12			

Total Returns for Different Periods Ending July 31, 1993

	Fund Total Return	Growth of $10,000
3 Months	3.39%	$10,339
6 Months	7.62	10,762
1 Year	21.24	12,124
3-Year Average	21.12	17,767
5-Year Average	18.49	23,354

Source: *Morningstar Mutual Funds*

Financial History

Figure 21.1 illustrates per-share data for a share outstanding throughout each period and selected ratio information for each year ended November 30.

Comments

Since its inception in 1987, this fund has developed an unparalleled performance record among convertible bond funds by positioning itself as an equity substitute—devoting up to one-fourth of its assets to high-growth common stocks for their tremendous upside potential. Recently, however, Andrew Offit decided to concentrate on the fund's current income; consequently, he reduced common stocks to less than 8 percent of assets. With 83 percent of the portfolio now in convertible securities, the fund became one of the few nearly pure convertible plays in the group.

Despite this new approach, however, Offit did not abandon his commitment to careful and informed security selection. Utilizing Fidelity's extensive research capabilities, he focuses on companies with clean balance sheets, sustainable earnings-growth potential and below-market price/earnings multiples. Most of these requirements have been met by small and mid-capitalization companies, of which there is a huge supply in the convertibles market; they currently represent one-third of the fund's portfolio.

FIGURE 21.1 Fidelity Convertible Securities Fund Per-Share Data and Selected Ratios

	1992	1991	1990	1989	1988	January 5, 1987 (commencement of operations) to November 30, 1987
	Years Ended November 30,					
1. Investment income	$ .80	$ .74	$ .79	$ .95	$ .79	$ .52
2. Expenses	.13	.14	.15	.15	.16	.12
3. Net investment income ..	.67	.60	.64	.80	.63	.40
4. Dividends from net investment income	(.64)	(.62)	(.77)	(.72)	(.60)	(.24)
5. Net realized and unrealized gain (loss) on investments ..	2.66	2.94	(1.15)	1.72	.93	(1.11)
6. Distributions from net realized gain on investments	(.37)	—	—	—	—	—
7. Increase (decrease) in net asset value	2.32	2.92	(1.28)	1.80	.96	(.95)
Net asset value:						
8. Beginning of period ...	13.45	10.53	11.81	10.01	9.05	10.00
9. End of period	$ 15.77	$ 13.45	$ 10.53	$ 11.81	$ 10.01	$ 9.05
10. Ratio of net investment income to average net assets	4.82%	4.99%	5.63%	7.48%	6.20%	5.45%*
11. Ratio of expenses to average net assets	.96%	1.17%	1.31%	1.38%	1.60%	1.60%*
12. Ratio of management fee to average net assets ..	.54%	.54%	.55%	.56%	.57%	.56%*
13. Portfolio turnover rate ...	258%	152%	223%	207%	191%	233%*
14. Shares outstanding at end of period (000 omitted)	26,148	9,385	5,431	5,048	4,456	4,364

* Annualized.

Source: Fidelity Convertible Securities Fund prospectus dated January 24, 1993

Such careful positioning has been a great boon to the fund's performance in recent years, as the market has become more oriented toward emerging companies. That trend continued in 1993, helping to keep the fund in its group's top quartile through the first half of the year. However, the true force behind the fund having a consistently spectacular performance is prudent investment decisions. For example, the fund sold off most of its ailing health-care securities in mid-1993 because of their drag on overall performance.

It would be difficult for an investor to find a better convertible fund than this one. It offers a competitive yield, average risk and stellar returns, making it a tough one to beat.

Portfolio

Total stocks: 9 as of May 31, 1993

Total fixed-income securities: 134 as of May 31, 1993

25 Largest Holdings

Security	Maturity
UAL Convertible Preferred 6.25%	
USAIR Group Class B Convertible Preferred 8.75%	
AMR Convertible Preferred $3	
Citicorp Convertible Preferred $5.375	
J Baker Convertible 7%	06/01/02
UNOCAL Convertible Preferred $3.50	
Blockbuster Entertainment Convertible 0%	
USAIR Group	
Centocor Convertible 7.25%	02/01/01
Mentor Euro Convertible 6.75%	07/22/02
Delta Air Line Convertible Preferred 3.5%	
Mark IV Industries Convertible 6.25%	02/15/07
Eastman Kodak Euro Convertible 6.375%	07/01/01
Primerica Convertible 5.5%	04/22/02
Freeport-McMoran Convertible Preferred $4.375	
Grumman Convertible 9.25%	08/15/09
Varity Class 1A Convertible Preferred $1.30	
Storage Technology Convertible Preferred $3.50	
USA Waste Services Convertible Preferred 8.5%	10/15/02
Whirlpool Convertible 0%	05/14/11
USF&G Class C Convertible Preferred $5	
Santa Fe Pacific	
Occidental Petroleum Convertible Preferred $3.875	
Sci-Med Life Systems	
Greyhound Lines Convertible 8.5%	03/31/07

Composition of Portfolio

As of June 30, 1993

Cash   12.2%

Stocks	4.0
Bonds	1.1
Convertibles	82.7

Other High-Performing Convertible Bond Funds

	Five-Year Growth of $10,000*
Gabelli Convertible Securities Fund	$ N/A
MainStay Convertible Fund	18,829
Pacific Horizon Capital Income Fund	23,519
Phoenix Convertible Fund Series	17,342
SBSF Convertible Securities Fund	**18,090**

*For period ending July 31, 1993

Funds listed in **bold type** are available by direct purchase.

N/A indicates that the fund has not had five full years of performance history.

Summary

The convertible bond group combines the elements of both stock and bond performance, providing income without sacrificing appreciation potential. Investors should note, however, that while convertibles offer the best features of bonds and stocks, they are also subject to the difficulties of interest rate fluctuations, credit risk or the failing strength of their underlying equities.

High-Yield Corporate Bond Funds

Usual Investment Objective of the Group

Funds included in the high-yield corporate bond group invest in lower-rated and unrated fixed-income securities, both domestic and foreign. These may include convertible and nonconvertible debt securities and preferred stocks. Many of the securities held by funds in this group would be categorized as "junk bonds."

Survey of the Group

High-yield bond funds have been through a dramatic series of events over the last several years. During the Great Debacle of 1989 and 1990, many investors deserted high-yield funds, as they encountered double-digit losses. As mutual fund shares were sold, managers were forced to sell into weakness to meet redemptions, pushing depressed bond prices even lower.

A spectacular comeback arrived in 1991, thanks to strong demand for higher-yielding issues and improving corporate balance sheets. Bond prices soared, causing the average high-yield fund to gain 37 percent for the year. While the group hasn't lost all its excitement, it has become a bit more mellow. Some aggressive funds, such as Dean Witter High-Yield Fund and Keystone Custodian B-4, continue to post outstanding returns. After outdistancing the Lehman Brothers Aggregate Index by about ten percentage points in 1992, the average high-yield fund surpassed the broad bond market by about five percentage points in the first half of 1993.

For the future, most portfolio managers are cautiously optimistic. They believe the default rate on high-yield bonds should remain low as long as the economy does not deteriorate. And while yield spreads have narrowed considerably from their peak of nearly 1,000 basis points, high-yield bonds still offer about 400 basis points more than the ten-year Treasury bond.

There are still some concerns, however. As issuers of high-yield securities have rushed to take advantage of a favorable interest rate climate, the market has been deluged with a supply of new issues. Most of the demand for these offerings comes from mutual funds, so if cash inflows to the funds fail to keep up with the supply, bond prices could come under pressure. On top of this, while credit quality remains decent overall, issuers have brought to market more and more deals with less than $100 million in principal value. This could create liquidity problems for the funds that buy them.

The following table indicates the historical average annual total return of the high-yield corporate bond group and the Lehman Brothers Aggregate Index for years ending December 31.

**High-Yield Corporate Bond Group versus
Lehman Brothers Aggregate Index**

	Group Total Return	LBA Index		Group Total Return	LBA Index
1983	15.96%	8.38%	1988	12.75%	7.88%
1984	8.30	15.16	1989	−0.50	14.54
1985	21.72	22.13	1990	−10.54	8.94
1986	12.71	15.25	1991	37.32	16.00
1987	1.38	2.76	1992	17.71	7.24

Source: *Morningstar Mutual Funds*

Recommended Fund

Fidelity Capital & Income Fund
82 Devonshire Street
Boston, MA 02109
800-544-8888

Portfolio manager: David Breazzano and Daniel Harmetz
Investment adviser: Fidelity Management & Research
Sales fees: No-load (1.5% fee if redeemed within 365 days)
Management fee: 0.72%
12b-1 fee: None
Other expenses: 0.37%
Total operating expense: 1.09%
Annual brokerage cost: 0.01%
Minimum initial purchase: $2,500 (additional: $250)
Minimum IRA purchase: $500 (additional: $250)
Date of inception: November 1, 1977
Net assets of fund as of July 31, 1993: $2.5 billion

Investment Objective
Fidelity Capital & Income Fund seeks to provide a combination of income and capital growth by investing primarily in debt instruments and common and preferred stocks.

Investment Policy
The fund may invest in any type or quality of debt or equity securities, but focuses on lower-rated debt securities and securities of companies with uncertain financial positions. These present higher

risks of untimely interest and principal payments, default and price volatility than higher-rated securities and may present problems of liquidity and valuation.

The fund has no fixed policy as to the allocation of its assets between debt and equity investments. However, the fund is expected to invest the majority of its assets in bonds and other interest-bearing debt instruments, with particular emphasis on lower-quality debt securities. The fund is designed as a long-term investment.

Performance

The tables below indicate annual total returns of Fidelity Capital & Income Fund for each year ending December 31 and comparative results for the Lehman Brothers Aggregate Index, followed by total returns and the growth of $10,000 invested for different periods ending July 31, 1993.

Fidelity Capital & Income Fund versus Lehman Brothers Aggregate Index

	Fund Total Return	LBA Index		Fund Total Return	LBA Index
1983	18.54%	8.38%	1988	12.59%	7.88%
1984	10.50	15.16	1989	-3.22	14.54
1985	25.54	22.13	1990	-3.84	8.94
1986	17.95	15.25	1991	29.82	16.00
1987	1.26	2.76	1992	28.05	7.24

Total Returns for Different Periods Ending July 31, 1993

	Fund Total Return	Growth of $10,000
3 Months	6.95%	$10,695
6 Months	13.61	11,361
1 Year	23.05	12,305
3-Year Average	22.49	18,380
5-Year Average	13.42	18,768
10-Year Average	13.79	36,394
15-Year Average	13.15	63,759

Source: *Morningstar Mutual Funds*

Financial History

Figure 21.2 illustrates per-share data for a share outstanding throughout each period and selected ratio information for each year ended April 30.

FIGURE 21.2 Fidelity Capital & Income Fund Per-Share Data and Selected Ratios

THE FUND'S FINANCIAL HISTORY

Per-Share Data and Ratios. The table below gives you information about the fund's financial history. It uses the fund's fiscal year (which ends April 30) and expresses the information in items one through ten in terms of a single share outstanding throughout each fiscal period. Effective December 30, 1990, the fund adopted a new investment objective and changed its name to Fidelity Capital & Income Fund. The information below may not be representative of the fund's operations under its new objective.

	1. Investment income	2. Expenses	3. Net investment income	4. Distributions from net investment income	5. Net realized and unrealized gain (loss) on investments	6. Redemption fees	7. Distributions from net realized gain on investments	8. Increase (decrease) in net asset value	9. Net asset value: Beginning of period	10. Net asset value: End of period	11. Ratio of net investment income to average net assets	12. Ratio of expenses to average net assets	13. Portfolio turnover rate**	14. Shares outstanding at end of period (000 omitted)
Years Ended April 30,														
1993	$ .723717	.078843	.644874	(.618697)	.942259	.011564	—	.980000	8.320000	$ 9.300000	7.45%	.91%	102%	228,469
1992	$ .784393	.059089	.725304	(.746090)	1.417530	.003256	—	1.400000	6.920000	$ 8.320000	9.77%	.80%	132%	189,872
1991	$ .773686	.052017	.721669	(.708290)	.196185	.000436	—	.210000	6.710000	$ 6.920000	11.26%	.81%	108%	137,568
1990	$1.057218	.063240	.993978	(.993978)	(1.620000)	—	—	(1.620000)	8.330000	$ 6.710000	12.70%	.81%	95%	158,304
1989	$1.090041	.066158	1.023883	(1.023883)	(.390000)	—	—	(.390000)	8.720000	$ 8.330000	11.96%	.77%	72%	208,947
1988	$1.110559	.080088	1.030471	(1.030471)	(.700000)	—	(.200000)	(.900000)	9.620000	$ 8.720000	11.38%	.88%	68%	175,451
1987***	$ .477644	.031840	.445804	(.445804)	(.060000)	—	(.260000)	(.320000)	9.940000	$ 9.620000	10.99%*	.78%*	116%*	178,817
Years Ended November 30,														
1986	$1.183121	.078470	1.104651	(1.104651)	.830000	—	(.130000)	.700000	9.240000	$ 9.940000	11.30%	.80%	104%	165,566
1985	$1.225991	.076336	1.149655	(1.149655)	.560000	—	—	.560000	8.680000	$ 9.240000	12.54%	.83%	157%	84,730
1984	$1.231634	.072751	1.158883	(1.158883)	(.330000)	—	—	(.330000)	9.010000	$ 8.680000	13.51%	.85%	71%	45,610
1983	$1.178525	.077165	1.101360	(1.101360)	.590000	—	—	.590000	8.420000	$ 9.010000	12.45%	.87%	129%	28,974

* Annualized

** In July 1985, the Securities and Exchange Commission adopted revisions to existing rules with respect to the calculation of portfolio turnover rate. The revised rules require the inclusion in the calculation of long-term U.S. government securities which, prior to these revisions, were excluded from the calculation. On January 23, 1987, the Board of Trustees approved a change in the fund's fiscal year-end to April 30.

*** Represents five months ended April 30, 1987.

Source: Fidelity Capital & Income Fund prospectus dated June 25, 1993

Comments

Fidelity Capital & Income Fund provides a good example of the difference between potential and actual risk. Despite the aggressive approach taken by its managers, the fund is considered to be relatively low in risk. About half of the portfolio is devoted to companies in default, distress or bankruptcy. Many of the issuers are unable to service their debt. As a result, the fund's distributed income yield, as well as the portfolio's credit quality, is among the lowest in the high-yield bond group.

Despite this aggressive management approach, the fund's downside volatility risk on a historical basis is considerably lower than that of the average junk bond fund. One reason for this is the fund's previous pursuit of a more conventional strategy. The fund adopted its new charter, with its adventurous style, just as the junk bond market bottomed out in late 1990. Since then it has enjoyed a very favorable market climate. The most speculative issues achieved the highest gains over the past two to three years.

Managers Breazzano and Harmetz further moderated the fund's risk by carefully examining cash flows, underlying assets and other key factors before buying each bond. Value has also been added through active involvement with corporate restructurings. Future problems could emerge if investors become nervous about lower-quality instruments. That certainly has not happened yet, as is indicated by the fund's stellar performance.

On balance, Fidelity Capital & Income offers appealing total returns and has good diversification. There is substantial risk, however, making the fund inappropriate for conservative investors.

Portfolio

Total stocks: 0 as of April 30, 1993

Total fixed-income securities: 229 as of April 30, 1993

25 Largest Holdings

Security	Maturity
Bally's Grand	04/15/96
E-II Holdings 12.85%	03/01/97
Revlon Worldwide 0%	03/15/98
Bally's Health/Tennis 13%	01/15/03
Mutual Benefit OVRS CMO 9.375%	02/01/96
TAK Communications (term loan)	
El Paso Funding 10.75%	04/01/13
Robin Media Group 11.125%	04/01/97

SPI Holding Reset PIK 11.5%	12/01/02
Ampex 14%	01/15/98
National Gypsum 11.375%	03/31/97
AFG Industries 12%	04/01/98
SCI TV (term loan) VRN	09/30/94
Kaiser Aluminum/Chemical 12.75%	02/01/03
E-II Holdings 13.05%	03/01/99
Lamonts Apparel 11.5%	11/01/99
American Annuity Group 11.125%	02/01/03
Hillsborough PIK 17%	01/01/96
USG (term loan) VRN	07/01/96
UNISYS 9.75%	09/15/96
Quantum Chemical 11%	07/01/18
American Financial 12%	09/03/99
Computervision 11.375%	08/15/99
Restaurant Enterprises 12.25%	12/15/96
Thermadyne Industries VRN	11/01/99

Composition of Portfolio
As of June 30, 1993

Cash	8.5%
Stocks	0.0
Bonds	78.3
Preferreds	9.2
Convertibles	2.1
Other	1.9

Other High-Yield Corporate Bond Funds

	Five-Year Growth of $10,000*
Advantage High-Yield Bond Fund	$ N/A
AIM High Yield Fund (C)	18,189
American High-Income Trust	18,374
Colonial High-Yield Securities Trust—Class A	17,123
Delaware Delchester Fund	16,991
Federated High-Yield Trust	**17,420**
Fidelity Advisor High-Yield Portfolio	**21,615**
Franklin AGE High-Income Fund	16,280
IDS Extra Income Fund	16,715
INVESCO High-Yield Fund	**15,853**
Kemper Diversified Income Fund	19,548

Kemper High-Yield Fund	17,121
Liberty High-Income Bond Fund	18,866
Lord Abbett Bond-Debenture Fund	17,727
Lutheran Brotherhood High-Yield Fund	17,319
MainStay High-Yield Corporate Bond Fund	16,932
Merrill Lynch Corporate Bond Fund High-Income	
Portfolio—Class A	19,195
Nicholas Income Fund	**15,584**
Northeast Investors Trust	**16,173**
Oppenheimer Champion High-Yield Fund	19,635
Oppenheimer High-Yield Fund	17,174
PaineWebber High-Income Fund—Class A	18,882
Phoenix High-Yield Fund Series	16,850
T. Rowe Price High-Yield Fund	**15,809**
Prudential High-Yield Fund—Class B	15,570
Putnam High-Yield Trust Advantage	17,894
Putnam High-Yield Trust—Class A	17,614
Seligman High-Yield Bond Series	17,558
Smith Barney Shearson High-Income Fund—Class B	15,558
Value Line Aggressive Income Trust	**15,984**
Vanguard Fixed-Income Securities High-Yield	
Corporate	**16,411**

*For the period ending July 31, 1993

Funds listed in **bold type** are available by direct purchase.

N/A indicates that the fund has not had five full years of performance history.

Summary

Funds in the high-yield corporate bond group are geared for the risk portion of an investor's portfolio. Share price, yield and total return will vary, and the market for lower-quality securities may be thinner and less active than other securities markets. These funds are not for conservative or short-term investors, nor for investors who plan to rely on them as their sole source of income. Rather, it is a way for sophisticated investors to obtain relatively high current income with the potential for growth of capital over the long term.

World Bond Funds

Usual Investment Objective of the Group

Mutual funds included in the world bond funds group seek current income with capital appreciation as a secondary objective by investing principally in debt securities issued anywhere in the world. Some funds are more restricted, such as Benham European Government Bond Fund, which invests primarily in bonds issued by European governments and agencies. Managers consider both yield and the potential for capital appreciation in making investments and will allocate fund assets among countries, geographic regions, and currency denominations in an attempt to achieve high total investment return.

Survey of the Group

Foreign currency–denominated bond markets have grown faster than the U.S. dollar–denominated bond market in terms of U.S. dollar market value and now represent more than half the value of the world's developed bond markets. Participants in the markets have grown in number, thereby providing better marketability. Further, a number of international bond markets have reduced barriers to entry to foreign investors by deregulation and by reducing their withholding taxes.

The 1992 currency crisis made Europe a turbulent place to invest, but this did not deter portfolio managers from making big bets on European bonds. Interest rate cuts begun by Germany led many investors to believe that it would continue to do so in an effort to stimulate the German economy. Lower German interest rates would enable other countries in the European Monetary System to bring down their rates, leading bond prices to appreciate. This outlook has led many world bond fund managers to invest at least 50 percent of their assets in European issues.

Of considerable concern to funds that invest in Europe is currency risk. If improving economic conditions cause U.S. interest rates to move up while European interest rates decline, dollar-denominated assets will become more attractive than European issues. European currencies would then probably decline relative to the dollar, reducing total returns for U.S.-based investors. Some fund managers have mitigated these problems by hedging their positions back into the U.S.

dollar. That was a costly strategy in the early part of 1993, however, as the dollar declined in the first quarter.

If European interest rates continue to decline, world bond funds will benefit. Funds heavily invested in Europe, such as Benham European Government Bond Fund, are well positioned to capitalize on interest rate declines. However, there could be some volatility along the way, so conservative investors may want to stay with a more diversified fund.

The following table indicates the historical average annual total returns of the world bond funds group and the Lehman Brothers Aggregate Bond Index for years ending December 31.

World Bond Funds Group versus Lehman Brothers Aggregate Bond Index

	Group Total Return	LBAB Index		Group Total Return	LBAB Index
1983	1.55%	8.38%	1988	4.53%	7.88%
1984	5.13	15.16	1989	6.21	14.54
1985	25.37	22.13	1990	12.67	8.94
1986	18.09	15.25	1991	13.52	16.00
1987	18.06	2.76	1992	2.31	7.24

Source: Morningstar Mutual Funds

Recommended Fund

Scudder International Bond Fund
175 Federal Street
Boston, MA 02110
800-225-2470

Portfolio manager: Adam Greshin/Larry Teitelbaum
Investment adviser: Scudder Stevens & Clark
Sales fees: No-load
Management fee: 0.73%
12b-1 fee: None
Other expenses: 0.52%
Total operating expense: 1.25%
Minimum initial purchase: $1,000 (additional: $100)
Minimum IRA purchase: $500 (additional: $50)

Date of inception: July 6, 1988
Net assets of fund as of March 31, 1993: $822 million

Investment Objective

Scudder International Bond Fund seeks income primarily by investing in high-grade bonds denominated in foreign currencies. As a secondary objective, the fund seeks protection and possible enhancement of principal value by actively managing currency, bond market and maturity exposure, and by security selection.

Investment Policy

The fund will invest primarily in a managed portfolio of high-grade international bonds that are denominated in foreign currencies, including bonds denominated in the European Currency Unit (ECU). Portfolio investments will be selected on the basis of yield, credit quality and the fundamental outlooks for currency and interest rate trends in different parts of the globe. Normally, at least 65 percent of its total assets will be in bonds denominated in foreign currencies.

The fund intends to have investments from a minimum of three different countries; however, it may invest substantially all of its assets in one country. Under normal conditions, the fund will not invest more than 35 percent of its assets in U.S. debt securities. For temporary defensive or emergency purposes, however, the fund may invest without limit in U.S. debt securities, including short-term money market securities. The fund actively manages currency, bond market and maturity exposure.

Performance

The tables below indicate annual total returns of Scudder International Bond Fund for each full year of operation ending December 31 and comparative results for the Lehman Brothers Aggregate Bond Index, followed by total returns and the growth of $10,000 invested in the fund for different periods ending August 31, 1993.

Scudder International Bond Fund versus Lehman Brothers Aggregate Bond Index

	Fund Total Return	*LBAB Index*		*Fund Total Return*	*LBAB Index*
1989	7.23%	14.54%	1991	22.23%	16.00%
1990	21.11	8.94	1992	7.63	7.24

Total Returns for Different Periods Ending August 31, 1993

	Fund Total Return	Growth of $10,000
3 Months	4.15%	$10,415
6 Months	10.78	11,078
1 Year	14.14	11,414
3-Year Average	17.68	16,297
5-Year Average	15.90	20,917

Source: *Morningstar Mutual Funds*

Financial History

Figure 21.3 provides historical per-share data and ratios on Scudder International Bond Fund. It is based on a single share outstanding throughout each fiscal year (which ends on the last day of June).

Comments

Scudder International Bond Fund is under new leadership. Larry Teitelbaum joined the fund as lead manager in early 1993 after having successfully led the Merrill Lynch Global Bond Fund since 1988.

The fund's nondollar exposure is high, with foreign denominated securities constituting 82 percent of the portfolio at the end of June 1993. The duration was an aggressive 6.7 years, anticipating a further decline in European interest rates. Portfolio exposure is well diversified, with securities being held from 13 foreign countries, as well as those denominated in European Currency Units. Holdings range from Australia to Japan to Great Britain and European countries.

The fund has traditionally invested aggressively and continues in that path, which it has found successful in the past.

Portfolio

Total fixed-income securities: 71 as of September 30, 1992

25 Top Holdings

Security	Maturity
Government of Japan 5.9%	09/20/12
Government of Netherlands 6.5%	01/15/99
Government of France 8.125%	05/25/99
Government of Netherlands 8.5%	06/01/06
KFW International Finance 6%	11/29/99
Government of Italy 9.25%	03/07/11
Government of Spain 11.6%	01/15/97
United Kingdom Treasury 11.75%	01/22/07

International Bank Reconstruction/ Development 5.25%	03/20/02
Government of Netherlands 7%	05/15/95
United Kingdom Treasury 3.5%	12/29/49
Kingdom of Sweden 10.25%	05/05/03
Venezuela FRN	12/18/07
Kingdom of Denmark 9%	11/15/96
Kingdom of Denmark 9%	11/15/00
Government of Sweden 10.75%	01/23/97
Government of Canada 9%	03/01/11
Kingdom of Belgium 6%	12/16/98
Government of Canada 8.25%	11/01/95
South Australia Finance 10%	01/15/03
Republic of Finland 11%	03/15/01
Government of France 9.5%	04/25/00
Republic of Italy Euro 10.5%	04/28/14
Government of Canada 9.25%	06/01/22
Government of Canada 9.25%	10/01/96

Composition of Portfolio

As of June 30, 1993

Cash	7.2%
U.S. Bonds	10.9
Foreign Bonds	81.9

Other World Bond Funds

	Five-Year Growth of $10,000*
Fidelity Global Bond Fund	**$17,152**
G.T. Global Government Income Fund—Class A	17,589
Merrill Lynch Global Bond Fund For Investment/Retirement—Class B	18,091
MFS World Governments Fund	17,683
PaineWebber Global Income Fund—Class B	16,235
Putnam Global Governmental Income Trust	17,768
Smith Barney Shearson Global Bond Fund—Class B	15,967
T. Rowe Price International Bond Fund	**17,136**
Templeton Income Fund	16,077
Van Eck World Income Fund	16,245

*For the period ending August 31, 1993

Funds listed in **bold type** are available by direct purchase.

FIGURE 21.3 Scudder International Bond Fund Per-Share Data and Selected Ratios

The following table includes selected data for a share outstanding throughout each period and other performance information derived from the audited financial statements. If you would like more detailed information concerning the Fund's performance, a complete portfolio listing and audited financial statements are available in the Fund's Annual Report dated June 30, 1993 and may be obtained without charge by writing or calling Scudder Investor Services, Inc.

	Years Ended June 30,				For the Period July 6, 1988 (commencement of operations) to June 30,
	1993	1992	1991	1990	1989
Net asset value, beginning of period	$13.68	$12.35	$12.08	$11.27	$12.00
Income from investment operations:					
Net investment income (a)	1.03	1.08	1.21	1.10	1.00
Net realized and unrealized gain (loss) on investments, options, futures contracts and foreign currency related transactions ÷	.52	2.15	.56	.80	(.73)
Total from investment operations	1.55	3.23	1.77	1.90	.27
Less distributions from:					
Net investment income	(1.04)	(1.09)	(1.21)	(1.09)	(1.00)
Net realized gains on investment transactions	(.62)	(.81)	(.29)	—	—
Total distributions	(1.66)	(1.90)	(1.50)	(1.09)	(1.00)
Net asset value, end of period	$13.57	$13.68	$12.35	$12.08	$11.27
Total Return (%)	12.24	28.25	14.88	17.59	2.16†

Source: Scudder, Stevens & Clark, Inc.; Scudder International Bond Fund prospectus, November 1, 1993

FIGURE 21.3 *(continued)*

Ratios and Supplemental Data

Net assets, end of period (millions)	$1,017	$542	$144	$73	$13
Ratio of operating expenses, net to average net assets (%) (a)	1.25	1.25	1.25	1.25	1.00*
Ratio of net investment income to average net assets (%)	7.69	8.31	9.48	9.57	8.58*
Portfolio turnover rate (%)	249.7	147.9	260.1	215.6	103.8*
(a) Reflects a per share amount of expenses, exclusive of management fees, reimbursed by the Adviser of	—	—	—	—	$ .39
Reflects a per share amount of management fee not imposed by the Adviser of	$ .02	$ .04	$ .06	$ .10	$ .10
Operating expense ratio including expenses reimbursed, management fee and other expenses not imposed (%) ..	1.37	1.57	1.75	2.51	5.59*

‡ Includes exchange gain (loss) of $.01, $.01 and ($.02) for the periods ended June 30, 1991, 1990 and 1989, previously included in net investment income.

* Annualized

† Not Annualized

Summary

World bond funds may provide, at times, higher investment returns than U.S. bonds. International bonds may provide higher current income than U.S. bonds, and/or the local price of international bonds can appreciate more than U.S. bonds. Fluctuations in foreign currencies relative to the U.S. dollar can potentially benefit investment returns. Of course, in each case, at any time the opposite may also be true. But a world bond fund can definitely have a place in a prudent investor's diversified portfolio.

Chapter 22

Investing in Corporate Bond Funds

General Corporate Bond Funds

Usual Investment Objective of the Group

General corporate bond funds seek income by investing in fixed-income securities, primarily corporate bonds. Funds in this group follow a diverse array of investment strategies. In addition to carrying large positions in corporate bonds with an average rating of AA, funds hold a full range of issues. Some funds will hold as much as 35 percent of their portfolios in junk bonds, others more than 60 percent in U.S. government–backed issues, and still others maintain nearly 35 percent in foreign-backed instruments.

Survey of the Group

Because funds in this group include in their portfolios issues from nearly all fixed-income sources, it makes sense to compare the performance of individual funds against high-yield bond funds, high-quality corporate bond funds, government and government-backed bond funds, and worldwide bond funds. Among these groups, results of the corporate bond group have been generally favorable, with their returns being above average over the long term.

Having a multifaceted and flexible investment policy has had a positive effect on the corporate bond group. Pure Treasury funds have done better as a result of their response to falling interest rates. In recent years, high-yield funds have also had better returns, but they have not done as well over the longer-term ten-year period. However, other groups have generally done worse. The mix of securities in general corporate bond funds helps, because when one area falls out of favor, the funds' other sectors can keep the overall performance up.

General corporate bond funds did particularly well in 1992 and early 1993. As the economy slowly picked up, more investors were willing to move down the credit-quality ladder to pick up better yields. The result of this increase in demand was higher prices.

There is a good deal of variation in the performance of different funds in this broad group. Some of the top performers in recent years have been funds with less than investment-grade–rated instruments. They enjoyed rising values along with the rally in junk bond issues. Also, as interest rates continued their downward trend to historic lows, those funds holding long maturity issues did better than their more cautious peers.

However, the investor should keep in mind that return is not the only criterion of importance. Many investors are looking to short-term bond funds for their low risk and their yields, which are above money market returns.

The following table indicates the historical average annual total return of the corporate bond group and the Lehman Brothers Corporate Bond Index for years ending December 31.

Corporate Bond Group versus Lehman Brothers Corporate Bond Index

	Group Total Return	LBCB Index		Group Total Return	LBCB Index
1983	9.04%	9.27%	1988	8.76%	9.22%
1984	12.67	16.62	1989	10.70	13.98
1985	21.57	24.06	1990	5.94	7.15
1986	14.20	16.54	1991	16.62	18.50
1987	1.91	2.56	1992	7.56	8.70

Source: *Morningstar Mutual Funds*, Morningstar, Inc., 225 W. Wacker Dr., Chicago, IL 60606; 312-696-6532

Recommended Fund

Harbor Bond Fund
One SeaGate
Toledo, OH 43666
800-422-1050

Portfolio manager: William G. Gross
Investment adviser: Harbor Capital Advisors
Sales fees: No-load
Management fee: 0.40%
12b-1 fee: None
Other expenses: 0.42%
Total operating expense: 0.82%
Annual brokerage cost: 0.00%
Minimum initial purchase: $2,000 (additional: $500)
Minimum IRA purchase: $500 (additional: $100)
Date of inception: December 29, 1987
Net assets of fund as of July 31, 1993: $140.9 million

Investment Objective

Harbor Bond Fund seeks to achieve maximum total return, consistent with the preservation of capital and prudent investment management, through investment in an actively managed portfolio of fixed-income securities.

Investment Policy

Under normal market conditions, Harbor Bond Fund will invest at least 65 percent of the value of its net assets in bonds, such as obligations issued or guaranteed by the U.S. government, its agencies or instrumentalities with maturities of at least five years; obligations issued or guaranteed by a foreign government or by supra-national organizations (such as the International Bank for Reconstruction and Development); obligations of domestic or foreign corporations and other entities; and mortgage-related and other asset-backed securities.

Normally, the fund invests at least 60 percent of its assets in domestic issues, and at least 80 percent is denominated in U.S. dollars. The fund's portfolio normally consists of securities with varying maturities; the fund intends to maintain a portfolio duration of three to six years.

FIGURE 22.1 Harbor Bond Fund Per-Share Data and Selected Ratios

Year (Period) Ended	Investment Income	Operating Expenses	Interest Expense
Harbor Bond Fund			
October 31, 1992	$.87	$.08*	—
October 31, 1991	.92	.09*	—
October 31, 1990	.96	.12*	—
October 31, 1989	.87	.11*	—
October 31, 1988**	.73	.13*	—

	Net Asset Value		Ratio of Operating Expenses to Average Net Assets (%)
	Beginning of Period	End of Period	
October 31, 1992			
October 31, 1991	$11.11	$11.35	0.77%*
October 31, 1990	10.03	11.11	0.86*
October 31, 1989	10.55	10.03	1.22*
October 31, 1988	10.26	10.55	1.21*
October 31, 1987***	10.00	10.26	1.55†*

Source: Harbor Fund prospectus dated June 25, 1993

Performance

The following tables indicate the total returns of Harbor Bond Fund for each full year of operation ending December 31 and comparative results for the Lehman Brothers Corporate Bond Index, followed by total returns and the growth of $10,000 invested for different periods ending July 31, 1993.

Harbor Bond Fund versus Lehman Brothers Corporate Bond Index

	Fund Total Return	LBCB Index		Fund Total Return	LBCB Index
1988	7.17%	9.22%	1991	19.65%	18.50%
1989	13.68	13.98	1992	9.11	8.70
1990	7.94	7.15			

FIGURE 22.1 *(continued)*

Net Investment Income	Dividends From		Net Realized and Unrealized Gains (Losses) on Investments Futures, Options and Forward Currency Contracts	Net Increase (Decrease) In Net Asset Value
	Net Investment Income	Net Realized Capital Gains		
$.79	$(.79)	$ (.26)	$ .50	$ .24
.83	(.84)	—	1.09	1.08
.84	(.83)	(.09)	(.44)	(.52)
.76	(.77)	(.07)	.37	.29
.60	(.51)	—	.17	.26

Ratio of Interest Expense to Average Net Assets (%)	Ratio of Net Investment Income to Average Net Assets (%)	Portfolio Turnover (%)	Number of Shares Outstanding at End of Period (000's)
—	7.30%*	52.54%	5,764
—	8.12*	58.45	3,643
—	8.30*	90.99	2,427
—	8.20*	91.17	2,012
—	7.42†*	124.15	1,094

Total Returns for Different Periods Ending July 31, 1993

	Fund Total Return	Growth of $10,000
3 Months	2.81%	$10,281
6 Months	7.07	10,707
1 Year	12.51	11,251
3-Year Average	14.05	14,833
5-Year Average	12.75	18,221

Source: *Morningstar Mutual Funds*

Financial History
Figure 22.1 illustrates per-share data for a share outstanding throughout each period and selected ratio information for each year ended October 31.

Comments

Harbor Bond Fund's interest rate outlook has recently changed from bullish to neutral. This is a big change for the fund, which achieved its good reputation with an optimistic rate stance. The fund is one of the few general corporate bond funds to place total returns ahead of income in importance. It has generally acted on the premise that greater gains could be made through appreciation than through income. That strategy was correct. The fund delivered moderate income, while becoming one of the top performers in total income through rising bond prices.

Management has now reevaluated its strategy, based on a belief that interest rates may have little further to go on the downside. The shift to a neutral interest rate position is reflected in a portfolio with 19 percent of its assets in intermediate- to long-term zero-coupon bonds, along with 40 percent in cash to hold back duration. The manager believes that zero-coupon instruments are undervalued.

Harbor Bond Fund has correctly followed the secular decline in interest rates to the advantage of its shareholders. There is no reason to think that it will not be able to handle as adroitly a possible rising interest rate environment.

Portfolio

Total stocks: 0 as of June 30, 1993

Total fixed-income securities: 78 as of June 30, 1993

25 Largest Holdings

Security	Maturity
FNMA 9%	11/01/09
Chrysler 12%	11/15/15
Sears Savings Bank 0%	05/25/32
FHLMC Forward 6.5%	01/01/99
Banmer 8%	07/07/98
Resolution Trust 0%	08/25/21
Banesto DEL 8.25%	07/28/02
Niagara Mohawk Power 8.875%	08/01/94
Housing Securities 8.35%	12/25/20
Commonwealth Edison 8%	10/15/03
Shearson Lehman Brothers 0%	03/18/96
FNMA CMO REMIC 9.2%	09/25/17
Residential Funding 9%	12/25/21
CMO Trust CMO 9%	04/20/17
Time Warner 0%	08/15/02
Ford Motor Credit 8.95%	01/31/95

AMR 10%	03/07/01
CTC Mansfield Funding 11.125%	09/30/16
Sears Roebuck 8.95%	02/15/95
Capstead Securities CMO 8.9%	12/25/21
AMR 7.6%	01/27/97
RJR Nabisco 0%	05/15/01
Structured Mortgage Asset Residential Trust 7.25%	10/25/02
Resolution Trust 0%	05/15/03
Discover Credit 0%	07/24/95

Composition of Portfolio
As of June 30, 1993

Cash	40.2%
Bonds	59.8

Other High-Performing Corporate Bond Funds

	Five-Year Growth of $10,000*
Bond Fund of America	$33,000
Boston Company Managed Income Fund—Retail Shares	**28,017**
Composite Income Fund	28,055
Fidelity Investment-Grade Bond Portfolio	**30,232**
Fidelity Short-Term Bond	**N/A**
FPA New Income	32,347
John Hancock Sovereign Bond Fund—Class A	31,121
Merrill Lynch Corporate Bond Fund Intermediate-Term Portfolio—Class A	28,677
Norwest Income Bond Fund—Investor Class A	N/A
PaineWebber Investment-Grade Income Fund— Class A	N/A
PIMCO Low-Duration Fund	**N/A**
PIMCO Total Return Fund	**N/A**
Strong Advantage Fund	**N/A**

*For the period ending July 31, 1993

Funds listed in **bold type** are available by direct purchase.

N/A indicates that the fund has not had five full years of performance history.

Summary

Funds in the corporate bond group have fared well over the past decade. As a group, they have not experienced any year with a negative total return. Other fund groups have done better for short periods of time during this period, but results of the corporate bond group have been favorable overall. Because there is such a variance in the investment policies of the funds in this group, its performance can logically be compared with that of other groups, such as high-yield funds, high-quality corporate funds, government bond funds and even worldwide bond funds.

High-Quality Corporate Bond Funds

Usual Investment Objective of the Group

Funds in the high-quality corporate bond group seek income by investing in fixed-income securities, 65 percent of which are rated A or higher.

Survey of the Group

Funds in the high-quality corporate bond group must invest at least 65 percent of their assets in fixed-income securities that are rated A or better. However, in recent years many funds in the high-quality group have invested a significant portion of their portfolios in lower-tier investment-grade or speculative high-yield bonds and have posted better returns than the group average. Such funds include Kemper Income and Capital Preservation Fund and Vanguard Fixed-Income Investment-Grade Corporate Portfolio (my recommended fund).

Some funds have also profited by being aggressive in choosing bonds with long-term maturities during the time that interest rates moved down toward the 6 percent mark. Included in this class were Dreyfus A Bonds Plus Fund, Vanguard Fixed-Income Investment-Grade Corporate and Security Income Corporate Bond. In 1993, all of these funds had average effective maturities of ten years or longer and were among the top of the corporate high-quality group, with each fund returning about three percentage points more than the average of its peers.

At some point, interest rates will no longer continue their downward movement, so some portfolio managers have reduced their long-term maturity stance in preparation for this and a possible rate increase. Security Income Corporate Bond Fund has already decreased the portfolio's average maturity by five years.

As interest rates in the economy have been declining over the last decade, so have the income dividends paid by mutual funds in the high-quality corporate bond group. In 1982 the average fund delivered an income return to shareholders of just over 13 percent. By 1993 this had fallen to under 6 percent. Investors who wish to achieve higher income dividends have been forced to look to funds that hold greater portions of their assets in lower-grade securities and maintain longer average maturities. This, of course, subjects the shareholder to increased credit-quality and interest-rate risk.

The following table indicates the historical average total return of the high-quality corporate bond group and of the Lehman Brothers Corporate Bond Index for years ending December 31.

High-Quality Corporate Bond Group versus Lehman Brothers Corporate Bond Index

	Group Total Return	LBCB Index		Group Total Return	LBCB Index
1983	8.00%	9.27%	1988	7.22%	9.22%
1984	13.02	16.62	1989	11.53	13.98
1985	19.62	24.06	1990	7.62	7.15
1986	13.11	16.54	1991	14.24	18.50
1987	2.51	2.56	1992	6.43	8.70

Source: *Morningstar Mutual Funds*

Recommended Fund

Vanguard Fixed-Income Securities Investment-Grade Corporate Portfolio
Vanguard Financial Center
P.O. Box 2600
Valley Forge, PA 19482
800-662-7447

Portfolio manager: Paul G. Sullivan
Investment adviser: Wellington Management

Sales fees: No-load
Management fee: 0.16%
12b-1 fee: None
Other expenses: 0.15%
Total operating expense: 0.31%
Minimum initial purchase: $3,000 (additional: $100)
Minimum IRA purchase: $500 (additional: $100)
Date of inception: July 9, 1973
Net assets of fund as of July 31, 1993: $3.257 billion

Investment Objective
Vanguard Fixed-Income Securities Investment-Grade Corporate Portfolio seeks to provide investors with a high level of current income consistent with the maintenance of principal and liquidity.

Investment Policy
The Vanguard Fixed-Income Investment-Grade Corporate Portfolio invests in a diversified portfolio of investment-grade corporate and government bonds. Under normal circumstances, at least 65 percent of the portfolio's assets are invested in straight-debt corporate bonds rated a minimum of Baa3 by Moody's or BBB- by Standard & Poor's at the time of purchase. Additionally, at least 80 percent of the portfolio's assets will normally be invested in a combination of investment-grade corporate bonds and securities of the U.S. government and its agencies and instrumentalities. The average weighted maturity of the portfolio is expected to range from 10 to 25 years.

The preponderance of the portfolio's holdings will be classified in the top three credit-rating categories. At least 70 percent of the portfolio's assets will be invested in the following securities:

1. Straight-debt corporate securities that, at the time of purchase, are rated a minimum of A3 by Moody's or A- by Standard & Poor's;
2. Securities issued by the U.S. government and its agencies and instrumentalities;
3. Commercial paper of companies having, at the time of purchase, outstanding debt securities rated as described in (1) or commercial paper rated P-1 or P-2 by Moody's or A-1 or A-2 by Standard & Poor's; and
4. Short-term fixed-income securities held as cash reserves, including U.S. Treasury or U.S. government agency securities,

certificates of deposit, bankers' acceptances or repurchase agreements collateralized by these securities.

Performance

The tables below indicate the annual total returns of the Vanguard Fixed-Income Securities Investment-Grade Corporate Portfolio and the comparative results of the Lehman Brothers Corporate Bond Index for years ending December 31, followed by total returns of the fund and the growth of $10,000 invested for different periods ending July 31, 1993.

Vanguard Fixed-Income Securities Investment-Grade Corporate Portfolio versus Lehman Brothers Corporate Bond Index

	Fund Total Return	LBCB Index		Fund Total Return	LBCB Index
1983	6.98%	9.27%	1988	9.70%	9.22%
1984	14.67	16.62	1989	15.18	13.98
1985	21.66	24.06	1990	6.21	7.15
1986	14.33	16.54	1991	20.90	18.50
1987	0.20	2.56	1992	9.78	8.70

Total Returns for Different Periods Ending July 31, 1993

	Fund Total Return	Growth of $10,000
3 Months	4.05%	$10,405
6 Months	8.57	10,857
1 Year	14.49	11,449
3-Year Average	15.04	15,224
5-Year Average	13.74	19,039
10-Year Average	12.60	32,757
15-Year Average	11.24	49,433

Source: *Morningstar Mutual Funds*

Financial History

Figure 22.2 illustrates selected per-share data and ratios for a share of Vanguard Fixed-Income Securities Investment-Grade Corporate Portfolio outstanding throughout each year ending January 31.

Comments

Vanguard Fixed-Income Securities Investment-Grade Corporate Portfolio has consistently ranked at the top of its peer group in terms of total return. By its charter, the fund's maturity ranges between 15 and 25 years. It holds callable securities to the extent of about 20

FIGURE 22.2 Vanguard Fixed-Income Securities Investment-Grade Corporate Portfolio Per-Share Data and Selected Ratios

| INVESTMENT GRADE CORPORATE PORTFOLIO | | | | | | | | | |
| Year Ended January 31, | | | | | | | | | |
	1993	1992	1991	1990	1989	1988	1987	1986	1985	1984
Net Asset Value, Beginning of Period	$8.63	$8.02	$8.00	$7.91	$8.11	$8.77	$8.42	$7.84	$7.84	$8.00
Investment Activities										
Income	.707	.732	.749	.759	.771	.800	.884	.97	1.01	1.01
Expenses	(.027)	(.026)	(.029)	(.027)	(.030)	(.030)	(.037)	(.05)	(.05)	(.06)
Net Investment Income	.680	.706	.720	.732	.741	.770	.847	.92	.96	.95
Net Realized and Unrealized Gain (Loss) on Investments	.561	.610	.020	.090	(.200)	(.660)	.473	.58	—	(.16)
Total from Investment Activities	1.241	1.316	.740	.822	.541	.110	1.32	1.50	.96	.79
Distributions										
Net Investment Income	(.680)	(.706)	(.720)	(.732)	(.741)	(.770)	(.847)	(.92)	(.96)	(.95)
Realized Net Gains	(.151)	—	—	—	—	—	(.123)	—	—	—
Total Distributions	(.831)	(.706)	(.720)	(.732)	(.741)	(.770)	(.970)	(.92)	(.96)	(.95)
Net Asset Value, End of Period	$9.04	$8.63	$8.02	$8.00	$7.91	$8.11	$8.77	$8.42	$7.84	$7.84
Ratio of Expenses to Average Net Assets	.31%	.31%	.37%	.34%	.38%	.37%	.41%	.55%	.62%	.67%
Ratio of Net Investment Income to Average Net Assets	7.68%	8.46%	9.16%	9.07%	9.40%	9.40%	9.41%	10.78%	12.50%	11.80%
Portfolio Turnover Rate	50%	72%	62%	70%	60%	63%	47%	56%	55%	62%
Number of Shares Outstanding, End of Period (Thousands)	305,501	230,796	156,410	119,270	92,839	81,949	85,882	37,807	13,589	8,755

Source: Vanguard Fixed-Income Securities Fund prospectus dated May 31, 1993

percent of its portfolio. But most of that isn't callable for five to ten years, so it doesn't represent much threat to maintaining the locked-in higher interest rates. The fund has typically had one of the longest maturities in the group, which tends to increase its volatility and, thus, risk.

When interest rates move up, as they did in 1987 and again in 1990, the fund's net asset value can drop substantially. Along with big downward moves, however, can come huge gains when rates drop, as they did in more recent years.

Maturity was scaled back from 22 years in 1992 to 17 years, as the portfolio manager came to believe that interest rates would finally begin to rise again. The duration of the portfolio—i.e., the average years left until bonds mature—also fell, from about nine years in early 1993 to eight years by mid-1993.

Despite the portfolio manager's relative caution in 1993, the fund's 15-year maturity limit means it will underperform other funds with shorter maturities when interest rates begin climbing again. Investors who can tolerate the volatility, however, will enjoy some of the best long-term returns in the high-quality bond group.

Portfolio

Total fixed-income securities: 146 as of June 30, 1993

25 Largest Holdings

Security	Maturity
GNMA 8.5%	06/15/23
U.S. Treasury Note 9.25%	01/15/96
TVA 7.75%	12/15/22
U.S. Treasury Note 6.375%	08/15/02
U.S. Treasury Note 6.25%	02/15/03
United Parcel Service 8.375%	04/01/20
Province of Nova Scotia 9.125%	05/01/21
Georgia-Pacific 9.875%	11/01/21
Long Island Lighting 9%	11/01/22
Union Pacific Railroad 8.625%	12/01/31
General Electric 8.125%	05/15/12
Westpac Banking 7.875%	10/15/02
Unocal 8.4%	01/15/99
Toys 'R Us 8.75%	09/01/21
EI Du Pont de Nemours 8.25%	01/15/22
Hydro-Quebec 8%	02/01/13
Arco Chemical 9.8%	02/01/20

General Reinsurance 9%	09/12/09
European Investment Bank 9.125%	06/01/02
Korea Development Bank 9.6%	12/01/00
Union Camp 9.25%	08/15/21
KFW International Finance 8.2%	06/01/06
Auburn Hills Trust 15.375%	05/01/20
Ford Motor Credit 6.875%	01/15/97
Chevron 9.375%	06/01/16

Composition of Portfolio
As of June 30, 1993

Cash	9.0%
Bonds	91.0

Other High-Performing High-Quality Corporate Bond Funds

	Five-Year Growth of $10,000*
AARP High-Quality Bond Fund	$16,666
Babson Bond Trust Portfolio L	17,049
Bernstein Intermediate Duration Portfolio	N/A
Columbia Fixed-Income Securities Fund	17,442
Dreyfus A Bonds Plus	17,897
IAI Bond Fund	17,526
IDS Selective Fund	17,459
Kemper Income & Capital Preservation Fund	16,655
Merrill Lynch Corporate Bond Fund High-Quality Portfolio—Class A	17,144
Portico Bond IMMDEX Fund	N/A
Scudder Income Fund	17,420
SteinRoe Intermediate Bond Fund	16,429
Vanguard Bond Index Fund	16,973

*For the period ending July 31, 1993

Funds listed in **bold type** are available by direct purchase.

N/A indicates that the fund has not had five full years of performance history.

Summary

Funds in the high-quality corporate bond group must invest at least 65 percent of their assets in fixed-income securities rated A or better. However, in recent years those funds that have also aggressively invested in lower-tier or speculative high-yield bonds have posted better returns than the group average. Investors willing to accept the volatility that accompanies such boldness may see higher income and total return, but with an increased amount of risk.

Short-Term World Income Funds

Usual Investment Objective of the Group

Short-term world income funds seek income and a stable net asset value (NAV) by investing primarily in a portfolio of various non-U.S. currency denominated bonds, usually with an average maturity of three years or less. These funds seek higher yield than a money market fund and less fluctuation of NAV than a long-term international bond fund. Funds in this group may engage in substantial hedging strategies to reduce fluctuation of NAV.

Survey of the Group

Short-term world income funds have been trying to rebuild their net asset values, which were hit hard during the currency crisis in 1992 when the European Exchange Rate Mechanism (ERM) fell apart. Because they had enjoyed rock-steady NAVs before the currency crisis, many investors had poured funds into these funds, happy to find a money market equivalent that still paid a decent yield. When NAVs started to fall, however, the incoming tide of shareholders ebbed, as they sought refuge elsewhere. Net assets of the group dropped from over $15 billion in 1991 to under $10 billion by the end of 1992.

To recover, many funds moved the bulk of their assets into U.S. dollar and dollar-bloc securities, keeping only a small portion of their European assets. Within that region, funds invested in longer debt instruments, hoping to benefit from declining interest rates. Funds that hedged their European exposure directly into the U.S. dollar generally succeeded. PaineWebber Global Short-Term Income Fund actually bettered the NAV level it carried before the crisis.

Interest rates in many countries are higher than our own domestic rates, which creates opportunities for income-oriented investors. Funds in the short-term world income group are appropriate for investors who seek the higher yields available from a global portfolio of debt securities, share price stability over the long term and a strong profile for credit quality.

The following table indicates the historical average annual total returns of the short-term world income group and the Lehman Brothers Aggregate Bond Index for years ending December 31.

**Short-Term World Income Group versus
Lehman Brothers Aggregate Bond Index**

	Group Total Return	LBAB Index		Group Total Return	LBAB Index
1987	−9.35%	2.76%	1990	2.74%	8.94%
1988	10.26	7.88	1991	7.40	16.00
1989	−13.80	14.54	1992	−0.94	7.24

Source: *Morningstar Mutual Funds*

Recommended Fund

Fidelity Short-Term World Income Fund
82 Devonshire Street
Boston, MA 02109
800-544-8888

Portfolio manager: Judy M. Pagliuca
Investment adviser: Fidelity Management & Research
Sales fees: No-load
Management fee: 0.59%
12b-1 fee: None
Other expenses: 0.65%
Total operating expense: 1.37%
Minimum initial purchase: $2,500 (additional: $250)
Minimum IRA purchase: $500 (additional: $250)
Date of inception: October 4, 1991
Net assets of fund as of March 31, 1993: $403.7 million

Investment Objective

Fidelity Short-Term World Income Fund seeks as high a level of income as is consistent with preservation of capital.

Investment Policy

The fund invests in high-quality short-term securities and money-market instruments issued anywhere in the world. It is normally invested in at least three different countries, one of which may be the United States. The fund will not invest in debt securities rated below A or equivalent quality.

Fidelity Short-Term World Income Fund is considered nondiversified. With respect to 50 percent of total assets, the fund may not invest more than 5 percent of its total assets in any one issuer. It may not invest more than 25 percent of its total assets in any one issuer, and it also may not invest more than 25 percent of its total assets in any one industry other than the financial services industry. These limitations do not apply to U.S. government securities. Under normal conditions, the fund may not invest less than 25 percent of its total assets in the financial services industry.

The fund may borrow up to one-third of its total assets for temporary or emergency purposes. It may make loans that, in the aggregate, do not exceed one-third of the fund's total assets.

Performance

Since Fidelity Short-Term World Income Fund was established only in the latter part of 1991, its performance record is very short. In 1992, its first full year of operation, the fund had a total return of 4.94 percent. This compared with an average return of minus 0.94 percent turned in by the other funds in the short-term world income group. In the first eight months of 1993, Fidelity had a total return of 9.42 percent, compared with the group's return of 3.69 percent.

In 1990 there were only three funds in the short-term world income arena. This increased to 16 in 1991, 29 in 1992 and 36 by the end of August 1993.

Financial History

Figure 22.3 details information about the financial history of Fidelity Short-Term World Income Fund. It uses the fund's fiscal year (which ends October 31) and expresses the information in terms of a single share outstanding throughout each fiscal period.

FIGURE 22.3 Fidelity Short-Term World Income Fund Per-Share Data and Selected Ratios

Short-Term World Income			
Per-share data and ratios			Two-month period ended
Fiscal years ended October 31	1991‡	1992	December 31, 1992
Interest income	$ .067	$ .936	$ .217
Expenses†	.006	.101	.026
Net interest income	.061	.835	.191
Distributions from net interest income	(.058)	(.737)	(.108)
Net realized & unrealized gain (loss) on investments	.037	(.338)	(.203)
Increase (decrease) in net asset value	.040	(.240)	(.120)
Net asset value (NAV) beginning of period	10.000	10.040	9.800
Net asset value at end of period	$10.040	$ 9.800	$9.680
Expenses borne by the investment adviser	$ .014†	$ —	$ .001†
Ratio of net interest income to average net assets	9.07%*	9.04%	8.63%*
Ratio of expenses to average net assets	1.00%*†	1.09%	1.20%*†
Ratio of expenses to average net assets before voluntary expense limitation	2.87%*†	1.09%	1.23%*†
Ratio of management fee to average net assets before voluntary expenses limitation	.62%*†	.62%	.62%*†
Portfolio turnover rate	62%*	154%	117%*
Shares outstanding at end period (000 omitted)	4,416	66,183	47,379

* Annualized
† During the periods shown, FMR voluntarily reimbursed the fund for total operating expenses (excluding interest, taxes, brokerage commissions and extraordinary expenses) above a certain rate of average net assets.
‡ From October 4, 1991 (commencement of operations) to October 31, 1991

Source: Fidelity Short-Term World Income Fund prospectus dated February 28, 1993

Comments

Although Fidelity Short-Term World Income Fund suffered a 2.32 percent loss when the Exchange Rate Mechanism collapsed in 1992, it still finished ahead of its peers. The entire portfolio was hedged back into dollars after Finland devalued the markka. In addition, money was made by shorting the lira and by cross-hedging deutsche marks with the pound. In early 1993 the fund's performance was even better, as it soared to the top of its group. According to *Morningstar Mutual Funds,* this was because the fund's manager extended duration in European holdings, most of which were hedged into dollars.

The fund also benefited from maintaining longer than average maturities in the United States and Canada, which together make up about 30 percent of its assets. Also contributing to returns is a 20 percent holding of high-yielding Mexican securities. An additional 20 percent of the fund is split between Australia and New Zealand, which is hedged with dollars, yen and deutsche marks. There is also an 18 percent stake in U.S. corporate securities.

Fidelity Short-Term World Income Fund has been successful so far in its brief history but has taken on some risk in pursuit of capital appreciation. Its average maturity is 2.6 years, one of the longest in the short-term group. This could cause problems if interest rates spike upward.

Portfolio

Total securities: 73 as of December 31, 1992

25 Largest Holdings

Security	Maturity
Government of Mexico CETES 0%	06/24/93
Ontario Hydro Euro 10.875%	01/08/96
Bancomer 0%	03/04/93
Banco Nacional Mexico 0%	03/04/93
Nacional Financiera 0%	06/15/93
Government of Sweden 10.75%	01/23/97
Government of France 8.5%	03/12/97
Government of Denmark Bullet 9%	11/15/96
Federal Republic of Germany 8.875%	07/20/95
Banca Serfin 0%	03/04/93
Republic of Italy 10.5%	10/01/95
Manufacturers Hanover 8.125%	01/15/97
Mellon Bank Euro FRN	11/29/96
Government of Denmark 9%	11/15/95
Swedish National Housing 13%	09/20/95
Federal Republic of Germany 6.5%	01/20/94
Government of Spain 13.45%	04/15/96
United Kingdom Treasury 12.25%	03/26/99
Toyota Motor Credit FRN	02/18/95
Government of Spain 13.65%	03/15/94
Government of New Zealand 10%	07/15/97
Texaco Capital 9%	10/01/94

Philip Morris 8.75%	11/15/94
U.S. Bancorp 8.46%	05/30/95
Household Finance 6.875%	11/15/94

Composition of Portfolio
As of December 31, 1993

Bonds   100.0%

Other Short-Term World Income Funds

Alliance Short-Term Multi-Market Trust—Class A
Blanchard Short-Term Global Income Fund
Eaton Vance Short-Term Global Income Fund
Kemper Short-Term Global Income Fund
Merrill Lynch Short-Term Global Income Fund—Class B
PaineWebber Short-Term Global Income Fund—Class A
Scudder Short-Term Global Income Fund
Shearson Lehman Brothers Short-Term World Income Fund—Class A

Funds listed in **bold type** are available by direct purchase.

Summary

Funds in the short-term world income group were hard-hit by the currency crisis in 1992, which followed the collapse of the European Exchange Rate Mechanism. This was a blow to the reputation for stable share prices that the funds had previously enjoyed. As a result, many funds in the group now emphasize capital appreciation. It may be too early to tell how successful they will be in this new strategy.

Chapter 23

Investing in Government Bond Funds

Government Bond—Adjustable-Rate Mortgage Funds

Usual Investment Objective of the Group

Mutual funds included in the government bond—adjustable-rate mortgage group seek current income with minimum fluctuation of share price by investing at least 65 percent of their assets in U.S. government–backed *adjustable-rate mortgages* (ARMs) or other adjustable-rate securities collateralized by mortgage securities.

Survey of the Group

ARM funds are normally bought by investors seeking a higher-yielding alternative to money market funds. Unlike money market instruments, ARMs are subject to principal fluctuation; their volatility roughly equals that of a one-year Treasury note. So investors are justified in using them as a low-risk way to achieve higher yields.

Investors should be aware, however, that while some funds do stick to the straight and narrow path by investing only in government-backed adjustable-rate mortgages, others reach out aggressively for higher yields and incur more risk than the average ARM fund investor is prepared for.

Of particular concern over the past couple of years has been the use of risky derivatives. Many funds bought interest-only STRIPS in 1992 as a hedge against rising interest rates and as a way to boost yield. The term *STRIPS* refers to stripped mortgage securities, in which the principal and interest payments on a pool of *collateralized mortgage obligations* (CMOs) are separated or "stripped" to create two classes of securities. The IO *(interest only)* class receives all interest and no principal payments, while the PO *(principal only)* class is entitled to receive all principal and no interest payments.

STRIPS can be extremely volatile and are acutely sensitive to fluctuations in interest rates and prepayment rates on the underlying mortgages. Because IOs get their sole value from the interest component of a mortgage pool, prepayments, which dry up the principal from which an IO's income is drawn, are a serious threat to IO prices. Funds that held a lot of IOs, such as Putnam Adjustable-Rate U.S. Government Trust, suffered in 1992 and early 1993 as rates fell and prepayments accelerated. Some funds offset prepayment risk with credit risk. Private ARMs don't have the U.S. government backing of agency ARMs, but they provide higher yields, which softens the effects of prepayments.

Because investors differ in their risk tolerance, they should determine the degree of aggressiveness that a fund employs before deciding to invest.

The following table compares the historical average annual total returns for funds in the government bond—adjustable rate mortgage group from 1986 (the first year a fund was established) through 1992 and the Lehman Brothers Aggregate Bond Index for years ending December 31.

Government Bond—Adjustable-Rate Mortgage Group versus Lehman Brothers Aggregate Bond Index

	Group Total Return	LBAB Index		Group Total Return	LBAB Index
1986	8.37%	15.25%	1990	8.27%	8.94%
1987	−1.39	2.76	1991	10.53	16.00
1988	5.95	7.88	1992	4.46	7.24
1989	12.33	14.54			

Source: *Morningstar Mutual Funds,* Morningstar, Inc., 225 W. Wacker Dr., Chicago, IL 60606; 312-696-6532

Recommended Fund

T. Rowe Price Adjustable-Rate U.S. Government Fund
100 East Pratt Street
Baltimore, MD 21202
800-638-5660

Portfolio manager: P. Van Dyke and H. Landon
Investment adviser: T. Rowe Price Associates
Sales fees: No-load
Management fee: 0.18%
12b-1 fee: None
Other expenses: 0.22%
Total operating expense: 0.40%
Minimum initial purchase: $2,500 (additional: $100)
Minimum IRA purchase: $1,000 (additional: $50)
Date of inception: September 30, 1991
Net assets of fund as of July 31, 1993: $331.9 million

Investment Objective

T. Rowe Price Adjustable-Rate U.S. Government Fund seeks high current income with minimum fluctuation of share price.

Investment Policy

The fund normally invests at least 65 percent of its assets in adjustable-rate securities that are issued or guaranteed by the U.S. government or its agencies. Such securities consist of adjustable-rate mortgages (ARMs) and adjustable-rate collateralized mortgage obligations (CMOs). The fund may also invest up to 10 percent of its assets in interest-only stripped mortgage securities (IOs), mainly for the purpose of reducing, or hedging against, the decline in principal value of mortgage securities that may occur as a result of increasing interest rates. IOs may also be purchased in anticipation of declining prepayment rates.

The fund will hold a portion of its assets in short-term money market securities maturing in one year or less. It may invest in high-quality debt securities of any type. It may invest up to 5 percent of its assets in futures contracts or options to hedge against changes in prevailing levels of interest rates.

As a fundamental policy, for the purpose of realizing additional income, the fund may lend securities with a value of up to 30 percent of its total assets to broker-dealers, institutional investors or other persons.

Performance

The tables below provide information for the short financial history of T. Rowe Price Adjustable-Rate U.S. Government Fund. Since the fund's date of inception was September 30, 1991, data is provided only for the year ending December 31, 1992, and the first seven months of 1993. Comparative returns are shown for the Lehman Brothers Aggregate Bond Index and a $10,000 investment in the fund.

T. Rowe Price Adjustable-Rate U.S. Government Fund versus Lehman Brothers Aggregate Bond Index

	Fund Total Return	LBAB Index		Fund Total Return	LBAB Index
1992	3.94%	7.24%	1993*	1.79%	7.51%

*For the period through July 31, 1993

Total Returns for the Period Ending July 31, 1993

	Fund Total Return	Growth of $10,000
3 Months	1.17%	$10,117
6 Months	1.59	10,159
1 Year	3.21	10,321

Source: *Morningstar Mutual Funds*

Financial History

Figure 23.1 illustrates per-share data for a share outstanding throughout each period and selected ratio information for each year ended February 28.

Comments

T. Rowe Price Adjustable-Rate U.S. Government Fund used to be one of the group's more aggressive ARM funds. Rather than relying on just government-backed securities, as most ARM funds do, this fund kept about a third of its portfolio in private ARMs. The main advantage of these private issues is that they are less expensive than government agency ARMs and, therefore, less hurt by falling interest rates and faster prepayments.

The fund also maintained a fairly large 5 percent investment in higher-yielding but risky interest-only STRIPS (IOs). These IOs, where the cash flow comes entirely from the interest component of the

FIGURE 23.1 T. Rowe Price Adjustable-Rate U.S. Government Fund Per-Share Data and Selected Ratios

	Investment Activities				Distributions			End of Period					
Year Ended, February 28	Net Asset Value, Beginning of Period	Net Investment Income	Net Realized and Unrealized Gain (Loss) on Investments	Total from Investment Activities	Net Investment Income	Net Realized Gain	Total Distributions	Net Asset Value, End of Period	Total Return	Net Assets (in thousands)	Ratio of Expenses to Average Net Assets	Ratio of Net Investment Income to Average Net Assets	Portfolio Turnover Rate
1992†*	$5.00	$.16	$(.03)	$.13	$(.16)	—	$(.16)	$4.97	6.2%††	$342,939	0.00%††††	7.45%	98.4%
1993	4.97	.29	(.13)	.16	(.30)	—	(.30)	4.83	3.3%	476,448	0.25%††††	5.96%	110.8%

† For the period September 30, 1991 (commencement of operations) to February 29, 1992.

†† An annualized, not actual, return. The Fund's average monthly return from inception to fiscal year-end was multiplied by 12 to provide an annualized (not compounded) return.

††† T. Rowe Price agreed to bear all expenses of the Fund through June 30, 1992. Excludes expenses in excess of a 0.20% voluntary expense limitation in effect July 1, 1992 through July 31, 1992, and a 0.30% voluntary expense limitation in effect August 1, 1992 through August 31, 1992, and a 0.40% voluntary expense limitation in effect September 1, 1992 through June 30, 1993.

* Year ended February 29.

Source: T. Rowe Price Adjustable-Rate U.S. Government Fund prospectus dated July 1, 1993

underlying mortgage pool, suffer severe price drops when prepayments eliminate the principal from which their income is derived.

In 1993 the fund drastically cut its investment in private ARMs (to about 6 percent of its portfolio as of the end of 1993) because of the difficulty in obtaining adequate information on them and because they had experienced high prepayment rates. The fund also got rid of all its IOs. When interest rates fell and prepayments rose over the past couple of years, IOs were some of the mortgage market's worst performers. Rather than suffer any more downside for the sake of higher yield or as a hedge against rising rates, management took the safer route by getting out.

To replace the private ARMs and IOs, the fund has been building its investment in government-backed agency ARMs. It has found that the GNMA ARMs are cheap and experience lower prepayment rates. These GNMAs had been boosted from 6 percent to 17 percent of assets in April 1993.

Even with the reduction of interest-only STRIPS and private adjustable-rate mortgages in the portfolio, the key thing that the fund needs to do is maintain good returns.

When considering a fund for purchase in the government bond—adjustable-rate mortgage group, an investor should pay particular attention to how low management is able to keep total operating expenses, as well as any sales fees that may be levied against the purchaser. This is a relatively new group with little historical performance to look at.

Portfolio
Total fixed-income securities: 23 as of March 31, 1993

Security	Maturity
FNMA ARM CMT	11/01/29
FHLMC ARM CMT	12/01/20
FNMA Bond ARM	09/01/26
FNMA ARM COF	05/01/31
FHLMC ARM COF	08/01/31
FNMA ARM CMT	02/20/23
Resolution Trust ARM CMT	01/25/22
GNMA 12%	05/15/15
Western Federal ARM COF	06/01/20
Western Federal ARM COF	03/01/19
U.S. Treasury Note 4.25%	01/31/95
Western Federal ARM COF	05/01/18

Resolution Trust ARM COF	07/27/20
Resolution Trust ARM COF	02/25/21
Great Western Bank ARM COF	08/15/17
Resolution Trust ARM CMT	11/15/20
Resolution Trust ARM COF	01/25/27
Salomon Brothers ARM COF	08/25/18
Rylan Mortgage ARM COF	05/25/17
Western Federal ARM COF	07/01/18
Resolution Trust ARM	04/25/21
Ryland Mercury ARM COF	10/15/18
Resolution Trust ARM CMT	12/26/20

Composition of Portfolio
As of June 30, 1993

Cash	97.0% (includes ARMs)
Bonds	3.0

Other Government Bond—Adjustable-Rate Funds

	Five-Year Growth of $10,000*
American Capital Federal Mortgage Trust—Class A	$14,574
Asset Management Fund Adjustable-Rate Mortgage Portfolio	N/A
Benham Adjustable-Rate Government Securities Fund	N/A
Federated ARMs Fund—Institutional Shares	15,839
Fortress Adjustable-Rate U.S. Government Fund	N/A
Franklin Adjustable U.S. Government Securities Fund	14,371
Goldman Sachs Adjustable-Rate Government Agency Fund	N/A
Merrill Lynch Adjustable-Rate Securities Fund— Class B	N/A
Overland Express Variable-Rate Government Fund	N/A
Putnam Adjustable-Rate U.S. Government Trust—Class A	13,591
TNE Adjustable-Rate U.S. Government Fund	N/A

*For the period ending July 31, 1993

Funds listed in **bold type** are available by direct purchase.

N/A indicates that the fund has not had five full years of performance history.

Summary

Funds in the government bond—adjustable-rate group are designed for investors who seek higher monthly dividend income than that provided by money market securities and who want minimal changes in share price. Investors should keep in mind, however, that some funds are willing to take on more risk to increase income and total return than many shareholders would like. Results for funds in this group are mixed, and because this is a fairly young investment category, the jury is still out in terms of assessing long-term results.

General Government Bond Funds

Usual Investment Objective of the Group

Mutual funds included in the general government bond funds group seek current income by investing primarily in securities issued or guaranteed by the U.S. government and its agencies or instrumentalities. Such funds have the flexibility to invest in securities ranging in maturity from short-term U.S. Treasury bills to longer-term notes and bonds. The funds' portfolios of high-quality, income-producing securities are designed to protect shareholders against credit risk.

Survey of the Group

General government bond funds are bought by investors looking for high yield with low credit risk. While fund shares are neither insured nor guaranteed by the U.S. government, there is essentially no credit risk related to securities issued or guaranteed by the government.

In recent years, U.S. Treasury bonds have been the place to be for funds in the general government bond group. As long-bond yields have tumbled to historic lows, funds that took on maximum interest rate risk by investing heavily in long-maturity obligations have been well rewarded for doing so. Treasury bonds are the ideal vehicle in a falling interest rate environment because they cannot be called away prior to their stated maturity dates. During this period, funds that were heavily weighted with long-maturity Treasuries turned in the best total-return performances. Advantage Government Securities, for example, did very well with 20 percent of its portfolio in aggressive zero-coupon bonds and an extremely long duration of over 18 years.

On the other hand, funds that tried to enhance yield by holding mortgage-backed securities found the going tougher. Because mortgages can always be refinanced, these bonds have fairly short expected lives; therefore, they tend to lag during bond rallies. While interest rates were falling in the last couple of years, many homeowners rushed to refinance their homes, and prepayments hit record levels. As a result, investors received their principal earlier than expected and were forced to reinvest at lower rates. This put pressure on the entire mortgage sector, causing their yield spreads to widen relative to Treasuries.

Many portfolio managers expect interest rates to remain low or decline even further, but if that doesn't happen, the funds that have extended their maturity duration to enjoy the bond market rally will absorb painful losses. Investors who aren't willing to take on that risk should stay with the group's shorter-duration funds, such as Dreyfus Short-Intermediate Government Fund and Fidelity Spartan Limited Maturity Government Fund.

The following table indicates historical average annual total returns of the general government bond group and the Lehman Brothers Government Bond Index for years ending December 31.

**General Government Bond Group versus
Lehman Brothers Government Bond Index**

	Group Total Return	LBGB Index		Group Total Return	LBGB Index
1983	7.42%	7.40%	1988	6.68%	7.23%
1984	12.94	14.50	1989	12.08	14.22
1985	17.66	20.43	1990	8.29	8.71
1986	12.06	15.31	1991	14.03	15.32
1987	1.31	2.20	1992	5.88	7.23

Source: *Morningstar Mutual Funds*

Recommended Fund

Strong Government Securities Fund
P.O. Box 2936
Milwaukee, WI 53201-2936
800-368-1030

Portfolio manager: Brad Tank and Jeff Koch
Investment adviser: Strong/Corneliuson Capital Management
Sales fees: No-load
Management fee: 0.60%
12b-1 fee: None
Other expenses: 0.57%
Total operating expense: 1.17%
Minimum initial purchase: $1,000 (additional: $50)
Minimum IRA purchase: $250 (additional: $50)
Date of inception: October 29, 1986
Net assets of fund as of July 31, 1993: $164 million

Investment Objective
Strong Government Securities Fund seeks a high level of current income.

Investment Policy
Strong Government Securities Fund is designed primarily for investors who seek higher yields than money market funds generally offer and the low credit risk that U.S. government securities generally carry, but who are also willing to accept some principal fluctuation in order to achieve that objective.

The fund normally invests at least 80 percent of its assets in government securities. The balance of assets may be invested in other investment-grade fixed-income securities. The fund may engage in hedging activities through the use of futures and options contracts. The fund expects a relatively high turnover rate, but it intends to limit turnover so that realized gains on securities held for less than three months do not exceed 30 percent of its gross income. The average weighted portfolio maturity varies in response to changing interest rates.

The fund does not invest in non-investment-grade securities. As a fundamental policy, for the purpose of realizing additional income, the fund may lend securities with a value of up to 30 percent of its total assets to broker-dealers, institutional investors, or other persons.

Performance
The following tables indicate historical average annual total returns of Strong Government Securities Fund and the Lehman Brothers Government Bond Index for years ending December 31, followed by total returns and the growth of $10,000 invested for different periods ending July 31, 1993.

Strong Government Securities Fund versus
Lehman Brothers Government Bond Index

	Fund Total Return	LBGB Index		Fund Total Return	LBGB Index
1987	3.46%	2.20%	1990	8.71%	8.71%
1988	10.51	7.23	1991	16.66	15.32
1989	9.97	14.22	1992	9.24	7.23

Total Returns for Different Periods Ending July 31, 1993

	Fund Total Return	Growth of $10,000
3 Months	2.57%	$10,257
6 Months	6.97	10,697
1 Year	13.56	11,356
3-Year Average	13.33	14,554
5-Year Average	11.67	17,366

Source: *Morningstar Mutual Funds*

Financial History

Figure 23.2 provides per-share data for a share outstanding throughout each period and selected ratio information for each fiscal year ending December 31.

Comments

Strong Government Securities Fund has consistently performed in the top 10 percent of its group. Based on total return since inception on October 29, 1986, the fund was ranked number 2 out of 51 funds in the general U.S. government category by Lipper Analytical Services.

The fund has kept its risk level well below average since shortly after Brad Tank was appointed portfolio manager in June of 1990. With co-manager Jeff Koch, he has invested the fund in some untypical investments to get an edge. These included a stake in FNMA cross-currency-linked notes in 1992, which the managers were able to buy cheaply after the European Exchange Rate Mechanism had problems in September of that year. The bond's floating-rate coupons rose and boosted the fund's returns before the issues were sold.

In 1993, the fund gained from a 15 percent commitment in corporate debt. The fund benefited from the higher coupons available from corporate bonds, reaping the profits of substantial price gains as yield spreads tightened under improving economic conditions and interest rates fell.

FIGURE 23.2 Strong Government Securities Fund Per-Share Data and
                Selected Ratios

Strong Government Securities Fund

	Year Ended December 31,						
	1986[1]	1987	1988	1989	1990	1991	1992
Investment Income	$ 0.14	$ 0.75	$0.72	$ 0.91	$ 0.85	$ 0.85	$ 0.88
Expenses	(0.01)	(0.10)	(0.04)	(0.13)	(0.13)	(0.08)	(0.08)
Net Investment Income	0.13	0.65	0.68	0.78	0.72	0.77	0.80
Dividends from Net Investment Income	(0.13)	(0.65)	(0.68)	(0.78)	(0.72)	(0.77)	(0.80)
Net Realized and Unrealized Gains or (Losses) on Investments	0.09	(0.34)	0.32	0.17	0.12	0.84	0.11
Distributions from Net Realized Gains and Other Capital Sources	-	-	(0.09)	(0.07)	(0.10)	(0.17)	(0.49)
Net Increase (Decrease) in Net Asset Value	0.09	(0.34)	0.23	0.10	0.02	0.67	(0.38)
Net Asset Value at Beginning of Period	10.00	10.09	9.75	9.98	10.08	10.10	10.77
Net Asset Value at End of Period	$10.09	$ 9.75	$9.98	$10.08	$10.10	$10.77	$10.39
Ratio of Expenses to Average Net Assets[2]	0.6%*	1.0%	0.4%	1.3%	1.3%	0.8%	0.7%
Ratio of Net Investment Income to Average Net Assets	7.2%*	6.6%	6.9%	7.6%	7.2%	7.5%	7.7%
Portfolio Turnover Rate	0.0%*	715.0%	1727.8%	421.6%	254.2%	292.9%	628.8%
Shares Outstanding at End of Period**	88	1,167	2,546	3,484	4,069	4,824	7,907

* Calculated on an annualized basis.
** In thousands.
(1) Inception date was October 29, 1986.
(2) The Advisor voluntarily waived its entire advisory fee from inception of the Fund through
    April 1989 and a portion of its advisory fee in 1990 and 1992. In addition, the Advisor vol-
    untarily waived its entire advisory fee for 1991. In 1988, 1989, and 1990, the Advisor also
    voluntarily absorbed certain other expenses of the Fund. Without these waivers and absorp-
    tions, the ratio of expenses to average net assets would have been 1.2%, 1.6%, 1.6%, 1.6%,
    1.5%, 1.4%, and 1.2% for the periods ended December 31, 1986, 1987, 1988, 1989, 1990,
    1991, and 1992, respectively.

Source: Strong Government Securities Fund prospectus dated May 1, 1993

The portfolio managers are not trying to predict where interest rates will go next, so the fund's duration is near the average for government bond funds. However, they are maintaining some long-term Treasury bonds in the portfolio to add some extra price appreciation potential for when interest rates may decline.

Strong Government Securities Fund has been one of the best total-return offerings in its group. It makes sense for investors who don't mind limited exposure to lower-quality bonds.

Portfolio

Total fixed-income securities: 49 as of March 31, 1993

25 Top Holdings

Security	Maturity
Postal Square 8.95%	06/15/22
U.S. Treasury Note 6%	11/30/97
FNMA CMO REMIC 4%	12/25/20
FHLMC 9.75%	08/01/02
FNMA 12%	02/01/19
U.S. Treasury Bond 8.125%	08/15/19
FNMA CMO REMIC PAC P/O 0%	11/25/15
NewsAmerica Holdings 9.25%	02/01/13
TKR Cable 10.5%	10/30/07
Time Warner 8.875%	10/01/02
Small Business Administration I/O 2.531%	12/15/18
Chrysler Financial FRN	05/15/96
FHLMC 14%	04/01/16
FNMA RESET 8.265%	08/19/02
U.S. Treasury Bond P/O 0%	08/15/20
GNMA 13%	11/15/14
U.S. Treasury Note 7.875%	02/15/96
FHLMC 12.25%	01/01/23
FHLMC 18.1%	11/15/20
U.S. Treasury Bond 12.75%	11/15/10
GNMA 14%	12/20/14
GNMA 13.5%	11/15/12
GNMA 14.5%	11/15/12
FNMA 12.5%	02/01/11
FHLMC 11.25%	01/01/01

Composition of Portfolio

As of June 30, 1993

Cash	9.2%
Bonds	90.8

Other General Government Bond Funds

	Five-Year Growth of $10,000*
AARP GNMA & U.S. Treasury Fund	**$16,082**
Advantage Government Securities	17,597
Bernstein Government Short-Duration Portfolio	**N/A**
Fidelity Government Securities Fund	**17,427**
Fidelity Spartan Limited Maturity Government Fund	**15,354**
Government Income Securities	**15,720**
Midwest Income Trust Intermediate-Term Government Fund	**16,018**
Smith Barney Shearson Government Securities Fund—Class B	16,859
State Street Research Government Income Fund—Class A	**16,694**

*For the period ending July 31, 1993

Funds listed in **bold type** are available by direct purchase.

N/A indicates that the fund has not had five full years of performance history.

Summary

Funds in the general government bond group are designed for investors who seek higher yields than money market funds usually offer and who want the low credit risk that U.S. government securities carry. Investors should be aware, however, that some funds are willing to take on more risk than many shareholders might feel comfortable with. Investors who want to avoid this additional risk should look at funds that are conservative in their choice of maturities and types of securities purchased for their portfolios.

Government Bond—Mortgage Funds

Usual Investment Objective of the Group

Mutual funds included in the government bond—mortgage funds group seek to provide current income along with preserving capital. These funds invest primarily in mortgage-backed securities guaranteed as to timely payment of principal and interest by the U.S. government and issued by its agencies or instrumentalities. Many of these funds have the flexibility to invest in other securities, such as intermediate- and long-term U.S. government bonds, privately issued mortgage-related securities and repurchase agreements collateralized by mortgage securities.

Survey of the Group

Prepayments have been a continuing problem for funds in the government bond—mortgage group, as refinancing of home mortgages have occurred in record numbers. In mid-1993 the Federal Home Loan Mortgage Corporation reported that prepayment speeds for securities carrying coupons of 7 percent and 7.5 percent were 20 percent faster than in the previous reporting period. With no sign of a slowdown, that trend will most likely continue if interest rates continue to fall.

Not all mortgage funds were suffering, however, as some managers circumvented prepayments by using precautionary measures. These included buying discount coupons that were not as susceptible to refinancings and purchasing mortgage-backed securities with lock-out provisions, such as GNMA graduated-payment mortgages and construction-loan certificates.

A popular safeguard strategy is the "dollar roll." This is done by selling securities forward with an agreement to buy them back within 30 or 60 days, and thus shifting to others the risk of holding mortgages vulnerable to prepayments. Portfolio managers have taken the proceeds from this transaction and invested them in safe short-term instruments, such as repurchase agreements. This strategy was successful for Managers Intermediate Mortgage Securities Fund and Alliance Mortgage Securities Income Fund.

Some funds that did not take advantage of protection strategies were hit hard in 1993. Such funds include Cardinal Government Obligations Fund, Colonial U.S. Government Trust and Federated Income Trust—

Institutional Shares. A continuing downtrend in interest rates can make life difficult for many funds in the government bond—mortgage group.

The following table indicates historical average annual total returns of the government bond—mortgage group and the Lehman Brothers Government Bond Index for years ending December 31.

Government Bond—Mortgage Group versus
Lehman Brothers Government Bond Index

	Group Total Return	LBGB Index		Group Total Return	LBGB Index
1983	8.12%	7.40%	1988	7.79%	7.03%
1984	13.36	14.50	1989	12.78	14.22
1985	19.13	20.43	1990	9.24	8.71
1986	11.07	15.31	1991	14.46	15.32
1987	2.11	2.20	1992	6.36	7.23

Source: *Morningstar Mutual Funds*

Recommended Fund

Vanguard Fixed-Income Securities GNMA Portfolio
Vanguard Financial Center
P.O. Box 2600
Valley Forge, PA 19482
800-662-7447

Portfolio manager: Paul G. Sullivan
Investment adviser: Wellington Management
Sales fees: No-load
Management fee: 0.13%
12b-1 fee: None
Other expenses: 0.16%
Total operating expense: 0.29%
Minimum initial purchase: $3,000 (additional: $100)
Minimum IRA purchase: $500 (additional: $50)
Date of inception: June 27, 1980
Net assets of fund as of March 31, 1993: $7.4 billion

Investment Objective
Vanguard Fixed-Income Securities GNMA Portfolio seeks a high level of current income consistent with safety of principal and maintenance of liquidity.

Investment Policy
The Vanguard GNMA Portfolio invests at least 80 percent of its assets in Government National Mortgage Association (GNMA or Ginnie Mae) pass-through certificates. The balance of the portfolio's assets may be invested in other U.S. Treasury or U.S. government agency securities, as well as in repurchase agreements collateralized by such securities. The portfolio may also be invested in bond (interest rate) futures and options to a limited extent.

The mortgage loans underlying GNMA certificates are either insured by the Federal Housing Administration (FHA) or guaranteed by the Department of Veterans Affairs (VA). They are issued by such lenders as mortgage bankers, commercial banks, and savings and loan associations. Each pool of mortgage loans must be approved by GNMA, a U.S. government corporation within the U.S. Department of Housing and Urban Development. Once GNMA approval is obtained, the timely payment of interest and principal on each underlying mortgage loan is guaranteed by the "full faith and credit" of the U.S. government.

Although stated maturities on GNMA certificates generally range from 25 to 30 years, effective maturities are usually much shorter due to the prepayment of the underlying mortgages by homeowners. On average, GNMA certificates are repaid within 12 years and so are classified as intermediate-term securities.

Performance
The following tables provide historical 12-month total returns for Vanguard Fixed-Income Securities GNMA Portfolio and the Lehman Brothers Government Bond Index for years ending December 31, followed by total returns and the growth of $10,000 invested for different periods ending March 31, 1993.

**Vanguard Fixed-Income Securities GNMA Portfolio
versus Lehman Brothers Government Bond Index**

	Fund Total Return	LBGB Index		Fund Total Return	LBGB Index
1983	9.65%	7.40%	1986	11.69%	15.31%
1984	14.03	14.50	1987	2.15	2.20
1985	20.68	20.43	1988	8.81	7.03

| 1989 | 14.77 | 14.22 | 1991 | 16.77 | 15.32 |
| 1990 | 10.32 | 8.71 | 1992 | 6.85 | 7.23 |

Total Returns for Different Periods Ending March 31, 1993

	Fund Total Return	Growth of $10,000
3 Months	2.67%	$10,267
6 Months	3.50	10,350
1 Year	11.46	11,146
3-Year Average	12.28	14,155
5-Year Average	11.07	16,904
10-Year Average	11.46	29,593

Source: *Morningstar Mutual Funds*

Financial History

Figure 23.3 provides historical per-share data on Vanguard Fixed-Income Securities GNMA Portfolio for a share outstanding throughout each period and selected ratio information for each year ended January 31.

Comments

Vanguard Fixed-Income Securities GNMA Portfolio has a risk/return ratio that is the highest of all GNMA funds, according to *Morningstar Mutual Funds,* and ranks second among all funds in the government bond—mortgage group as a whole. The fund has shown consistently high returns over the years. Its returns have never fallen below the group average over the past 12 years.

The fund's top returns result largely from its very low expense ratio of 0.29 percent. The most obvious benefit of such low expenses is the approximately 60-basis-point advantage the fund has over its more expensive peers. The average expense ratio for the group was 0.92 percent in 1992. That dropped to 0.84 percent in mid-1993. Low expenses also mean that the portfolio manager does not need to hold premium coupons to provide a competitive yield, but can invest in more discount coupons than his competitors when he thinks interest rates will fall. As a result, the fund has more flexibility in different market environments.

Flexibility does not extend to selection of securities. Although the fund's charter permits it to hold up to 20 percent of its assets in other securities, Paul Sullivan has traditionally kept the entire portfolio in Ginnie Maes, not even Treasury bonds. This policy can limit the fund

FIGURE 23.3 Vanguard Fixed-Income Securities GNMA Portfolio Per-Share Data and Selected Ratios

GNMA PORTFOLIO
Year Ended January 31,

	1993	1992	1991	1990	1989	1988	1987	1986	1985	1984
Net Asset Value, Beginning of Period	$10.25	$ 9.85	$9.54	$9.34	$9.69	$10.10	$ 9.92	$9.25	$9.20	$9.21
Investment Activities										
Income	.808	.860	.887	.907	.916	.922	1.004	1.09	1.13	1.12
Expenses	(.030)	(.029)	(.032)	(.029)	(.034)	(.033)	(.039)	(.05)	(.05)	(.05)
Net Investment Income	.778	.831	.855	.878	.882	.889	.965	1.04	1.08	1.07
Net Realized and Unrealized Gain (Loss) on Investments	.250	.400	.310	.200	(.350)	(.410)	.186	.67	.05	(.01)
Total From Investment Activities	1.028	1.231	1.165	1.078	.532	.479	1.151	1.71	1.13	1.06
Distributions										
Net Investment Income	(.778)	(.831)	(.855)	(.878)	(.882)	(.889)	(.965)	(1.04)	(1.08)	(1.07)
Realized Net Gains	—	—	—	—	—	—	(.006)	—	—	—
Total Distributions	(.778)	(.831)	(.855)	(.878)	(.882)	(.889)	(.971)	(1.04)	(1.08)	(1.07)
Net Asset Value, End of Period	$10.50	$10.25	$9.85	$9.54	$9.34	$ 9.69	$10.10	$9.92	$9.25	$9.20
Ratio of Expenses to Average Net Assets	.29%	.29%	.34%	.31%	.35%	.35%	.38%	.50%	.58%	.58%
Ratio of Net Investment Income to Average Net Assets	7.38%	8.22%	8.95%	9.25%	9.35%	9.35%	9.41%	10.16%	11.90%	11.31%
Portfolio Turnover Rate	7%	1%	1%	9%	8%	22%	28%	32%	23%	21%
Number of Shares Outstanding, End of Period (Thousands)	682,855	508,101	275,309	223,172	204,237	196,967	235,673	127,230	32,311	18,736

Source: Vanguard Fixed-Income Securities GNMA Portfolio prospectus dated May 31, 1993

at times, such as when rates dropped sharply in the first quarter of 1993 and the fund's performance lagged its peers.

Vanguard Fixed-Income Securities GNMA Portfolio has done an impressive job of staying ahead of the group's average, making the fund a good investment for investors who want pure Ginnie Mae exposure.

Portfolio
Total fixed-income securities: 36
as of December 31, 1993

25 Top Holdings

Security	Maturity
GNMA 9%	04/15/22
GNMA 9.5%	06/15/22
GNMA 8.5%	06/15/22
GNMA 10%	07/15/22
GNMA 8%	03/15/22
GNMA 7.5%	06/15/21
GNMA 10.5%	03/15/21
GNMA 9.25%	10/01/23
GNMA 11%	02/15/16
GNMA 12%	09/15/15
GNMA 8.75%	08/15/24
GNMA 15-Year 9%	07/15/01
GNMA 12.5%	08/15/15
GNMA 7%	01/15/19
GNMA 8.25%	07/15/08
GNMA 11.5%	12/15/15
GNMA 13%	06/15/15
GNMA GPM 9.25%	05/15/18
GNMA GPM 11.5%	08/15/13
GNMA GPM 11.25%	02/20/16
GNMA 15.25%	08/15/14
GNMA GPM 11%	09/15/10
GNMA 13.5%	12/15/14
GNMA GPM 12%	02/15/13
GNMA GPM 13%	01/15/13

Composition of Portfolio
As of March 31, 1993

Cash	6.0%
Bonds	94.0

Other Highly Regarded Government Bond—Mortgage Funds

	Five-Year Growth of $10,000*
Alliance Mortgage Securities Income Fund—Class A	$16,504
Benham GNMA Income Fund	**16,662**
Dreyfus GNMA Fund	**15,771**
Federated GNMA Trust—Institutional Shares	**16,760**
Fidelity Mortgage Securities Portfolio	**15,706**
Franklin U.S. Government Securities Series	16,311
Lexington GNMA Income Fund	**16,467**
Managers Intermediate Mortgage Securities Fund	**18,433**
Scudder GNMA Fund	**16,259**
SEI Cash+Plus Trust GNMA Portfolio—Class A	**16,805**
T. Rowe Price GNMA Fund	**16,171**

*For the period ending March 31, 1993

Funds listed in **bold type** are available by direct purchase.

Summary

Funds in the government bond—mortgage group are designed for investors who seek high yields with little or no credit risk. Funds that invest primarily in Government National Mortgage Association securities have historically been rewarded with high returns. However, they have suffered in recent years as prepayments on residential mortgages have eroded much of the returns investors had become accustomed to in 1992 and 1993.

Government Bond—Treasury Funds

Usual Investment Objective of the Group

Mutual funds included in the government bond—Treasury group have a variety of investment objectives. AIM Limited Maturity Treasury Shares seeks liquidity with minimum fluctuation of principal value and the highest total return possible, while Benham Treasury Note Fund (my recommended fund) seeks the highest level of current income consistent with the conservation of assets. Most funds look for current income and protection of capital, with varying degrees of emphasis.

To be included in the group, a fund must have a preponderance of its assets invested in U.S. Treasury bills, notes and bonds, and other "full faith and credit" obligations of the U.S. government.

Survey of the Group

The U.S. Treasury and government securities market, which includes Treasury bills, notes, bonds, zeros, agency securities and mortgage-backed instruments, is by far the largest securities market in the world. It has a daily trading volume that exceeds $100 billion. The basic attraction for this market is safety. For 200 years the U.S. government has made timely interest and principal payments on the funds it borrows. The "full faith and credit" pledge of the U.S. government is the best credit guarantee an investor can receive.

Funds in the government bond—Treasury group invest primarily in securities issued by the U.S. Treasury, rather than securities guaranteed by the U.S. government or its agencies.

One feature of Treasuries is that they are not callable. Because they have no call risk, they are highly sensitive to interest rate changes and therefore are very volatile. Long-term Treasury bonds are particularly volatile, which means that funds with heavy portfolio positions in long bonds are subject to significant price fluctuation.

The volatility of funds with large positions in long Treasury bonds resulted in handsome returns during the time when interest rates were falling in the last few years. For example, Benham Target Maturities 2015 Portfolio had outstanding total returns in 1989, 1991 and the first quarter of 1993, when interest rates were in steep declines. The fund is made up entirely of zero-coupon obligations and had returns of 34.7, 16.4 and 7.3 percent, respectively, in those periods. This volatility has a flip side, however; in 1987, when interest rates spiked upward, the fund had a negative total return of 18.49 percent.

Many investors, skeptical that interest rates would fall much farther, began moving out of the volatile Benham fund and such long-duration funds as the Vanguard Fixed-Income Securities Fund Long-Term U.S. Treasury Portfolio in early 1993 in favor of the relative safety of shorter bond funds. These included AIM Limited Maturity Treasury Shares, Federated Short-Intermediate Government Trust and Vanguard Short-Term U.S. Treasury Portfolio. The attraction of the shorter-term funds is that they offer investors a yield that beats money market funds with no credit risk and only moderate interest rate sensitivity.

The following table indicates historical average annual total returns of the Government Bond—Treasury Group and of the Lehman Brothers Government Bond Index for years ending December 31.

Government Bond—Treasury Group versus
Lehman Brothers Government Bond Index

	Group Total Return	LBGB Index		Group Total Return	LBGB Index
1983	7.52%	7.40%	1988	10.12%	7.03%
1984	13.09	14.50	1989	14.52	14.22
1985	17.91	20.43	1990	7.33	8.71
1986	27.09	15.31	1991	14.98	15.32
1987	−0.04	2.20	1992	6.47	7.23

Source: *Morningstar Mutual Funds*

Recommended Fund

Benham Treasury Note Fund
1665 Charleston Road
Mountain View, CA 94043
800-472-3389

Portfolio manager: David W. Schroeder
Investment adviser: Benham Management
Sales fees: No-load
Management fee: 0.26%
12b-1 fee: None
Other expenses: 0.27%
Total operating expense: 0.53%
Minimum initial purchase: $1,000 (additional: $100)
Minimum IRA purchase: $100 (additional: $25)
Date of inception: May 16, 1980
Net assets of fund as of March 31, 1993: $390 million

Investment Objective
Benham Treasury Note Fund seeks to earn and distribute the highest level of current income consistent with the conservation of assets and the safety provided by U.S. Treasury notes, bills and bonds.

Investment Policy

The fund will invest at least 65 percent of its total net assets in U.S. Treasury notes. The remaining 35 percent may be invested in any combination of Treasury bills and bonds. The fund may not invest in repurchase agreements, making it a complete Treasury fund. The fund's weighted average portfolio maturity ranges from 13 months to ten years.

Performance

The tables below indicate annual total returns of Benham Treasury Note Fund for each year ending December 31 and comparative results for the Lehman Brothers Government Bond Index, followed by total returns and the growth of $10,000 invested for different periods ending August 31, 1993.

**Benham Treasury Note Fund versus
Lehman Brothers Government Bond Index**

	Fund Total Return	LBGB Index		Fund Total Return	LBGB Index
1983	7.52%	7.40%	1988	5.22%	7.03%
1984	12.32	14.50	1989	11.92	14.22
1985	17.67	20.43	1990	9.20	8.71
1986	13.32	15.31	1991	13.74	15.32
1987	−1.01	2.20	1992	6.56	7.23

Total Returns for Different Periods Ending August 31, 1993

	Fund Total Return	Growth of $10,000
3 Months	3.18%	$10,318
6 Months	3.98	10,398
1 Year	8.50	10,850
3-Year Average	11.10	13,713
5-Year Average	10.19	16,242
10-Year Average	10.18	26,359

Source: *Morningstar Mutual Funds*

Financial History

Figure 23.4 provides historical per-share data and ratios on Benham Treasury Note Fund. It is based on a single share outstanding throughout each fiscal year (which ends on the last day of September, except as noted).

FIGURE 23.4 Benham Treasury Note Fund Per-Share Data and
Selected Ratios

BENHAM TREASURY NOTE FUND
Years ended March 31

	1984	1985	1986	1987	1988	1989	1990	1991	1992	1993
Investment Income	$1.06	1.09	1.01	.81	.83	.83	.84	.82	.75	.62
Net Expenses	(.10)	(.10)	(.11)	(.10)	(.08)	(.07)	(.07)	(.07)	(.06)	(.06)
Net Investment Income	.96	.99	.90	.71	.75	.76	.77	.75	.69	.56
Distributions from Net Investment Income	(1.03)	(.93)	(.83)	(.89)	(.92)	(.75)	(.77)	(.75)	(.69)	(.56)
Distributions from Net Realized Gains	0	0	0	(.80)	(.03)	0	0	0	0	(.48)
Net Realized and Unrealized Gains (Losses) on Investments	(.15)	.16	1.55	(.08)	(.60)	(.49)	.24	.36	.29	.69
Net Asset Value at Beginning of Period	10.35	10.13	10.35	11.97	10.91	10.11	9.63	9.87	10.23	10.52
Net Asset Value at End of Period	$10.13	10.35	11.97	10.91	10.11	9.63	9.87	10.23	10.52	10.73
Ratio of Net Expenses to Average Daily Net Assets	1.00%	1.00%	1.00%	.93%	.75%	.75%	.75%	.73%	.59%	.53%
Ratio of Net Investment Income to Average Daily Net Assets	9.44%	9.76%	8.42%	6.26%	7.36%	7.67%	7.66%	7.49%	6.55%	5.18%
Portfolio Turnover Rate	N/A*	52.51%	293.90%	395.91%	465.35%	386.46%	216.84%	69.72%	148.75%	299.29%
Shares Outstanding at End of Period (in Thousands)	912	1,209	2,377	3,964	5,359	7,441	9,826	15,509	28,779	36,499

* U.S. government securities were excluded from the portfolio turnover rate calculation for years prior to 1985.

Source: Benham U.S. Treasury & Government Funds prospectus dated June 1, 1993

Comments

Benham Treasury Note Fund adopted the Merrill Lynch One- to Ten-Year Treasury Index as its benchmark in 1988, moderating its riskiness. Prior to that time the fund had often made big interest rate bets, which resulted in a high degree of share price risk. Since 1988, risk has been decreasing and now ranks well below the Treasury group average, according to *Morningstar Mutual Funds.*

The main reason for the fund's improving risk stance is its short maturity. While the fund's charter permits it to extend its average maturity out as far as ten years, it has recently tended to keep maturity between two and five years. With little downside potential in shorter-term Treasury notes, the fund's moderate posture has reduced its interest-rate sensitivity relative to its longer-maturity peers in the group.

The fund compares well with other funds that maintain similar maturity parameters. Its risk is slightly lower, yet its total returns have been a bit higher. While its yield is somewhat below that of the average fund in the Treasury group, it compares well against it shorter-maturity peers.

Apparently shareholders like the fund's more conservative stance. Its net assets have grown from some $66 million in 1988 to $129 million in 1990 and $390 million by March of 1993. Benham Treasury Note Fund is not likely to soar during bond rallies, but it has held up better in down markets than its more aggressive competitors. Finally, expenses have been decreasing in recent years, from 1 percent in 1986 to 0.53 percent as reported in the June 1, 1993 prospectus.

Portfolio

Total fixed-income securities: 21 Holdings
as of December 31, 1992

25 Top Holdings

Security	Maturity
U.S. Treasury Note 4.625%	12/31/94
U.S. Treasury Note 8.625%	01/15/95
U.S. Treasury Note 6.875%	04/30/97
U.S. Treasury Note 7.875%	02/15/96
U.S. Treasury Note 7.5%	11/15/01
U.S. Treasury Note 4.625%	11/30/94
U.S. Treasury Note 7.75%	03/31/96
U.S. Treasury Note 7.875%	04/15/98
U.S. Treasury Note 6.875%	03/31/97

U.S. Treasury Note 8.875%	11/15/98
U.S. Treasury Note 7.625%	04/30/96
U.S. Treasury Note 0%	08/15/97
U.S. Treasury Note 10.5%	02/15/95
U.S. Treasury Note 8.875%	02/15/99
U.S. Treasury Note 7.875%	08/15/01
U.S. Treasury Note 8%	05/15/01
U.S. Treasury Note 8.25%	07/15/98
U.S. Treasury Note 9.25%	08/15/98
U.S. Treasury Note 8.75%	08/15/00
U.S. Treasury Note 8.5%	02/15/00
U.S. Treasury Note 5.125%	11/15/95

Composition of Portfolio
As of March 31, 1993

Bonds   100%

Other Government Bond—Treasury Funds

	Five-Year Growth of $10,000*
AIM Limited Maturity Treasury Shares	**$14,707**
Benham Target Maturities Trust 2015	**19,466**
Federated Intermediate Government Trust—Institutional Shares	**15,699**
Federated Short-Intermediate Government Trust Institutional Shares	**14,707**
ISI Total Return U.S. Treasury Fund	N/A
Midwest Income Trust Intermediate-Term Government Fund	**15,592**
Vanguard Fixed-Income Securities Fund Long-Term U.S. Treasury Portfolio	**16,805** **17,647**
Vanguard Fixed-Income Securities Fund Short-Term U.S. Treasury Portfolio	**N/A**

*For the period ending March 31, 1993

Funds listed in **bold type** are available by direct purchase.
N/A indicates that the fund has not had five full years of operation.

Summary

Funds in the government bond—Treasury group offer the potential for higher yields than money market funds to investors willing to accept some market risk. But investors should be aware that risk is relative, and that some funds in this group are more aggressive than others and can be quite volatile. Such funds can produce high total returns in declining markets, but may give back much of the gains when interest rates spike back up.

Chapter 24

Investing in Municipal Bond Funds

Municipal Bond Funds

Usual Investment Objective of the Group

Mutual funds in the municipal bond funds group seek income by investing primarily in tax-free bonds issued by any state or municipality. These municipal bonds, similar to bonds issued by a corporation or the U.S. government, obligate the issuer to pay bondholders a fixed amount of interest periodically, and to repay the principal value of the bond on a specific maturity date. Municipal bonds are considered fixed-income securities; they offer a steady rate of interest income. They are often called debt obligations, becuase they represent a loan to the bond issuer.

Survey of the Group

The main appeal of municipal bonds to investors is the fact that they provide income that is exempt from federal income taxes and, in some cases, from state and local taxes.

An added appeal of municipal bonds is diversification. Bonds have characteristics that are quite different from those of common stocks. Although they can be sharply volatile in price, bonds are generally considered more conservative than stocks, and they provide a way to diversify a portfolio heavily weighted toward equities.

Like other mutual funds, municipal bond funds deliver an investment return in two forms: income return (yield) and capital return. Together, they provide the total return.

A municipal bond's yield is its interest income expressed as a percentage of its purchase price. For example, a bond that costs $1,000 and pays $70 each year provides a 7 percent yield. The capital return is a measure of the appreciation or depreciation in a bond's market price. Thus, if a $1,000 bond declines in price to $980, the capital return would be minus 2 percent.

The income return of a municipal bond is determined primarily by two factors: credit quality and maturity.

Credit quality assessments are made by independent organizations and are denoted by letter rating (see Chapter 4, "How Bonds Are Rated for Safety"). In general, you will earn a higher yield from a lower-quality municipal bond. For example, a B-rated bond generally provides a higher yield than an A-rated bond, and municipal bond funds carrying lower-rated bonds will pay higher yields than more conservative funds.

The *maturity* of a bond is set by its issuer and is expressed in days or years. You will earn a higher yield from a bond with a longer maturity, among bonds of similar quality. For example, a 30-year A-rated municipal bond generally delivers a higher yield than a 3-year A-rated bond.

The gain or loss you experience as a result of changes in a municipal bond's price—your capital return—is determined mainly by changes in interest rates. Bond prices tend to move inversely with interest rates. When interest rates go up, bond prices go down, and when rates go down, bond prices go up. In addition, greater price changes are experienced by longer-maturity municipal bonds than by shorter-term bonds. The table below shows the relationship of bond prices and interest rates.

Bond Prices and Interest Rates
Initial Principal of $1,000 and Yield of 7%

Bond Maturity	1% Rise in Rates		1% Decline in Rates	
Short-term (2.5-year maturity)	$978	–2.2%	$1,023	+ 2.3%
Intermediate-term (7-year maturity)	947	–5.3	1,056	+ 5.6
Long-term (20-year Maturity)	901	–9.9	1,116	+11.6

Source: The Vanguard Group *(How To Select a Tax-Free Bond),* 1993

Therefore, an investor should assess both market risk and credit risk before investing in a municipal bond fund.

Market risk is the degree at which you tolerate price fluctuations as a result of changes in interest rates, keeping in mind that bonds with longer maturities generally offer higher yields but also have the potential for greater price swings than bonds with shorter maturities.

Credit risk is the chance a bond will default as to interest or principal payments. Lower-quality bonds generally offer higher yields but also have greater risk of default.

The following table indicates the historical average annual total return of the municipal bond group and the Lehman Brothers Municipal Bond Index for years ending December 31.

Municipal Bond Group versus
Lehman Brothers Municipal Bond Index

	Group Total Return	*LBMB Index*		*Group Total Return*	*LBMB Index*
1983	9.90%	8.04%	1988	10.55%	10.17%
1984	9.00	10.55	1989	9.34	10.78
1985	18.20	20.03	1990	6.18	7.30
1986	16.66	19.31	1991	11.31	12.14
1987	-0.23	1.51	1992	8.41	8.81

Source: *Morningstar Mutual Funds,* Morningstar, Inc., 225 W. Wacker Dr., Chicago, IL 60606; 312-696-6532

Tax Effect of a Municipal Bond Fund

Before deciding on a specific tax-exempt investment, such as a municipal bond fund, you should determine whether taxable or tax-free income is better in your tax bracket. This can be done by calculating the "taxable equivalent yield" for the municipal bond fund you are considering and comparing it with the yield of a taxable fund with similar credit and maturity standards.

The taxable equivalent yield for a municipal bond fund is based upon the fund's current tax-exempt yield and your tax bracket. The formula is:

$$\frac{\text{Fund's Tax-Free Yield}}{100\% - \text{Your Tax Bracket}} = \frac{\text{Your Taxable}}{\text{Equivalent Yield}}$$

For example, if you are in the 28 percent federal tax bracket and can earn a tax-free yield of 6 percent, the taxable equivalent yield would be 8.33 percent.

$$\frac{6.0\%}{100\% - 28\%} = 8.33\%$$

Recommended Fund

Vanguard Municipal Bond Fund Intermediate-Term Portfolio
Vanguard Financial Center
P.O. Box 2600
Valley Forge, PA 19482
800-662-7447

Portfolio manager: Ian MacKinnon and Christopher Ryon
Investment adviser: Vanguard's Fixed-Income Group
Sales fees: No-load
Management fee: 0.11%
Investment advisory fee: 0.01%
12b-1 fee: None
Other expenses: 0.11%
Total operating expense: 0.23%
Minimum initial purchase: $3,000 (additional: $100)
Date of inception: September 1, 1977
Net assets of fund as of April 30, 1993: $4.284 billion

Investment Objective
Vanguard Municipal Bond Fund Intermediate-Term Portfolio seeks the highest level of income that is exempt from federal income tax and is consistent with preservation of capital.

Investment Policy
The fund invests primarily in municipal securities and expects to maintain a dollar-weighted average maturity between 7 and 12 years. There is no limit on the maturity of any individual security in the portfolio.

At least 95 percent of the municipal securities held in the portfolio must be rated a minimum of Baa (or BBB) by Moody's (or Standard & Poor's). No more than 20 percent of the portfolio will be held in the lowest investment grade rating.

Performance

The tables below indicate annual total returns of Vanguard Municipal Bond Fund Intermediate-Term Portfolio and the Lehman Brothers Municipal Bond Index for years ending December 31, followed by total returns and the growth of $10,000 invested for different periods ending April 30, 1993.

Vanguard Municipal Bond Fund Intermediate-Term Portfolio versus Lehman Brothers Municipal Bond Index

	Fund Total Return	LBMB Index		Fund Total Return	LBMB Index
1983	6.48%	8.04%	1988	10.00%	10.17%
1984	9.54	10.55	1989	10.00	10.78
1985	17.33	20.03	1990	7.20	7.30
1986	16.22	19.31	1991	12.16	12.14
1987	1.64	1.51	1992	8.86	8.81

Total Returns for Different Periods Ending April 30, 1993

	Fund Total Return	Growth of $10,000
3 Months	3.36%	$10,336
6 Months	8.40	10,840
1 Year	12.70	11,270
3-Year Average	11.17	13,739
5-Year Average	9.77	15,937
10-Year Average	9.60	25,009
15-Year Average	7.34	28,935

Source: *Morningstar Mutual Funds*

Financial History

Figure 24.1 details information about the financial history of Vanguard Municipal Bond Fund Intermediate-Term Portfolio. It uses the fund's fiscal year (which ends August 31) and expresses the information in terms of a single share outstanding throughout each fiscal period.

Comments

Vanguard Municipal Bond Fund Intermediate-Term Portfolio has achieved exceptional returns. It stands out among funds that label themselves intermediate-term. The fund has consistently ranked among the top performers over the last several years. Over the past five

FIGURE 24.1 Vanguard Municipal Bond Fund Intermediate-Term Portfolio Per-Share Data and Selected Ratios

Intermediate-Term Portfolio

	Year Ended August 31,									
	1992	1991	1990	1989	1988	1987	1986	1985	1984	1983
Net Asset Value Beginning of Year	$12.41	$11.90	$12.08	$11.71	$11.79	$12.15	$10.98	$10.44	$10.54	$10.14
Income	.776	.821	.852	.871	.834	.865	.931	.961	.937	.917
Expenses	(.029)	(.030)	(.030)	(.032)	(.034)	(.031)	(.039)	(.042)	(.042)	(.049)
Net Investment Income	.747	.791	.822	.839	.800	.834	.892	.919	.895	.868
Net Realized and Unrealized Gain (Loss) on Investments	.516	.605	(.114)	.370	.012	(.360)	1.190	.540	(.100)	.400
Total From Investment Activities	1.263	1.396	.708	1.209	.812	.474	2.082	1.459	.795	1.268
Distributions Net Investment Income	(.747)	(.791)	(.822)	(.839)	(.800)	(.834)	(.892)	(.919)	(.895)	(.868)
Realized Net Gain	(.076)	(.095)	(.066)	—	(.092)	—	(.020)	—	—	—
Total Distributions	(.823)	(.886)	(.888)	(.839)	(.892)	(.834)	(.912)	(.919)	(.895)	(.868)
Net Asset Value End of Year	$12.85	$12.41	$11.90	$12.08	$11.71	$11.79	$12.15	$10.98	$10.44	$10.54
Ratio of Expenses to Average Net Assets	.23%	.25%	.25%	.27%	.29%	.26%	.33%	.39%	.41%	.46%
Ratio of Net Investment Income to Average Net Assets	5.91%	6.49%	6.83%	7.03%	6.88%	6.94%	7.66%	8.53%	8.58%	7.85%
Portfolio Turnover Rate	32%	27%	54%	56%	89%	57%	13%	26%	55%	117%
Number of Shares Outstanding End of Year (Thousands)	241,400	161,630	105,787	83,226	67,857	78,034	66,824	37,506	20,031	14,245

Source: Vanguard Municipal Bond Fund prospectus dated April 3, 1993

years, it compounded annual returns at 9.77 percent, compared with 8.54 percent for the average intermediate-term offering.

The fund's success is based on two factors. First, it assumes more interest rate risk than many of its peers, because it emphasizes lower-coupon bonds with good call protection. This provided additional interest rate sensitivity, which boosted performance during a period of a sustained decline in interest rates. Second, the fund's expense ratio is 58 basis points lower than the norm of municipal bond funds nationally. This gives it a significant advantage.

The investment managers are neither bullish nor bearish on the bond market and are keeping the fund's maturity duration neutral. Since they believe the yield curve will not flatten significantly, assets remain laddered among bonds with different maturities. Credit quality remains fairly high, with 41 percent of assets in AAA-rated bonds and only a small portion of the fund in lower than investment-grade BBB-rated issues.

The fund is more volatile than most intermediate-term bond funds, and it will lose money if interest rates rise sharply. However, in the long term, it should continue to deliver a competitive yield and solid long-term returns.

Portfolio

Total stocks: 0 as of August 31, 1992

Total fixed-income securities: 251 as of August 31, 1992

20 Largest Holdings

Security	Maturity
MA Water Resource Authority 6.5%	07/15/19
NY Triborough Bridge & Tunnel Authority 6.6%	01/01/10
CA Los Angeles Transportation Commission Sales Tax 6.5%	07/01/10
GA State General Obligation 7%	11/01/07
NJ Turnpike Authority 6.5%	01/01/09
NJ Camden Utility Authority FGIC 0%	09/01/03
WI State General Obligation 6.25%	05/01/08
NJ Turnpike Authority 4.75%	01/01/06
TX Houston General Obligation 7%	03/01/08
MO New Madrid Revenue Electric 5.75%	06/01/03
TX Municipal Power Agency MBIA 6.1%	09/01/08
AZ Tucson USD FGIC 7.5%	07/01/08
PA State General Obligation 6.5%	11/01/07
RI Depositors Economic Protection 6.55%	08/01/10

NY Dormitory Authority University FGIC 6.375%	07/01/07
MA Rev Incl Finance Agency Biomedical Research 7.1%	08/01/99
IN University Student Fee 6.8%	08/01/04
IL Metro Pier & Exposition Authority 6.75%	06/01/10
FL Hillsborough General Obligation School District 7.1%	08/15/03
NY New York City Municipal Assistance 4.25%	01/15/94

Composition of Portfolio
As of March 31, 1993

Cash	10.0%
Bonds	90.0

Sector Weightings

General Obligation	25.29%	Education	11.04%
Utility	14.16	Transportation	17.35
Health	6.34	Lease	1.23
Water/Waste	7.15	Private	5.99
Housing	0.05	Miscellaneous	11.39

Other High-Performing Municipal Bond Funds

	Five-Year Growth of $10,000*
Fidelity Advisor High-Income Municipal Portfolio	**$17,951**
General Municipal Bond Fund	**17,657**
INVESCO Tax-Free Long-Term Bond Fund	**17,135**
SAFECO Municipal Bond Fund	16,970
Scudder High-Yield Tax-Free Fund	**17,081**
Scudder Managed Municipal Bonds	**16,841**
USAA Tax-Exempt Intermediate-Term Fund	**15,691**
Vanguard Municipal Bond Fund—High-Yield Portfolio	**17,273**
Vanguard Municipal Bond Fund Insured Long-Term Portfolio	**16,872**
Vanguard Municipal Bond Fund Long-Term Portfolio	**17,150**
Vista Tax-Free Income Fund	17,950

*For the period ending August 31, 1993

Funds listed in **bold type** are available by direct purchase.

Summary

Funds in the municipal bond group have experienced good total returns over the last ten years, benefiting from the long secular downtrend in interest rates. The municipal bond market won't always be as friendly as it has been lately, and investors may want to consider short- and medium-term bond funds that will not be as adversely affected by a possible future rise in interest rates. Short-term funds take on little risk but still offer fairly attractive returns.

Appendix

Mutual Fund Companies Whose Funds You Can Buy Directly—Without a Broker

This directory provides the addresses and telephone numbers of the mutual fund companies whose funds are available to investors by direct purchase.

AARP Funds
160 Federal Street
Boston, MA 02110
800-253-2277

Acorn Funds
227 West Monroe Street
Chicago, IL 60606
312-634-1900
800-922-6769

Advantage Funds
60 State Street
Boston, MA 02109
617-742-9858
800-523-5903

Afuture Fund, Inc.
251 Royal Palm Way
Palm Beach, FL 33480
407-822-3353
800-947-6984

Alger Funds
75 Maiden Lane
New York, NY 10038
212-806-8800
800-992-3863

Amana Mutual Fund Trust
101 Prospect Street
Bellingham, WA 98227-2838
206-734-9900
800-728-8762

Babson Funds
2440 Pershing Road
Kansas City, MO 64108
816-471-5200
800-422-2766

Bartlett Capital Trust
36 East Fourth Street
Cincinnati, OH 45202
513-621-4612
800-800-4612

Bascom Hill Funds
6411 Mineral Point Road
Madison, WI 53705
608-273-2020
800-767-0300

Beacon Hill Mutual Fund
75 Federal Street
Boston, MA 02100-1904
617-482-0795

The Benham Group
1665 Charleston Road
Mountain View, CA 94043-1211
415-965-8300
800-472-3389

Berger Funds
210 University Boulevard
Denver, CO 80206
303-329-0200
800-333-1001

Bernstein Funds
767 Fifth Avenue
New York, NY 10153
212-756-4097

Blanchard Funds
41 Madision Avenue
New York, NY 10010
212-779-7979
800-922-7771

Bond Portfolio for Endowments
Four Embarcadero Center
San Francisco, CA 94120-7650
415-421-9360
800-421-0180

Boston Company Funds
One Boston Place
Boston, MA 02109
617-956-9740
800-225-5267

Brandywine Fund
P.O. Box 4166
Greenville, DE 19807
302-656-6200

Brundage, Story and Rose
Investment Trust
312 Walnut Street
Cincinnati, OH 45202-3874
513-629-2000
800-543-0407

Bull & Bear Funds
11 Hanover Square
New York, NY 10005-3401
212-785-0900
800-847-4200

Century Shares Trust
1 Liberty Square
Boston, MA 02109
617-482-3060
800-321-1928

CGM Funds
222 Berkeley Street
Boston, MA 02116
617-859-7714
800-345-4048

Charter Capital Funds
4920 West Vliet Street
Milwaukee, WI 53208
414-257-1842

Clipper Fund
9601 Wilshire Boulevard
Beverly Hills, CA 90210-5291
310-247-3940

Cohen & Steer Realty Shares
757 Third Avenue
New York, NY 10017
212-832-9912
800-437-9912

Columbia Funds
P.O. Box 1350
Portland, OR 97207-1350
503-222-3600
800-547-1707

Cornerstone Funds
1500 Forest Avenue
Richmond, VA 23229
800-728-0670

Crabbe Huson Funds
121 Southwest Morrison
Portland, OR 97204
503-295-0919
800-541-9732

DFA Funds
1299 Ocean Avenue
Santa Monica, CA 90401
310-395-8005

Dodge & Cox Funds
One Sansome Street
San Francisco, CA 94104-5277
415-981-1710

Dreman Funds
10 Exchange Place
Jersey City, NJ 07302
201-434-0700
800-533-1608

Dreyfus Funds
144 Glenn Curtiss Boulevard
Uniondale, NY 11556-0144
718-895-1206
800-645-6561

Eclipse Funds
144 East 30th Street
New York, NY 10016
212-696-4130
800-872-2710

Elite Group
1206 IBM Building
Seattle, WA 98101
206-624-5863
800-423-1068

Endowment Funds
Four Embarcadero Center
San Francisco, CA 94120-7650
415-421-9360
800-421-0180

Evergreen Funds
2500 Westchester Avenue
Purchase, NY 10577-2555
914-694-2020
800-235-0064

FAM Value Fund
P.O. Box 399
Cobleskill, NY 12043
518-234-7543
800-932-3271

Fasciano Fund
190 South La Salle Street
Chicago, IL 60603
312-444-6050
800-848-6050

Federated Funds
Federated Investors Tower
Pittsburgh, PA 15222-3779
412-288-1900
800-245-2423

Fidelity Funds
82 Devonshire Street
Boston, MA 02109-3605
800-544-8888
617-570-7000

Fiduciary Management Associates
1345 Avenue of the Americas
New York, NY 10105
212-969-1000
800-221-5672

Financial Funds
7800 East Union Avenue
Denver, CO 80237-2756
303-779-1233
800-525-8085

First Eagle Fund
45 Broadway
New York, NY 10006-3094
212-943-9200
800-451-3623

Flex-Funds
P.O. Box 7177
Dublin, OH 43017-0777
614-766-7000
800-325-FLEX

Fontaine Capital Appreciation
210 West Pennsylvania Avenue
Towson, MD 21204
410-825-7894
800-247-1550

44 Wall Street Funds
26 Broadway
New York, NY 10004
212-248-8080
800-543-2620

Founders Funds
2930 East Third Avenue
Denver, CO 80206
303-394-4404
800-525-2440

Fremont Funds
50 Fremont Street
San Francisco, CA 94105-2239
415-768-9000
800-548-4539

Gabelli Funds
One Corporate Center
Rye, NY 10580-1434
914-921-5000
800-422-3554

Gateway Funds
400 TechneCenter Drive
Milford, OH 45150
513-248-2700
800-354-6339

General Funds
144 Glenn Curtiss Boulevard
Uniondale, NY 11556-0144
718-895-1396
800-242-8671

Gintel Funds
Greenwich Office Park, #6
Greenwich, CT 06831
203-622-6400
800-243-5808

GIT Funds
1655 Fort Myer Drive
Arlington, VA 22209-3108
703-528-6500
800-336-3063

Greenspring Fund
2330 Joppa Road
Lutherville, MD 21093-4641
410-823-5353
800-366-3863

Harbor Funds
One Seagate
Toledo, OH 43666
419-247-2477
800-422-1050

Helmsman Funds
680 East Swedesford Road
Wayne, PA 19087-1658
800-338-4345

IBM Mutual Funds
290 Harbor Drive
Stamford, CT 06904-2399
203-973-5050
800-IBM-9876

Institutional International Funds
100 East Pratt Street
Baltimore, MD 21202-1090
410-547-2000
800-638-5660

Investment Series Trust
Federated Investors Tower
Pittsburgh, PA 15222-3779
412-288-1900
800-245-2423

Janus Funds
P.O. Box 173375
Denver, CO 80217-3375
303-333-3863
800-525-3713

Japan Fund
345 Park Avenue
New York, NY 10154-0010
212-326-6200
800-225-2470

Kaufman Fund
17 Battery Place
New York, NY 10004
212-344-2661

Kleinwort Benson Funds
200 Park Avenue
New York, NY 10166
212-687-2515
800-237-4218

Landmark Funds
6 St. James Avenue
Boston, MA 02116
617-423-1679
800-331-1792

Lazard Funds
1 Rockefeller Plaza
New York, NY 10020
212-632-6873
800-228-0203

Lepercq-Istel Fund
1675 Broadway
New York, NY 10019
212-698-0700
800-338-1579

Lexington Funds
P.O. Box 1515
Saddlebrook, NJ 07662-5812
201-845-7300
800-526-0057

LMH Fund
P.O. Box 830
Westport, CT 06881-0830
203-226-4768
800-847-6002

Loomis Sayles Funds
One Financial Center
Boston, MA 02111
617-482-2450
800-626-9390

Mairs & Power Funds
W-2062 First National Bank
    Building
St. Paul, MN 55101
612-222-8478

Mathers Fund
100 Corporate North
Bannockburn, IL 60015
708-295-7400
800-962-3863

Maxus Funds
18601 Chagrin Boulevard
Cleveland, OH 44122
216-292-3434
800-446-2987

Meridian Fund
60 East Sir Francis Drake
    Boulevard
Larkspur, CA 94939-1714
415-461-6237
800-446-6662

Merriman Funds
1200 Westlake Avenue North
Seattle, WA 98109-3530
206-285-8877
800-423-4893

MIM Mutual Funds
4500 Rockside Road
Independence, OH 44131-6809
216-642-3000
800-233-1240

Monetta Fund
1776-A S. Naperville Road
Wheaton, Il. 60187
708-462-9800
800-MONETTA

Mutual Series Fund
51 J.F. Kennedy Parkway
Short Hills, NJ 07078
201-912-2100
800-448-3863

Neuberger & Berman Funds
605 Third Avenue
New York, NY 10158-3698
212-476-9000
800-877-9700

Nicholas Funds
700 North Water Street
Milwaukee, WI 53202
414-272-6133

Nomura Pacific Basin Fund
Two World Financial Center
New York, NY 10281-1198
212-509-8181
800-833-0018

Northeast Investors Funds
50 Congress Street
Boston, MA 02109
617-523-3588
800-225-6704

Nottingham Investment Trust
105 North Washington Street
Rocky Mount, NC 27802-0069
919-972-9922
800-525-FUND

Olympic Funds
800 West Sixth Street
Los Angeles, CA 90017-2708
213-362-8900
800-346-7301

Papp Funds
4400 North 32nd Street
Phoenix, AZ 85018
602-956-0980

Parnassus Fund
244 California Street
San Francisco, CA 94111
415-362-3505
800-999-3505

Pax World Fund
224 State Street
Portsmouth, NH 03801
603-431-8022
800-767-1729

Perritt Capital Growth Fund
680 North Lake Shore Drive
Chicago, IL 60611-4402
312-649-6940
800-338-1579

Portico Funds
207 East Buffalo Street
Milwaukee, WI 53202
414-287-3808
800-228-1024

PRA Real Estate Securities Fund
900 North Michigan Avenue
Chicago, IL 60611
312-915-3600

Preferred Group of Mutual Funds
100 Northeast Adams Street
Peoria, IL, 61629-5330
309-675-4999
800-662-GROW

Price (T. Rowe) Funds
100 East Pratt Street
Baltimore, MD 21202-1090
410-547-2000
800-638-5660

Primary Trend Fund
700 North Water Street
Milwaukee, WI 53202
414-271-7870
800-443-6544

Reich & Tang Fund
100 Park Avenue
New York, NY 10017
212-476-5050
800-221-3079

SAFECO Funds
P.O. Box 34890
Seattle, WA 98124-1890
206-545-5530
800-426-6730

Salomon Brothers Funds
Seven World Trade Center
New York, NY 10048
212-783-7000
800-725-6666

SBSF Funds
45 Rockefeller Plaza
New York, NY 10111
212-903-1200
800-422-7273

Schafer Value Fund
645 Fifth Avenue
New York, NY 10022
212-644-1800
800-338-1579

Schroder Capital Funds
787 Seventh Avenue
New York, NY 10019
212-841-3830
800-344-8332

Scudder Funds
175 Federal Street
Boston, MA 02110-1706
617-439-4640
800-225-2470

Selected Funds
120 South Riverside Plaza
Chicago, IL 60606
312-669-7700

Sentry Fund
1800 North Point Drive
Stevens Point, WI 54481
715-346-6000
800-533-7827

Sherman Dean Fund
6061 Northwest Expressway
San Antonio, TX 78201-2107
512-735-7700

Sit Funds
90 South Seventh Street
Minneapolis, MN 55402-4130
612-334-5888
800-332-5580

Sound Shore Fund
61 Broadway
New York, NY 10006
203-629-1980
800-551-1980

Southeastern Asset Management
  Funds
800 Ridgelake Boulevard
Memphis, TN 38120
901-761-2474
800-445-9469

Spartan Funds
82 Devonshire Street
Boston, MA 02109-3605
617-570-7000
800-544-8888

Special Portfolio
Box 64284
St. Paul, MN 55164
612-738-4000
800-872-2638

State Farm Funds
One State Farm Plaza
Bloomington, IL 61710-0001
309-766-2029

SteinRoe Funds
300 West Adams Street
Chicago, IL 60606-5101
800-338-2550

Stratton Funds
610 West Germantown Pike
Plymouth Meeting, PA 19462-1050
215-941-0255
800-634-5726

Strong Funds
P.O. Box 2936
Milwaukee, WI 53201-2936
414-359-3400
800-368-3863

Thompson, Unger & Plumb Fund
8201 Excelsior Drive
Madison, WI 53717-1788
608-831-1300

Tocqueville Fund
1675 Broadway
New York, NY 10019-5820
212-698-0800

Twentieth Century Funds
P.O. Box 419200
Kansas City, MO 64141-6200
816-531-5575
800-345-2021

UMB Funds
2440 Pershing Road
Kansas City, MO 64108
816-471-5200
800-422-2766

Unified Funds
429 North Pennsylvania Street
Indianapolis, IN 46206-6110
317-634-3300
800-862-7283

United Services Funds
P.O. Box 29467
San Antonio, TX 78229-0467
512-308-1234
800-873-8637

USAA Funds
USAA Building
San Antonio, TX 78288-0227
512-498-8000
800-531-8181

U.S. Boston Investment Company
Lincoln North
Lincoln, MA 01773
617-259-1144
800-872-7866

Valley Forge Fund
P.O. Box 262
Valley Forge, PA 19481
215-688-6839
800-548-1942

Value Line Funds
711 Third Avenue
New York, NY 10017
212-687-3965
800-223-0818

Vanguard Funds
P.O. Box 2600
Valley Forge, PA 19482-2600
215-669-1000
800-662-7447

Variable Funds
P.O. Box 1978
Boston, MA 02105
404-892-0896
800-554-1156

Volumetric Fund
87 Violet Drive
Pearl River, NY 10965-1258
914-623-7637
800-541-3863

Warburg, Pincus Funds
466 Lexington Avenue
New York, NY 10017-3147
212-878-0600
800-888-6878

Wasatch Advisors Funds
68 South Main Street
Salt Lake City, UT 84101-9984
801-533-0777
800-551-1700

Wayne Hummer Funds
300 South Wacker Drive
Chicago, IL 60606
312-431-1700
800-621-4477

Weiss Peck & Greer Funds
One New York Plaza
New York, NY 10004-1950
212-908-9582
800-223-3332

Weitz Funds
9290 West Dodge Road #405
Omaha, NE 68114-3323
402-391-1980
800-232-4161

Wellesley Fund
P.O. Box 2600
Valley Forge, PA 19482-2600
215-669-1000
800-662-7447

Wellington Fund
P.O. Box 2600
Valley Forge, PA 19482
215-669-1000
800-662-7447

Wells Fargo Funds
111 Sutter Street
San Francisco, CA 94104
415-396-7690
800-572-7797

William Blair Funds
135 South La Salle Street
Chicago, IL 60603
312-853-2424
800-742-7272

Windsor Funds
P.O. Box 2600
Valley Forge, PA 19482
215-669-1000
800-662-7447

WPG Funds
One New York Plaza
New York, NY 10004
212-908-9582
800-223-3332

Wright Funds
24 Federal Street
Boston, MA 02110-2575
617-482-8260
800-225-6265

Glossary

account registration form Accompanies a prospectus and is completed by a prospective investor to provide a mutual fund with account name, address, Social Security number and other pertinent data.

account statement A statement sent by a mutual fund to each shareholder at least annually. It indicates the shareholder's registration, account number, tax ID number and shares owned. It also lists the account activity and a summary of dividends and distributions paid during the statement period.

accumulation plan An arrangement whereby an investor makes regular purchases of mutual fund shares in large or small amounts.

accumulation unit A measure of ownership interest in a variable annuity contract prior to the annuity date.

adviser *See* investment management company.

annuitant The person whose life is used to determine the duration of annuity payments.

annuity unit The unit of measure used to calculate variable annuity payments.

anticipated growth rate In a zero-coupon bond fund, the anticipated rate at which a share of the fund will grow from the date of purchase to a particular date during the maturity year.

anticipated value at maturity In a zero-coupon bond fund, the anticipated value of the fund's net assets on a particular date during the maturity year.

asked price The price at which the buyer may purchase shares of a mutual fund (the net asset value per share plus the sales charge, if any).

average cost–double category Permits calculation of investment cost by averaging costs of shares held for a short term with those held long-term.

average cost–single category Permits calculation of investment cost by averaging the cost of all shares regardless of the holding period.

back-end load A redemption fee charged to an investor in certain mutual funds when shares are redeemed within a specified number of years after purchase.

balanced fund A mutual fund that at all times holds bonds and/or preferred stocks in varying ratios to common stocks to maintain relatively greater stability of both capital and income.

bank draft plan A periodic cash investment made through a shareholder's checking account via bank drafts for the purpose of regular share accumulation.

bid price The price at which the holder of open-end mutual fund shares may redeem his or her shares. In most cases, it is the net asset value (NAV) per share. For closed-end fund shares, it is the highest price then offered for stock in the public market. It may be more or less than the NAV per share.

blue chip The common stock of large, well-known companies with a relatively stable record of earnings and dividend payments over many years.

blue-sky laws Laws of the various states regulating the sale of securities, including mutual fund shares, and the activities of brokers and dealers.

bond A security representing debt; a loan from the bondholder to the corporation.

bond anticipation notes Securities that provide interim financing in advance of an issue of bonds or notes, the proceeds of which are used to repay the anticipation notes.

break-point In the purchase of mutual fund shares, the dollar value level at which the percentage of the sales charge becomes lower. A sales charge schedule typically contains five or six break-points.

broker A person in the business of effecting security purchase and sale transactions for the accounts of others. He or she receives a commission for those services.

business day A day when the New York Stock Exchange is open for trading.

buying a dividend Purchasing shares of a mutual fund just in time to receive the current income or capital gains distribution. This practice results in receiving a portion of the investment back as a taxable distribution.

call (1) The exercise by an issuer of its right to retire outstanding securities; (2) an option contract that gives the holder the right to purchase a particular security from another person at a specified price during a specified period of time.

call price The price that an issuer of preferred stock or bonds must voluntarily pay to retire such securities.

capital (1) The assets of a business, including plant and equipment, inventories, cash and receivables; (2) the financial assets of an investor.

capital gains Profits realized from the sale of securities.

capital gains distribution A distribution to shareholders from net capital gains realized by a mutual fund on the sale of portfolio securities.

capital growth An increase in the market value of securities.

cash equivalent Includes U.S. government securities, short-term commercial paper, and short-term municipal and corporate bonds and notes.

cash position Includes cash plus cash equivalent minus current liabilities.

certificates of deposit (CDs) Interest-bearing certificates issued by commercial banks or savings and loan associations against funds deposited in the issuing institutions.

check-writing privilege A service offered by some mutual funds (particularly money market funds) permitting shareholders of such funds to write checks against their fund holdings. The holdings continue to earn dividends until the checks are cashed.

closed-end fund An investment company with a relatively fixed amount of capital whose shares are traded on a securities exchange or in the over-the-counter market.

commercial paper   Short-term, unsecured promissory notes issued by corporations to finance short-term credit needs. The maturity at the time of issuance normally does not exceed nine months.

common stock   A security representing ownership of a corporation's assets. The right to common stock dividends comes after the requirements of bonds, debentures and preferred stocks. Shares of common stock generally carry voting rights.

common stock fund   A mutual fund whose portfolio consists primarily of common stocks. Such a fund may at times take defensive positions in cash, bonds and other senior securities.

common trust fund   A mutual fund organized and administered by a bank or trust company for the benefit of its own trust account customers.

contractual plans   A type of accumulation plan under which the total intended investment amount is specified in advance, with a stated paying-in period and provision for regular monthly or quarterly investments. A substantial amount of the applicable sales charge is deducted from the first year's payments.

controlled affiliate   A mutual fund company in which there is any direct or indirect ownership of 25 percent or more of the outstanding voting securities.

convertible securities   Securities carrying the right to exchange them for other securities of the issuer (under certain conditions). This normally applies to preferred stock or bonds carrying the right to exchange for given amounts of common stock.

corporate (master or prototype) retirement plan   A plan and trust agreement that qualifies for special tax treatment available to a corporation or other organization whereby it can purchase the shares of a fund for the benefit of plan participants.

current assets   In a mutual fund, includes cash plus cash equivalent less current liabilities.

current liabilities   Obligations due within one year or less.

custodian   The bank or trust company that holds all cash and securities owned by a mutual fund. It may also act as transfer agent and dividend disbursing agent but has no responsibility regarding portfolio policies.

dealer   A person or firm that buys and sells securities to others as a regular part of its business. Mutual fund shares with a sales charge are usually purchased through dealers.

debenture   A bond secured only by the general credit of the corporation.

declaration of trust   A document that identifies a specific fund and declares that it is being held in trust for a specified beneficiary.

defensive stock   A stock that is expected to hold up relatively well in declining markets because of the nature of the business represented.

direct purchase fund   A mutual fund whose shares are purchased directly from the fund at a low charge or no charge at all. The investor deals directly with the fund rather than through a broker or dealer.

discount   The percentage below net asset value at which the shares of a closed-end mutual fund sell.

distributions   Dividends paid from net investment income and payments made from realized capital gains.

diversification   Investment in a number of different security issues for the purpose of spreading and reducing the risks that are inherent in all investing.

diversified investment company   A company that, under the Investment Company Act, in respect to 75 percent of total assets, has invested not more than 5 percent of its total assets in any one company and holds not more than 10 percent of the outstanding voting securities of any one company.

dividend   A payment from income on a share of common or preferred stock.

dollar cost averaging   A method of automatic capital accumulation that provides for regular purchases of equal dollar amounts of securities and results in an average cost per share lower than the average price at which purchases have been made.

dual-purpose fund   A type of closed-end mutual fund that is designed to serve the needs of two distinct types of investors: (1) those interested only in income and (2) those interested only in possible capital gains. It has two separate classes of shares.

earnings   In respect to common stock, net income after all charges (including preferred dividend requirements) divided by the number of common shares outstanding.

equity securities   The securities in a corporation that represent ownership of the company's assets (generally common stocks).

exchange privilege   The right to exchange the shares of one open-end mutual fund for those of another under the same fund group at a nominal charge (or no charge) or at a reduced sales charge. For tax purposes, such an exchange is considered a taxable event.

expense ratio The proportion that annual expenses, including all costs of operation, bear to average net assets for the year.

fiduciary A person who has legal rights and powers to be exercised for the benefit of another person.

first in, first out (FIFO) An accounting method for determining cost basis that assumes the first shares sold are the first shares purchased.

fixed-income security A preferred stock or debt instrument with a stated percentage or dollar income return.

forward averaging A special tax treatment available for certain lump-sum distributions from qualified retirement plans.

forward pricing The pricing of mutual fund shares for sale, redemption or repurchase at the next computed price after the receipt of an order. Pricing is usually done at 4:00 P.M. when the New York Stock Exchange closes.

front-end load A sales fee charged investors in certain mutual funds at the time shares are purchased.

general obligation bonds Bonds that are backed by the full taxing power of a state or municipality.

government agency issues Debt securities issued by government-sponsored enterprises, federal agencies and international institutions. Such securities are not direct obligations of the Treasury but involve government guarantees or sponsorship.

growth stock A stock that has shown better than average growth in earnings and is expected to continue to do so as a result of additional resources, new products or expanded markets.

hedge fund A mutual fund that hedges its market commitments by holding securities it believes are likely to increase in value and at the same time is "short" other securities it believes are likely to decrease in value. The only objective is capital appreciation.

incentive compensation A fee paid to an investment adviser that is based wholly or in part on management performance in relation to specified market indexes.

income The total amount of dividends and interest received from a fund's investments before deduction of any expenses.

income fund A mutual fund whose primary objective is current income.

individual retirement account (IRA)   A tax-saving retirement program for individuals, established under the Employee Retirement Income Security Act of 1974.

industrial revenue bond   A type of revenue bond backed by the credit and security of a private issuer; may involve greater risk.

inflation   A persistent upward movement in the general price level of goods and services that results in a decline in the purchasing power of money.

investment adviser   *See* investment management company.

investment company   A corporation or trust through which investors pool their money to obtain supervision and diversification of their investments.

Investment Company Act of 1940   A federal statute enacted by Congress in 1940 for the registration and regulation of investment companies.

investment management company   An organization employed to advise the directors or trustees of an investment company in selecting and supervising the company's assets.

investment objective   The goal of an investor or investment company. It may be growth of capital and income, current income, relative stability of capital or some combination of these aims.

investment policies   The means or management techniques that an investment manager employs in an attempt to achieve his or her investment objective.

investment trust   Same as investment company.

junior securities   Common stocks and other issues whose claims to assets and earnings are contingent on the satisfaction of the claims of prior obligations.

Keogh plan   A tax-favored retirement program for self-employed persons and their employees (also known as H.R. 10 Plan or Self-Employed Retirement Plan).

letter of intention   A pledge to purchase a sufficient amount of mutual fund shares within a limited period (usually 13 months) to qualify for the reduced selling charge that would apply to a comparable lump-sum purchase.

leverage   The effect of using borrowed money or other senior capital to magnify changes in the assets and earnings available for junior issues.

liquid   Assets that are easily converted into cash or exchanged for other assets.

living trust   A trust instrument made effective during the lifetime of the creator, in contrast to a testamentary trust, which is created under a will.

load   *See* selling charge.

low-load   Indicates that the sales fee charged to investors in certain mutual funds is approximately 1–3 percent of the amount invested.

management company   *See* investment management company.

management fee   The charge made to an investment company for supervision of its portfolio. It frequently includes various other services and is usually a fixed or reducing percentage of average assets at market value.

management record   A statistical measure, expressed as an index, of what an investment company management has accomplished with the funds at its disposal.

money market fund   A mutual fund whose investments are in short-term debt securities, designed to maximize current income with liquidity and capital preservation.

money purchase pension plan   A retirement program to which a percentage of the earnings of participating employees is contributed each year. The pension amount received by a participant at retirement depends on the amount contributed and earnings achieved on the funds over the period of participation.

municipal bonds   Debt instruments issued to raise money for various public purposes by state and local governments.

municipal bond fund   A mutual fund that invests in diversified holdings of tax-exempt securities, the income from which is exempt from federal taxes.

mutual fund   Same as open-end investment company.

National Association of Securities Dealers (NASD)   An organization of brokers and dealers in the over-the-counter securities market that administers rules of fair practice and rules to prevent fraudulent acts for the protection of the investing public.

net asset value (NAV)   Total resources at market value less current liabilities.

no-load fund   *See* direct purchase fund.

offering price   *See* asked price.

open account   An account in which a shareholder, by virtue of his or her initial investment in a fund, automatically has reinvestment privileges and the right to make additional purchases.

open-end investment company   An investment company whose shares are redeemable at any time at approximate net asset value. In most cases, new shares are offered for sale continuously.

option   A right to buy or sell specific securities at a specified price within a specified period of time.

optional distribution   A payment from realized capital gains or investment income that an investment company shareholder may elect to take either in cash or additional shares.

payroll deduction plan   An arrangement between a fund and an employer under which money is deducted from the employee's salary to purchase shares in the fund.

pension plan   A retirement program based on a definite formula that provides fixed benefits to be paid to employees for their lifetime upon the attainment of a stated retirement age.

pension rollover   The opportunity to take distributions from a qualified pension or profit-sharing plan and, within 60 days from the date of distribution, reinvest them in an individual retirement account.

performance   *See* management record.

performance fund   An investment company that appears to emphasize short-term results and that usually has had rapid turnover of portfolio holdings. It may also refer to any fund that has had an outstanding record of capital growth.

periodic payment plan   *See* accumulation plan.

portfolio   The securities owned by an investment company.

portfolio turnover   The dollar value of purchases and sales of portfolio securities, not including transactions in U.S. government obligations and commercial paper.

preferred stock   An equity security, generally carrying a fixed dividend, whose claim to earnings and assets must be paid before common stock is entitled to share.

premium   The percentage above net asset value at which the shares of a closed-end fund trade.

private activity municipal bonds   Bonds issued to finance housing projects, student loans, and privately owned solid waste disposal and water and sewage treatment facilities.

profit-sharing retirement plan   A retirement program to which a percentage of the profits of a company is contributed each year for the benefit of the plan's participants.

prospectus The official document that describes the shares of a new issue. This document must be provided to each purchaser, under the Securities Act of 1933. It applies to closed-end funds only when new capital is raised.

prototype retirement plan A retirement plan document that has been determined by the Internal Revenue Service to satisfy the requirements in the tax laws for qualified retirement plans.

prudent man rule The law governing the investment of trust funds in those states that give broad discretion to the trustee.

put An option contract that gives the holder the right to sell a particular security to another person at a specified price during a specified period of time.

qualified plans Retirement plans that meet the requirements of Section 401(a), 403(a) or 403(b) of the Internal Revenue Code, or the Self-Employed Individuals Tax Retirement Act.

redemption in kind Redemption of investment company shares for which payment is made in portfolio securities rather than cash. It is permissible for many mutual funds and tax-free exchange funds.

redemption price *See* bid price.

reduction-of-tax-basis dividend Payment by an investment company that is nontaxable as current income but must be used to reduce the tax cost of the shares.

registered investment company An investment company that has filed a registration statement with the Securities and Exchange Commission under the requirements of the Investment Company Act of 1940.

registration statement Document containing full and accurate information that must be filed with the Securities and Exchange Commission before new securities can be sold to the public.

regular account A lump-sum purchase of mutual fund shares without provision for automatic dividend reinvestment or planned periodic additions or withdrawals.

regulated investment company An investment company that has elected to qualify for the special tax treatment provided by Subchapter M of the Internal Revenue Code.

reinvestment privilege A service offered by most mutual funds and some closed-end investment companies through which dividends from investment income may be automatically invested in additional full and fractional shares.

reinvestment risk The risk that lower interest rates in the future will make it impossible for interest payments on a debt security to be reinvested at the same rate as the instrument from which they have been paid.

repurchase agreement Refers to the purchase of a security at one price and simultaneous agreement to sell it back at a higher price.

repurchases Refers to the voluntary open-market purchases by closed-end funds of their own shares. In mutual funds, the term represents shares taken back at their approximate net asset value.

revenue bond A bond that is backed by the revenues of a specific tax, project or facility.

right of accumulation The application of reduced sales charges to quantity purchases of mutual fund shares made over an extended period of time.

sales commission *See* selling charge.

Securities and Exchange Commission (SEC) An independent agency of the U.S. government that administers the various federal securities laws.

selling charge An amount that, when added to the net asset value of mutual fund shares, determines the offering price. It covers commissions and other costs and is generally stated as a percentage of the offering price.

senior securities Notes, bonds, debentures or preferred stocks. These issues have a claim ahead of common stock as to assets and earnings.

separate account In a variable annuity plan, assets that are segregated by the insurance company and invested in mutual fund portfolios.

shareholder experience A measure of the investment results that would have been obtained by an actual mutual fund shareholder. It is usually expressed in terms of a hypothetical $10,000 investment.

short sale The sale of a security that is not owned (but is borrowed) in the hope that the price will go down so that it can be repurchased at a profit.

simplified employee pension (SEP) plan A retirement plan whereby employers can make deductible contributions to Individual Retirement Accounts established for their employees.

specialty or specialized fund An investment company concentrating its holdings in specific industry groups.

specific shares An accounting method for determining cost basis that lets the investor identify the specific shares being sold.

sponsor Usually refers to the principal underwriter of an investment company's shares.

statement of additional information Contains more complete information than is found in a prospectus and is on file with the Securities and Exchange Commission.

subaccount In a variable annuity plan, the portion of the separate account that invests in shares of a single investment portfolio.

swap fund *See* tax-free exchange fund.

tax-exempt commercial paper short-term securities issued by municipalities to help finance short-term capital or operating needs.

tax-free exchange fund An investment company organized to permit investors holding individual securities selling at appreciated prices to exchange such securities for shares of the fund without payment of capital gains tax.

total return A statistical measure of performance reflecting the reinvestment of both capital gains and income dividends.

Treasury bill A non-interest-bearing security issued by the U.S. Treasury and sold at a discount, with a maturity of one year or less.

turnover ratio The extent to which an investment company's portfolio (exclusive of U.S. government obligations and commercial paper) is turned over during the course of a year.

12b-1 fee The fee charged by some funds, permitted under a 1980 Securities and Exchange Commission rule (for which it is named), to pay for distribution costs, such as advertising, or for commissions paid to brokers.

uncertificated shares Fund shares credited to a shareholder's account without the issuance of stock certificates.

unrealized appreciation or depreciation The amount by which the market value of portfolio holdings exceed or fall short of their cost.

U.S. government securities Various types of marketable securities issued by the U.S. Treasury, consisting of bills, notes and bonds.

volatility The relative rate at which a security or fund share tends to move up or down in price as compared with some market index.

voluntary plan An accumulation plan without any stated duration or specific requirements. Sales charges are applicable to each purchase made.

warrant An option to buy a specified number of shares of the issuing company's stock at a specified price, usually for a specified time.

withdrawal plan   An arrangement provided by many mutual funds by which an investor can receive periodic payments in a designated amount that may be more or less than the actual investment income.

yield   Income received from investments, usually expressed as a percentage of the market price.

yield to maturity   The rate of return on a debt security held to maturity. Both interest payments and capital gain or loss are taken into account.

Index of Mutual Funds

Index